W9-DDJ-892

# SHARING

## our stories, our selves, our success

*an anthology*
*of women's empowerment stories*

**SHARING:** *our stories, our selves, our success*
*an anthology of women's empowerment stories*

Copyright @ 2013
All copyrights are retained by the individual authors.
No part of this book may be reproduced or transmitted in any part
by any means without the express written permission of the author.

Canadian Cataloguing in Publication Data

SHARING: *our stories, our selves, our success*
ISBN No. 978-0-9920831-1-3


Editing, Layout and Design by
*words ... along the path*
a branch of One Thousand Trees


Printed in Guelph, Ontario, Canada by
M & T Printing Group

*Our deepest fear is not that we are inadequate. Our deepest fear is that we are powerful beyond measure. It is our light, not our darkness that most frightens us. We ask ourselves, Who am I to be brilliant, gorgeous, talented, fabulous? Actually, who are you not to be? You are a child of God. Your playing small does not serve the world. There is nothing enlightened about shrinking so that other people won't feel insecure around you. We are all meant to shine, as children do. We were born to make manifest the glory of God that is within us. It's not just in some of us; it's in everyone. And as we let our own light shine, we unconsciously give other people permission to do the same. As we are liberated from our own fear, our presence automatically liberates others.*

Marianne Williamson

# Words of Gratitude

The words of Marianne Williamson, as printed on the previous page, have always been one of my favourite quotes. *"Our deepest fear is not that we are inadequate. Our deepest fear is that we are powerful beyond measure."* For so many women, it is an inherent sense of unworthiness (which is different than inadequacy) that holds us back, and contriburors to a fear of success.

I have heard it, time and time again. "What if I become really successful? Eventually, I am going to mess up, and people will discover that I am nothing but a fraud."

It is as if their authentic self and their shadow side are engaged in a battle of wills, each one determined to conquer the other.

Through the writing, and publishing, of their stories, the women in this book have challenged and defeated their shadow side. They have discovered the power that comes from standing up and speaking their truth.

We all have a story. Everyone in this life has faced adversity and challenge, to one degree or another. It is only when we face our challenges, with an underlying faith that we will come through them stronger and more aligned with our authentic selves than ever before, that we give ourselves permission to shine.

Words are so powerful, when we hear them, when we read them, AND when we write them. I am so proud of each and every woman whose story graces the pages of this book. I am so very grateful to be in the company of a group of extraordinary women. Going through the writing and discerning process with them has been an absolute blessing.

Lisa Browning

# Words of Love

You are invited to read these stories with an open and gentle heart. The words are strong and true and have remained unedited to accurately portray each Author's experiences ... experiences which, though often intensely difficult, have created the strength and beauty of soul and spirit of each courageous woman whose story appears within these pages. Their words remind us that it is not for us to feel sadness for the trials we experience in Life, but to celebrate with unbridled joy who we have become through our life's experiences. It is our deepest wish that these real stories of trial through to triumph will inspire courage, hope and forward moving direction upon the pathway of Life in all who read them.

# Contents

# The Lion's Roar
## by Nicole Odelle Morrison

It was the middle of the night and a young woman got up to go to the bathroom only to discover that she couldn't return to her upright position. Her husband and daughter were both sound asleep. She did not want to wake her husband since he had just returned from work a few short hours ago. The young lady made her way to the kitchen and grabbed the emergency ten dollar bill that was always stored under the dinner plates in case anyone got sick. Without letting anyone know, she called the local taxi service to take her to the hospital.

The young woman was nine months pregnant but had not yet considered that her inability to stand back up might be linked to labour. She saw the world in a very simplistic way, not always able to see the fullness of a situation. When she arrived at the hospital and had been assessed by the doctor he asked, "Do you have any pain?" The young woman explained that she did not have any pain, just could not stand upright. The doctor informed her that she was in labour. The young woman delivered a baby girl naturally. Nicole Odelle graced the world with no pain given and with a genuine peace within her.

Within her first year of life, Nicole's mother took her to the doctor because she was concerned that there was something wrong with her. Nicole just smiled. There was no crying or fussiness, which is unlike most other babies. The young mother thought that her sweet baby's mind must be simple. The doctor examined her and informed the young woman that she just had the most content baby he had ever seen. This baby knew the truth deep inside when others had forgotten. The picture that is kept in the family album is Nicole at one day old with 20 or more energy bubbles hovering over top of her hospital cot.

* * *

*By o' baby bunting, Daddy's gone a hunting, hunting for a rabbit skin to wrap Colie's baby in….* is the song I loved to hear my daddy sing to me throughout my childhood. My older sister called me Colie instead of Nicole, and that became the name my family knew me by. I was completely in love with my Daddy. He was my God on earth to me. He was intelligent, creative, had charisma, and it seemed that there wasn't anything that my

Daddy couldn't do. I always loved to hear stories about my father when he was young. Dad was quite handsome as a young man. The girls were always interested in him. I remember an old photo of him with his thick black hair swooped up and slicked back with his leather jacket on and jeans much like the greasers from the 1960s. Mom would say that the girls would line up at the dances to be his partner for the Jive. There were so many things my father could do that came so naturally to him. For instance, he built an indoor bathroom for his parents, could talk baseball or politics when he had never even played or kept up with it, he could cook deliciously, and he could bring together a good party of music, guitar, singing, food, drinks, and laughter. But he could also shut it all down in a moment. When drunk Dad had a way of pushing social norms and by being grossly cruel and filthy with his words and actions. Many a night I would wake up to find my dad slumped over in his chair, leather coat still on, hat barely on his head, with a broken nose or black eyes starting to show themselves. Often it was a punch from a man whose girl dad had been rude to or it was a cowboy boot to the face from someone Dad just loved to get riled up. It seemed like a form of self-abuse to me as if he had set himself up to be beaten. I never could understand it. I chose not to include these episodes of drunken misbehaviour as a part of my character summary of my Dad. I kept that drunk man separate in my mind. He was not my Dad. I chose to see only the good in him because I knew that to be his true self.

* * *

It was a quiet Sunday morning. My mother and sister were in bed still; as usual, Dad was still passed out in his chair. I tiptoed around the house so as not to wake anyone. It felt so surreal, as if everything was frozen in time and I had the freedom to move around not affecting anything. I could see the clues to last night's events; overflowing ashtrays, the smell of spilt liquor and pop, Dad's headphones still playing fiddle tunes as they lay beside him where they fell off his head when he passed out. The chair thrown to the side where he put it when he tried to get to my mother as she screamed "No! Stop!" Our coats and boots at the bottom of the stairs where we left them when we snuck back in late last night. How many times we've played out the same scene weekend after weekend.

This night was no different. We were enjoying his early drinking since it made him loosen up and be more playful. As a family, we played poker and Scat for change and penny candies. Dad drank more and more and his playful nature soon turned to teasing and then to ridicule and abuse. My

2

sister and I ended up in tears and Mom sent us off to bed. Then the fighting started. First with insults to my mother and then sexual advances that were not loving in nature. I could hear her fighting him off. I crawled out of bed and put my ear to the vent. I was so afraid for my Mom but also mad at her.

"Just shut up!" I thought. "Don't argue with him. Get out of there!" When I heard the argument escalate I would start to pack my stuff. Even though I knew the seriousness of the threat to my Mom there was this notion within me that none of this was real and I would play along with the adventure. I knew which steps creaked and the corner to step on so the creaky step did not whine. I would climb over the banister with my sister's and my stuff, enough for a night or two, and leave the bags at the door. I would quietly sneak back up to my room. I would have clothes on under my nightgown so I was ready for a quick getaway. Standing at the door, which was open a crack for me to hear, I would hear the familiar "No don't hurt me!" that my mother would shout. I felt the tightening in my tummy and a lump in my throat knowing what was coming.

I heard the whack he gave her in the face and I yelled from my bedroom, "Don't hurt my Mom! Don't hurt my Mom!" She yelped from the blow and she cried, "You Fucking Bastard!" He kicked her out of the house and told her to leave the kids. The staircase ran the length of our hallway so I could see her as she left. She looked me straight in the eye and mouthed, "I will be back for you girls." As I sobbed I knew it to be true because she always came back when it was safe to get us.

I was the one that could get away with the most when it came to Dad. I was not his favourite target. So I went out and tested the waters to see if he had passed out yet. When he was out cold my sister and I shimmied down the stairs to meet our Mom and grab our supplies. We three walked the night streets wondering who could take us in this time. Sometimes it was old friends we hadn't seen in years, sometimes friends of Mom's that we did not know. Some places were nicer than others. Some smelled of urine-filled sheets. Some had food and some had little but they all took us in and provided us with safety. We tried not to be a burden on people. Sometimes we would just walk for hours or visit people for a bit until we knew he was out cold and then sneak back in. ….. This particular morning as I moved freely through last night's rubble, I looked at Dad with his hair a mess and head slumped to the side. I could feel and smell the fog of fear. I saw his vulnerability, pain, misery, and his despair and told him secretly in my mind and heart, "I love you. I'm sorry that your heart hurts so much." If only he could have seen himself as I saw him through my loving eyes he could have been the man I knew he was. I tiptoed back to bed and snuggled into my sheets and waited for my family to wake.

* * *

It took several pushes and then his head rose and his eyes opened, revealing that glossy-eyed look he wore when drunk, that always put a tight knot in my stomach. He started to talk and I could smell the rye on his breath that made me nauseous and triggered memories of drunken nights of fear that were stored deep within my cells. These recollections were filled with fear for my family's safety and also for my Dad for within those glossy-eyes I always saw a fearful and wounded child. I worked hard to protect and care for that child.

This night, I am six years old and in the kitchen checking to see if my Dad is alive. He opened his eyes and hugged me way too tight and long because he had passed out again briefly holding me in a bear hug that I cannot seem to wiggle myself free from. I remembered thinking how strong he was and how that made me nervous, scared that I will be trapped here until he wakes again. I called his name a few times with no response. I tried to wiggle out again and could not even peel his fingers off his opposite forearm to loosen his grip. I began to cry and slumped myself into the hold, hoping to make it more comfortable. After fifteen minutes he opened his eyes and freed me.

"Nikki… sit down." He said in a drawn-out slur and I obeyed, afraid not to even though it was three in the morning and I should have been in bed.

"Yes Daddy?" I asked, waiting for the sad story to begin. Even at this young age I was accustomed to being my Dad's witness to his infliction and his ideas of life. I would brighten my eyes, settle into the chair, and be ready to listen and impart love, acceptance, and wisdom to this frightened child. Maybe my love could heal him, is the thought I had, as most naïve children believe. I still thought my dolls could not breathe when my Mom put them in the toy barrel, and I would run to rescue them from their plight.

"Nikki." My name would be drawn out like it went on for mile. "Why did God give me you? I don't deserve you." This question would hang heavily between us like a dark cloud that blurred our vision.

4

With great love in my heart and an eagerness to teach I replied, "Daddy maybe God gave you to me so that I could learn from you." We both knew I was speaking about his demons, not the skills and abilities that he could teach.

"Maybe, Nikki," he said with lit-up eyes, the way he looked when I would say something wise that would surprise him. He sat up straight and mulled the idea over in his mind. Then he put the headphones back on his ears as the full volume fiddle tunes still were playing throughout our exchange. He looked up to the ceiling as he always did, as he shook his feet that were propped up on another chair to the beat, and he re-entered his world of make-believe and memories that he escaped to each weekend when the liquid he ingested flowed through his veins and provided an escape from reality, or his sense of it. Some inner part of me knew it to be true that I was to learn from him.

* * *

As a child, school was where I escaped to. I was fortunate that academics came quite naturally to me. My academic intelligence anchored my worth. I aimed to please and please I sure did. I had close to the top marks in all my grades, was trusted by the teachers and Principal to answer the phone, have access to the key to the supply room in the basement, and with running copies on the old crank and turn ditto copy machine. I wasn't the typical teacher's pet. I didn't work hard for these privileges; the adults just knew they could rely on me. I was kind and friendly with my peers and for the most part was well-liked.

My teachers believed in my abilities. They believed that I would go to university some day and do something grand with my life. This belief fueled my spirit and provided hope that things could someday be different for me. School was also where I could just play and be a kid. On occasion, a police car would visit my house to deal with the domestic abuse. I am not sure who would call; whether it was my Mom for help or a neighbour that could hear the disturbance. Needless to say, the police would escort my mother and us girls out of the house and into the cruiser leaving my father who was drunk and behaving abusively in the comfort of his own house. I remembered looking around and seeing my friends and their families silently watching on as we were removed from our home and taken to a family member's home for safety. What was so amazing was that when I returned to school not one child from my school would ever speak of it. It was like an unwritten code: whatever happens in our homes stays there and when we are together we escape through play and love of friendship. There were some kids that got beaten. There were some that had little food or clean clothes. Some kids had undiagnosed learning problems that led them to get them into trouble a lot, and some who could not keep their desks tidied if their lives depended on it. And then some who had safe and nurturing homes. However, we were all friends. We played tag, square ball, rode our bikes, and played twenty-one. No one ever spoke of what went on when we were not together. They were my saving grace. I could just be me and they liked me.

I always held the belief that there must be a better way; a more nurturing and loving way to be with one another that brought out the best in each of us instead of the fear. I would get excited when thinking about the possibilities and how I would create a different, healthier life for myself and the children that I brought into the world.

At eight years old I vowed to myself that I would never be with a man who abused me or anyone in any way. This promise was like a root that buried deep within myself so deep that it could never be plucked from me. I searched for all of God's helpers that I could find to support me. I tried to notice them all and heed their warnings and store their teachings. From that point on, I became a support sponge soaking in all genuine love and guidance that I could recognize so that I could create that better life I knew was available to me. I heard messages in exchanges that others would overlook. I saw kindness and safety in certain people for whom I was grateful. I looked, I paid attention, I listened deeply, and I stored. When I was present with these teachers I knew that I wasn't alone.

It was the simple things that taught me so much. One morning in particular, while sleeping over at a friend's house, I rose early as she slept to sit and have hot chocolate with her parents while they enjoyed their coffee on the front stoop. Her family was so loving and close. I absorbed the family energy, taking mental notes of how they spoke to each other, how love was shown in words and in deeds, how they would ask me about my week, my thoughts on things, and include me in all of the family things. I felt like a student of love and togetherness.

"I love when people look me in the eye and genuinely care what I have to say. They even had questions about what I said so they must have been really listening. Ahhh, that's what feeling valued and included feels like. I like this feeling. I will have this and so will my children." I took down that mental note and stored it deep to protect it.

\* \* \*

"Fuck you all!!!!" And then a loud bellowing lion's ROAR ignited within me. And as I opened my mouth to roar, FEAR snuck in and I swallowed it. Fear was like a dark fog that permeated every nook and cranny of my existence, both inside and outside, like a parasite overtaking its host. It covered my eyes so heavily like a dense fog that all I could see was Fear. Even the good stories were now tainted by Fear. The hopes and dreams for the future were polluted with Fear. It was like the fog moved throughout my mind changing the form of everything; every thought, every memory. I was seething and I ROARed again!

My parents were separating. Sure, it was good for them and my sister because none of them got along. But me? I loved them all and I was close with each of them. I was devastated; not only with the separation but with each one of them going their separate ways and living their own lives without me. I spent so much energy throughout my childhood trying to keep everyone happy and to show them the beauty in each one of them. They couldn't hear me or see themselves as I did. It was if they were walking in a world that was covered with a dense fog that distorted their truth. And now I have swallowed that same fog of Fear and rage. That's when the darkness fell and I joined the others that felt forsaken and abandoned.

\* \* \*

I knew not where I belonged anymore in my life. I was starting high school and I was no longer the smart kid. I was lost in the sea of students and couldn't find where I fit or anyone to help me feel safe. I had made some good friends initially but soon their regular lifestyles with curfews, expectations, family gatherings, and normalcy did not fit my life. My Dad had set the rules clearly from the start when I moved in with him; that is, he would drink Thursday to Sunday so I was to do my thing without it interrupting his. This schedule required a shift in friends because I needed friends that had very lenient rules such as mine. Those friends became like family to me. Some served as good homes for me to be at. Many were lost souls with similar fears to mine; that we were not loved, not worthy or good enough, that we were alone and discarded, and that we were broken and less than. These friends "got me". They understood and needed a companion in their misery as much as I did. This led to nights on the street supporting each other when one or the other could not bear to go home. This led to drinking to escape and drug use to numb the pain and loneliness.

The drugs and alcohol would allow my body to finally relax when it was accustomed to being on high alert. I would smile and giggle the whole night through. I missed feeling carefree and playful. How I loved this sensation. Sometimes I would feel this powerful energy surge through me and I would swear I could run faster than a train and lift up cars. I could do anything! I was invincible! I would do this again and again just to feel the euphoria that came with it and the false sense of power and security that I felt in those moments.

As one would expect, school became less important. High school was no longer that safe place or refuge that elementary school was. It did not have the same family feel where I felt seen, valued, and invested in. Teachers only saw my pain and thought my Lion's roar was the real me. They did not take the time to learn that I was an all-star student in all ways throughout my entire elementary days. That I was quiet and polite and always helped others around me. That people believed that I would do great things in this world. And that now I am no longer operating in this manner. RED FLAG!!! GIRL IN CRISIS!!!

"Please don't be afraid of my pain and anger. I need you!!" This was the cry of the Lioness within me. But instead I was judged, harassed, and ignored by most teachers. When I would will myself to school from under my fog of fear and depression to try again, I would be greeted with sarcasm. "You finally decided to join us?" I would turn around immediately and could hear the door slam closed behind me.

"Do you know how hard it was to get myself here today?" I would scream in my head as tears welled up. "I don't need this shit from you. I already live with a bastard. I don't need to pull myself up from a debilitating dense fog, shower, dress, and bus to school to be in the presence of another bastard. Do you know I was up most of the night planning my escape out of a one bedroom apartment on the fifth floor in case he came in again in some psychotic state? Or that I slept on the floor because Dad said it was best since he had a dirty whore in my bed last night. Fuck. Are you all that stupid? I fucking need you. I need someone to see me. SEE ME. I'm under here and I'm drowning."

\* \* \*

The phone rang. I answered only to discover that it was my Vice-Principal on the other end of the line. He, in his usual sarcastic tone, asked if I was going to show up at school tomorrow.

"You can speak to me Monday through Friday between nine and three. Otherwise this is my own time." I hung up. This was not the usual manner in which I spoke to people. I had become truant at school since I was still roaring like a Lion and saying *Fuck you!* to the world. I had given up on most adults; I saw them as useless.

I told my Vice Principal, "I missed Fridays at school because my Dad drinks Thursday nights and gets paranoid in the middle of the night and kicks me out for whatever reason his diseased mind creates in his pretend world. I walk the streets in the wee hours of the morning alone in the dark crying and terrified until enough time has elapsed for him to re-enter his world of make-believe and memories while listening to his music on his headphones. His eyes are open but he is not present, so I can walk by him without him even noticing. However, when this happens I am given the gift of swollen eyes in the morning from the crying. So swollen that they are just slits that I look out from and need to ice them for a day or two." When my VP heard this truth from me he gave me his usual grin of disbelief and then assigned detentions. Silently I say, "Fucker. And you wonder why I hate you." I throw the detention slip in the garbage.

I never was one to see hierarchy. Just because someone held a higher position or had more responsibility than me did not determine their worth. We were equal and that was that. I would be respectful to them as I would anyone whatever their position, socioeconomic status, religion, race, culture, and beliefs, whatever. I could not see the difference. However, if they were clearly wrong in their perception of me or my loved ones I felt completely justified to impart my wisdom and truth onto them. However, as an angry teenaged Lioness my delivery could cut clear through to the bone.

\* \* \*

How many nights of tears and swollen eyes must one girl endure? Rocking back and forth on my bed while grasping my hair in fists on either side, crying begging for an answer to WHY? Why must my life be like this? I would start to question out loud through gritted teeth, "Why? Why must he be such a bastard?" Then more tears fell and so did my heart.

9

"I fucking hate him, I fucking hate him, I fucking hate him!" These words would spew from my lips while I rocked back and forth. I started to scare myself and think that maybe it was me who was crazy since everyone around me was not reacting to my situation. No one was helping me. Maybe they were all sane and I was the insane one? Then I caught the sight of myself in the mirror, rocking with my fisted hands in hair, eyes big and swollen and tears streaming down my face. I looked the clear picture of crazy.

"I hate you. I hate you. You are pathetic. You are weak." I said to my reflection with conviction and disgust. And I cried myself to sleep that night at the edge of my bed fully clothed with my drunk ass father on the other side of the door and not another soul around to help me. My final thoughts before a crash, "Fuck. I'm so alone."

* * *

The shame I felt around not going to school was debilitating. I believed that I was letting myself and everyone else down. The dense fog of fear that I had swallowed was now a putrid vile substance that coursed through my veins, making my body have its own purpose separate from my mind. I knew that I must return to school and get myself back on track but it was like there was this menace inside my veins that would laugh in its evil voice and mock me. I would lay in bed trying to will my body to move but my limbs were like dead weight. I lost the control of my body. I did not understand then that this was the depths of depression.

Today, for a reason unknown to me, the menace was distracted and my mind was able to get me up so I could begin again. I avoided the class where I would be met with sarcasm and judgement and waited for English class. I had missed an insane amount of classes already but still was passing everything. But this day I was going to where I felt safe. I started walking out to the portable where my teacher was standing in the doorway greeting each student. I loved that about him. Then he spotted me. His eyes lit up and he smiled. I grinned and blushed in shyness.

"Welcome." The first words I heard as I started back to class. He gestured towards the door for me to enter, came in and pulled out my chair for me, which I was unaccustomed to, and then he squatted down and privately caught me up on what they had been doing so that I could participate. My grade nine English teacher always included me. He didn't care about my burgundy bangs that covered my face or that the shirt of my uniform was not tucked in, or that I had not been there in weeks. He took the time he had with me and made the most of it.

On one occasion I had done an assignment for class; to write a piece that would sell readers on the book *A Tale of Two Cities*. I had done this silly piece on the phone with a friend really hamming it up. When I went to hand it in I was a bit unsure of the piece since it was pretty silly. He then made me stand up in front of the class. I knew I was in shit for sure. He held up my paper in front of him with both hands.

"This is the best piece of writing I have ever had." He said in the most serious and proud tone. That was unexpected. The students that had been there day in and day out and didn't participate in my kind of extracurricular activities showed with their expressions that it was unexpected to them as well. I returned to my seat quickly and tried to hide both my pleasure and my vulnerability.

"He SEES ME."

My heart started stirring. I felt a warm sensation moving throughout my body. I wondered what it was. "Hmmmm. I think I'm happy." And as I continued to experience this witnessing of my truth by this man and as I experienced his genuine care and support I promised myself that I would try to live up to his vision of me. He didn't see me as broken. He saw me as whole and I liked that. He was my mirror of wholeness. I liked me the way he saw me. Something shifted inside of me at that moment and I allowed an inkling of love to sneak in and to flow again.

\* \* \*

My back was up against the hard wall. My head was spinning and the scene in front of me was a blur. I slowly slid down the wall and sat with my legs straight out in front of me. My vision steadied but it was like I was the observer inside of my head looking out examining myself; as if there was me and then this other presence but the other presence was me too. I was high this evening and was at a friend's house where several of us "friends" gathered. In the drug world, if you were sharing dope then you were "friends". Outside of that you might not be friends. But that night everyone was my "friend". I sat and watched the scene in front of me move in what seemed to be a choppy kind of slow motion where the sounds were muffled and distorted, the people's movements and reactions exaggerated.

I thought to myself in a most disgusted tone, "Do I look as stupid as they do?"

And the other voice in my head answered, "Yep." I watched and became more and more disgusted in their behaviour and their interactions as they continued ingesting more and more drugs and thinking they were cool shit.

"Really? I look that ridiculous?" I queried.

"You got it." The voice continued. "You've got a choice to make here Nicole. You can continue down this path you are on and look like these fools or you can get your shit together. You see that you are powerful in creating this shit-ass existence. You can use the same power to create that better life you've always known to be out there." I pondered this dilemma for what felt like hours but the scene in front of me made me aware that I was in the same moment still.

"Hmmmmm….the one choice seems like so much work." I thought.

The other voice chimed in, "You know you are capable of better than this. You've said *Fuck the World* long enough. No one's listening. Your life's not better for it. Look around you." It was the first time that I saw my "friends" and myself in this light. I looked again at myself from the observer's eyes and saw how pathetic I looked. I couldn't stand it any longer and made the courageous choice that night to go down the other path even though it seemed like such a monumental journey with no map or directions.

Fear took a big blow that night and that familiar tingle of remembering and of love for self ran through my body again. That presence reminded me that I was not broken; I had just taken a sabbatical from reality. I was capable of creating a different life. And the Lioness breathed and settled. Then in my mind's eye I saw her; that little girl that I had always loved. She was smart, spunky, carefree, and confident in the love she knew and saw the world through. I had forgotten her. Then I realized that I had missed her so much! Her eyes lit up when I spotted her. I could see her cheesy grin and bubbles dancing all around her and I started to remember. That night against the wall, I knew I had to walk this life my way even though I had no clue what that was. I had to let my parents and my sister be responsible for their own lives and me, for mine. They were all in my life still but less enmeshed. Eventually I trusted something bigger and grander than me to be in charge of all of our lives, that would protect and guide us. Once I decided to focus on my healing, all sorts of teachers in all kinds of disguises began to show up.

For the most part, I was getting my life on track; attending school, honour roll, drug free, and had a good circle of friends. I had even started seeing a young man that fit all the promises I had made about a man when I was eight. My days fluctuated with light and fog since I still struggled with my family issues. There were negative messages that had built up over time that competed with the messages of love that new relationships had begun to gift me. I was in grade 14. This was difficult since my new friends and my new boyfriend were in university and I was left behind to clean up my academic mess.

This day was especially foggy. I had gotten glasses for the first time and not one person, student nor teacher, recognized this change. It was a pretty big deal in my life. As I walked the halls at the end of the day I thought to myself, "What's the point if no one even sees me? I could not be alive today and no one would have noticed."

The fog of fear started to grow. It knew I was vulnerable at that moment. My heart began to sink and tears began to well up in the corners of my eyes. Then he showed up. My grade nine English teacher walked by and said, "Hello Miss MacDonald." That was my surname at the time. My mouth and my heart started to smile in return.

"How did he remember my name after so long?" I wondered. That made me feel special. As I continued to walk I felt a tap on my shoulder. I turned to see it was him again. "You got new glasses. They look great on you." He smiled and his eyes lit up. I smiled so large and tears of love and gratitude replaced the tears of fear. I silently said to him, "I needed you today. I so needed you." Once again, he SAW ME and reminded me that I had value and wasn't invisible like I had thought. Thank God for the Earth Angels that were sent my way to lighten my path.

\* \* \*

I dial his number. He picks up and I am unsure of how he will receive me since I closed the door tightly on his support a year ago. *"Yes?"*

"Hello Bruce?"

*"Yeeeees?"*

"Can you help me?"

*"Why should I help you Nicole?"*

"Because I'm ready to do my work now." I take a breath, nervous of his reply.

*"What's the fear?"*

"Well the other day this….." I started.

He interrupts, *"No. What's the fear?"*

"I'm trying to tell you." I say with frustration building.

*"No you're telling me a story, what's the fear?"*

Frustrated I say, "But I'm trying…"

*"What's the fear?"* He waivers not in his questioning.

"I don't know!"

*"Yes you do. What's the fear?"* The silence sits between us as I ask myself the honest question.

"I'm afraid that I'm not good enough."

*"FEAR. False Evidence Appearing Real."* The definition stopped me in my tracks. I had never heard this before. He continued to teach. *"Evidence – You are no good because you've been treated as such. False evidence because what happened was a projection of other people's shit on you. Appears real because there was emotion, sensation, sound, memories, etc. attached to it so it felt real. So, how people treat you is not a reflection of your worth but instead an indication of what is happening within them."*

"So they are acting on False Evidence too that they bought into when they were young right? So none of it was about me?" He smiled. "WOW!"

*"Ready to live in Trust instead of Fear my dear?"* He smiled his Cheshire Cat-like grin that said, "Come on. You know this to be true Nicole, now do it."

So the cleanup of erroneous beliefs began. The first steps towards freedom and seeing through the illusion into the truth of who I am... whole, beautiful, loved, good enough, and wanted. My whole vision of the world shifted that day. I now could see everyone's internal world being shared with me and no longer saw it as the reflection of my value in the world. I left the illusions with their owners and sent love in hope for their eyes to be opened like mine were. Bruce SAW ME in my purest form and that ignited the Lion's Roar deep inside of me again; this time fuelled by the knowledge of my truth, love of self, and Grace. As I continued to fear less and trust more my teachers arrived to greet me at each step and I was grateful for each one.

* * *

*Nicole is a teacher of love. From a very young age Nicole could see the beauty in people no matter what role they were portraying in the world. She uses this unique ability to coach teens in remembering the Truth of who they are and how to live according to those Truths.*

*Nicole is the Founder of Inspire Counselling & Therapeutic Services where she uses a combination of counselling strategies, Energy Healing, and Hypnotherapy. When you change your mind, you change your experience of the world. She lives in Guelph, Ontario. For more information please go to www.inspirecounselling.ca*

*The Lion's Roar is a sampling of a larger piece of work in progress.*

# Leaning in to Find the Light
## by Alex MacEachern

"Must we all talk about our eating disorders?[1]

I feel this way sometimes, like I really want to talk about the things I have overcome in my life. I want to tell people that my first memories in life are peppered with anxiety, I want to tell them how much I suffered with my eating disorder and at the same time felt really happy, on top of the world even. I want to share my stories, especially the painful ones. But I often wonder, when do I let them rest? When should I put them down, throw up my hands and just stop? Stop the telling, stop the remembering and the reminding, stop finding the space within me that feels like a victim. I return to this place because it is safe and then people will really love me, right? If they know how hard I work and how hard things have been, even though my life is shiny and bright on the outside, then they will have to love me, right? Maybe this is it. Maybe this is the moment and I have been given one last chance to lay my cards out, bear my soul and be heard, to be seen, really. I think all I want is to be seen in my entirety and this is my chance. So yes, we do need to talk about our eating disorders and all that lies beneath them, until we feel heard and it is our time to stop and let them lie. This is my time.

I now understand that it is important for women with a platform to talk about all of the things that lurk in the grey, that come out at night, that taunt and haunt us while we are awake and shake our soul in such a serious way that, when it is over, we wonder how we ever let it happen. Women with a platform are easier to hear but I recognize the importance of hearing all women who are made powerful by finding the courage to share their stories of fear and growth and triumph. And yes, I use triumph quite deliberately because coming out of a cycle of self-loathing and personal harm, whether physically or emotionally, is a triumph and should not be taken lightly; people should dance and sing and celebrate and hold the hands of the one who is brave enough to reach the bottom of the pit, or fall as it may be, and lie in the dark and eventually reach for the light on the other side; to begin the painful and tricky and slippery process of finding a voice and a space and a community that can hold your hand and be your mirror to remind you of how far you have come and just how lovely you are.

[1] A question raised in response to New York City mayoral candidate Christine Quinn's admission that she has struggled with alcoholism and an eating disorder.

16

So here I begin. This is a story of a beautiful, full life, with a loving family, plenty of opportunities, a strong and supple body and mind, and a belief that left me, from a young age, with the complete understanding that there was something wrong with me. From the outside my life growing up was idyllic ~ a close-knit family with four kids, we lived in a large city and enjoyed life in the country on weekends. I had stable parents with a loving relationship who had been together since they were teenagers, who had us all rally as a family and "show up" for each other. I was the youngest by a mile with 14 years between my eldest sibling and myself and 9 years to my closest sister; when I was little, they were off being busy with the joys and angst of teenage life.

My earliest memories are filled with anxiety; a deep unshakeable sense that something was not right in the world despite all that seemed so good. I knew I was different from the age of about four. I used to cry myself to sleep. I worried that my Mum would die in a car crash, that was the most frequent of all my worries. But other kids have tears too, worries even, but I knew that I had no words for my tears and the clawing and gnawing that took place inside of me when I went to bed. I kept my tears to myself, crying quietly, knowing if I reached out I would be asked the cause of the tears. My little self understood that I had no words to describe the rattle and hum that were constants in my life.

I was a home body, feeling that if I was close to home I could keep all those I loved safe and so the cycle began of intertwining this deep-seated fear for my family's safety with an overactive sense of responsibility. This fear continued throughout my childhood, into adolescence and, let's face it, even early adulthood. I had a litany of excuses to shift situations to help reduce my anxiety or to keep the tears at bay when they were more than I could handle; please turn down that emotionally charged music, it's hurting the cat's ears; even telling a teacher my Grandma had died to justify the unstoppable tears I cried when September inevitably came and I had to go back to school. I needed to escape holiday dinners to throw up which stemmed from my overwhelming anxiety, the worry that one day someone I loved would be missing from the table; my Dad and my paternal Grandma were the main source of concern for me. I threw up often when out for family dinners, always with a huge amount of emotion or worry attached to it. Because so much of my anxiety went undetected, my tiny self made leaps and connections from all of this undercover worrying. I began to believe that I was unseen and that somehow my invisibility, my quiet sickness was okay.

My small body and big heart were wracked with nervous energy, big feelings, feelings of being different and just wanting it all to stop. I wanted each day to run on fast forward so I would finally be free of these unbearable feelings that invaded my cells like a disease. My leaving for university was filled with a painful disentanglement from my Mum, and a breakdown of all of the coping mechanisms I had set in place to manage my anxiety and keep my family safe. How can you save your Dad's life when you are not there? I was terrified. The first photo I have at university is one my sister took, I am sitting on my bed with red swollen eyes and tear marks all down the front of my shirt, not the experience of many students who are happily sending their folks off and diving into their new independence. I struggled immensely. One important tipping point happened when I ran panicked across campus to the university psychologist whom I had called out of desperation in the midst of a panic attack. I somehow in my attempt for relief seemed to even fool her and was prescribed sleeping pills, because lack of sleep must have been the cause of my anxiety and homesickness. Once again, I faded into the background and evaded the opportunity to find the words to ask for the help I so desperately needed.

I finally had to come clean to my parents that something was not right. I found the courage to seek help because a family friend's son was seeing a therapist and that normalized the process enough for me. I engaged in talk therapy for four years with a lovely therapist who offered me moments of peace, even though there were no lasting results or major changes in my sadness. One of my only specific memories of working with him was when he asked me if he could offer me a pill (not antidepressants, this is a large powerful hypothetical pill) to get rid of this high level of sensitivity that contributed to my anxiety, would I take it? I sat quietly in thought and through a flood of tears I said no. This was both a heartbreaking and enlightening process, knowing I would have to find a way through all of these feelings but also allowing myself to see this spirit I had as something to cherish and nurture, rather than continuing to chastise myself for it. Wouldn't it be lovely if this is the end of my struggle and I felt okay? Yes it would be lovely, but I have to tell you it got worse before it got better.

When I was taking my Masters degree I had the incredible -- or shall I say life-changing, blow your socks off, earth shattering, limit-shattering -- experience of being introduced to an energy worker named Susan. I was introduced to her by a friend and I went on my hands and knees, desperate, having had enough and needing to find some peace. I remember those first sessions well, feeling the energy shift and change, dissipate and return, always in a different form, shedding layers like a snake, emerging new and yet the same and somehow in my more true form. The connection with EFT[2] was instant. This form of energy therapy clears energetic blockages on a cellular and spiritual level without re-traumatization. This deep work began to bring me moments of peace while I worked with this remarkable woman, but my stories ran deep and there was a lot of work to be done.

During this time I struggled with anxiety-driven underemployment and a relationship that was deeply unsatisfying. I spent most of my life in long term relationships, nourishing the belief that I couldn't be on my own, that I wasn't brave enough, capable enough, strong enough to leave when I knew I wasn't deeply loved. Maybe this was just a reinforcement that I wasn't enough and this was all I deserved in my life; never really being able to reach my potential; always settling for second best; always stepping back and letting others shine; supporting and enabling, while what I could become slowly died. I accepted that these were the cards I was dealt in this life and so I quietly accepted.

I remember so vividly Susan speaking of the amazing shifts that can take place as the layers of self-doubt, loathing, trauma, hurt, sadness and the stories we create to protect ourselves drift away because of this remarkable technique. People changing jobs, cities, personal style, body shape, negative patterns of behavior, posture, hobbies and spouses, all through shedding the way we believe we are. We emerge from how we have constructed ourselves and allow our true selves, free from the burdens of our histories, to shine free. I worked with Susan over a period of four years, shifting the energy and working with deep-seated beliefs, but my anxiety remained. There was a knowledge deep in my body that knew something wasn't right, something needed to shift that I just wouldn't allow myself to touch. I needed to address my fear of being alone and confront the relationship I knew would inevitably fail, but it was so overwhelming. How can you shift something that you have so thoroughly intertwined into every aspect of your life? We owned a house, parts of our work overlapped, we were ingrained in each other's families after years spent together, we lived in the same community and more than anything, I truly believed I couldn't be on my own; so I stayed until he left me.

The details of the separation are not newsworthy; however, the most remarkable thing happened to me. For the first time in my life, my anxiety

---

[2] *EFT is the Energy Freedom Technique. For more information on this work visit Susan Bushell's website at www.freeyouremotions.com.*

stopped. There was a beautiful silence within my heartbreak and grief. That clawing, gnawing feeling that had shaken me all of my life, left my jaw tense and my insides shaking, was gone and I mean really and truly gone and it was remarkable! There were many tears and the usual angst that comes with separating out of a long-term relationship but I dove deeply into the energy work, feeling desperate for some direction and relief from my sadness, all the while living with a beautiful quiet inside. And I began to change my shape and form. I found a whole new me that I didn't know existed; friendships deepened and flourished, I loved working out and taking care of myself, I bought clothes that I never thought looked good on me, I found confidence to venture out on my own, travel alone, close my business, move cities, buy my house from my ex, rent it out, get a financially stable job and change and grow into the person I couldn't have imagined I would become.

But from this place of rapid change and this immensely light and jovial woman I had found inside me, I discovered a new layer that needed to be looked at. I developed an eating disorder. There was just so much darn change and I was feeling oh so good in many ways, but the speed of all of this change left me with a tiny toehold of ground to hang on to as my old life slipped away, but before the new me had roots deep enough to hold me during all of this change. And I wasn't engaging in my energy work as often as I should because I was feeling so good! I was getting high from running, exercise, walking everywhere and, to top it all off, I had created skinny legs the shape of which I never could have before imagined. I looked in the mirror and thought "damn girl, you are looking good". But there was a wise old soul within me that told me the skinny me looking back from the mirror was suffering, but I ignored that wise part of me because my skinny legs spoke louder, as did people's compliments. Many of these compliments sadly came from women who praised my skinniness, but there was nothing enviable about being hungry and boney. My Dad commented on how skinny I was and I said, "Thanks, I work really hard at it".

But once the rapid pace of change began to slow, I realized I was hungry. I was into my new job and my new city, my life had taken a new form and I felt I should be able to maintain the ferocious pace of exercise and fun that existed in the past few months. But I had to work really hard to resist eating. I began reading every label on the food I bought, making my rice really watery so it was "filling" but a bit less caloric, I denied myself tiny bites of food as I prepared my lunch for the next day. I drank a lot of coffee so I could continue to work out six days a week but it was becoming a struggle rather than the high it had been while all of the changes were happening. I would come home from a hard workout, shower and then do more sit ups at home before bed and, although I continued to engage in these behaviours, it broke my heart knowing what I was doing to myself. I would lift up my shirt every time I went to the bathroom to see if I was any fatter than I had been an hour before. The constant analysis of my shape and reflection was exhausting. Calf-raises at work, taking the stairs two at a time, the barrage on my body was endless. I scrubbed my body every night, I used baking soda on my teeth, I gargled with so much apple cider vinegar ("trying to aid my digestion") to the point that the skin peeled off the inside of my mouth. What was I really trying to do? Was it about being thin or having white teeth or smooth skin? In hindsight I see it was not. I was like a snake, trying to shed my old skin and my old life in any way I could. In this modern era many of us are not equipped with the skills to shed the old and become new; we lost this when we lost our connection with nature and our quieter selves, so I did the best I could.

One of the most profound moments for me was standing in front of the full-length mirror I had in my apartment. I had been crying because the internal dialogue of needing to be skinnier was relentless, reminded me that nothing I did was quite good enough and that no matter how hard I work my body isn't quite what it could be. In this moment I realized that I would never speak to another person with such poisonous words and would never let someone else speak to me this way, so why was I allowing myself such an assault? I made myself stand in front of my mirror and watched the tears that resulted from the endless barrage. I watched the tears fall, my body shake and I was brought to my knees, crying for all of the changes I had gone through, for everything I had let go, for all there was to figure out, for being a source of violence towards myself and for having created another secret that I needed to work through. I just wanted to be done with all of this growing and changing and just be at the end point where I am a new me and I don't have to work so bloody hard!

I finally told my Mum that I had some eating issues going on; I am pretty sure I used some vague language like this and I slowly began to acknowledge what was happening. I will digress for a moment and say that, during this time when I was travelling on my own, I met an amazing man in Guatemala. I came home after knowing him for nine days and said that I had never felt more adored in my life. He lived in England and, during this massive transition, we had kept in close contact, he had come to visit me and I was scheduled to head to England to see him. I told him about my eating issues and my worry that he wouldn't be as attracted to me if I gained weight. And you know what, the most remarkable thing happened, my concerns were met with compassion and reassurance. He is a breath of fresh air in my life, a cool drink of water on a hot day. Because we met after my anxiety shifted, he doesn't know me as the anxious person I spent so many years being and therefore he acts as a reflection of my true, un-anxious self. He sees me without the layers that I worked so hard to shed, and that is truly a gift.

In a recent skype session with Susan, she asked me how I would feel if I didn't need to find the words to identify all of the hurt, sadness and worry that I have felt in my life? What if I can heal these wounds and lay down my cards, and let go and move forward without having to find words for that kid who couldn't find her voice. And I cried, a deep soulful cry that let me know that my little self is being cleared and released from years of not feeling like she is enough, or okay just as she is. And I looked up to see Susan smiling at me. I am deeply comforted knowing she can see the beauty in this work and understands how deeply I will be rewarded for finding this buried sadness.

There is more work to be done and more layers to shed. I still from time to time fall into the old stomach analyzing patterns of seeing how fat I have become in the last 20 minutes, which usually happens when I am worried about money or the future mostly, the big questions of what I am going to do with my life. When I lack abundance in one area of my life, I want to eat. Or should I say, I have a heightened and judgmental awareness of my eating which has the tendency to bring up old habits. I hope with time I become better at being gentle with myself and letting go of the fear that these old habits will return. I strive for offering myself a simple acknowledgement that my life is a work in progress and I don't have to aim for perfection all of the time.

I recently had a gathering of friends, young and older, all of whom I love and have had such an impact on my life. It was a gift to sink in with these old friends and feel so grateful for the life I have been given and the friendships I have. One of my wise friends wondered aloud to me what would happen if I was a really good friend to myself? The deeply attentive, compassionate and steadfast friend that I am to others? Needless to say, I got the message. This friend, who I adore and respect and is oh so wise, offered me an olive branch to extend to myself and, because I was buoyed by all of the love of these amazing people who had come to see me, I got it. It sunk in and dug deep and grew roots deep enough to sustain this amazing idea of self-compassion. So I move forward glowing and shining and ready to listen to the quiet voice that knows all and has always known. The voice that has loved and cared for me even when I have been unable to love myself. The voice that will never lead me astray if I promise to hear the true messages and not what I hope will come of my life. Anything but the path that this crystal clear voice will lead me on is just not the right choice.

And so here I am living in England with an amazing man that I love so deeply, working through lessons that continue to show up, clearing what needs to be let go of and honouring who I am now, have been and am becoming. I am finding my voice and have been given a platform to share my story. I am sure my story seems quite average compared to the lives of many but it is a story which has been deeply challenging, nourishing and enlightening for me to live. I am standing on this platform sharing my story, not because it is exceptional, but because I think we all deserve a place to be heard. And here I am laying down my cards, letting go of the story that has shaped me into the person I am, and I am giving myself permission to move on and stop living the old and spend more time building the new. So much of the painful work is done and I am going to let it lie and know it is okay to move forward; that I will still be loved by many even if I free myself from this story of pain and hard work and struggle. What I am learning is that the growth never stops but the old stories can. I will spend the rest of my life pushing, stretching, moving, dancing, groaning, pulling, resisting, giving in, leaning into the darkness and reveling in the light. I continue to find peace and opportunities for growth and, for this, I am grateful with every part of my being.

\* \* \*

*Alex's background was inspired by her upbringing on a farm and her love of cooking. A master's degree in Sociology and a catering business followed, bridging her passion for organic food and small farms. Making the most of her transition to the UK, Alex has retrained and is now a Reiki and Flower Essence practitioner. She resides in London, England.*

# Earth School 101
## by Franziska Boon

There are so many journeys within my life that have tried and tested me, shaping me into who I am today. Yet I have been filled time and again with euphoric ecstasy, bursting with love and joy.

In this very moment I stand in a place of reflection; drawing back within myself to try and piece together my experiences in a cohesive fashion. It's difficult though, as epiphanies can dawn in a flash, offering new insights while obliterating the concept of space and time. So here I sit as I tentatively weave the tale of my unfolding and the blossoming of my spiritual self, limited only by self-imposed restrictions through the fear of standing fully in my truth as a Divine spark of light.

About ten years ago, around the age of 30, I had a very profound astral experience. I was lying down on my bed listening to a Magpie singing the most beautiful melody. At the time we were living in a rickety old cottage that we were renting at the foot of the Dandenong Ranges in Australia. The most majestic Oak tree stood outside my bedroom window. I was by myself and clean of any drugs or alcohol.

I felt my body become very relaxed while my mind remained sharp and alert. For an instant everything went black; however, I felt totally safe and secure. Then I was completely enveloped by the brightest white light. It had a slightly blue tinge, kind of like the "cool" white lighting choices within a hardware store. I was completely aware of being within my own consciousness and yet I was also aware of being connected with all other independent consciousnesses simultaneously. I realized that I was the source of my own light, even though I was connected to all the others. I sensed I was in the process of planning a major event as I was very busy communicating with the other sparks of light, asking for their assistance to fulfill various roles. I was planning my incarnation of the life that I am experiencing now.

It was hard to comprehend as our thought processes are somewhat limited within this three dimensional reality. We perceive things from a more linear perspective; however, what I was experiencing was beyond this. I witnessed myself in my light-form asking for assistance from other independent light-forms, even though we were all connected as a whole. I had criteria I wanted to achieve and here I was as an etheric form excitedly brainstorming how this lifetime would unfold.

My mind was so expansive as there were no limits. What a ride!!! You'd think I was Jerry Garcia from "The Grateful Dead" tripping on LSD. At one point I recognized my father and brother from my current life. I was passionately asking my father to be malicious towards me. I really wanted him to fulfill his role within my journey. He obliged and remained one of the most amplified parts of this astral journey upon recall.

When I came to, I was shocked as I pondered exactly what this meant within the context of the reality I had known as opposed to the one that would be forever altered if I allowed myself to expand with the insights I had been given. My whole world was turned upside down. There was so much to reflect upon, revaluate and let go of. This meant I couldn't be a victim anymore after knowing I had chosen to enrol in Earth School 101.

I began to see reflections about myself within all of my relationships, be they through blood, friends, acquaintances or randoms. The anger I had carried within me no longer had a place other than to serve as my attachment to the pattern I had become familiar living with. This was some very heavy shit to consider as it placed responsibility for myself within self. I didn't know if I was ready for this, or if I wanted to become Mary Fucking Poppins!

I was confused because my life had held so much emotional pain, and to rise above that physical experience and take the higher spiritual road meant doing a hell of a lot of inner work to release my limitations. How do you do that? How do you wipe away all the perceived wrongs, abuse, abandonment issues, betrayal, disappointment, mistrust and lack of self-worth? How? How do you share this epiphany with someone who probably has never considered what has prompted you to explore yourself on a deeper level inspired by cosmic surrender? I was lost; I felt even more alone because I knew that it was going to be a long road of self -discovery, healing and forgiveness.

The irony is that my father is the very one I pleaded with most to be a really destructive force within my life. I kept shaking my head knowing that I had ultimately created this. The wounds were so deep and the painful memories so raw. I still feel the sadness well up within me as I write these words, showing me I have more layers to move through so I may heal and liberate myself. It's funny because I've had many good memories with my

Dad; however, the ones that impacted me most are the ones that spring forward first. How sad that we can allow ourselves to be restricted by our pain. It takes so much energy to hold onto the pain because of the fear we have about facing our demons and truly letting go. Forgiveness is so much more than just a word. Why do I allow myself to be stuck and depleted by the misery of my past? Why do I struggle to implement what I know I need to do? These are just a few of the merry-go-round thoughts that recycle through my head. The perpetual onion full of layers.

My earliest recall of accepting a negative program within my belief system came forward in my early twenties during a kinesiology session I had with my Doctor. The Physician I was seeing had actually delivered me as an infant. Sheila had given up her regular medical practice and was inspired by Louise Hay's work.

We were focusing on core believes around self-worth, trying to go back to the earliest implant about myself. I was able to clairvoyantly see throughout the process with my insights being validated through the muscle testing technique performed by Sheila. I saw myself in utero at eight months gestation. I was aware of my mother feeling incredibly sad, rejected, angry and hurt. I expanded my awareness to see what caused her emotional reaction. I became aware of my mother standing in the lobby of a hotel during the day. I saw a phone in her hand. I heard my father's voice on the other end. She told him that she was in the lobby of the hotel and she knew he was having sex with his secretary. He didn't deny the fact.

In that moment I felt all of my mother's emotion and accepted it as my own. I adopted a program which impacted my self-worth as a female. It created a handicap which filtered through my perception of the world. My mother was a devote Irish Catholic in a foreign country about to birth her first child. Her ideal had been shattered and, because of her indoctrination, she believed she had to grin and bear it.

My next earliest memory was when I was an infant. I was in a cot, however I wasn't stringing words together yet. I could clearly see my yellow room with my cot placed close to the window with sheer billowy curtains. I was upset and crying my eyes out because no one would come in and pick me up. It seemed like hours had passed. An incredible rage built up within me. I felt abandoned and neglected by my mother. Later in life I learned that my mother would often leave me alone to do shopping up the street while I was having a nap. I shared what I had recalled with my mother, expressing how that made me feel emotionally; feelings she quickly dismissed.

I know my parents love me; however, I've become more aware of how my perceived shortcomings have been due to their need to fulfil their own souls' contracts for whatever level of personal growth. This insight offers me an opportunity to try and remain objective while alleviating so many emotions. However, being able to integrate this through your being and consciousness is quite a different story filled with many chapters and evolving sequels as a human being.

As a small child I was very striking to look at, with nearly white hair, big brown eyes and a rosebud mouth. People would often stop and comment on how beautiful I was. My father was proud to show me off. He could connect with small children and animals in such a kind and loving way. I used to spend hours as a toddler floating in an inflatable boat watching the birds in the sky. Sometimes I would even crawl out of the house without anyone knowing, only to be found in the pool to everyone's shock horror ... which earned me the nickname Sneaker.

I was memorized by all creatures great and small, and I loved the water. Apparently Mum's little Poodle, Putzi, wouldn't acknowledge me for the first six weeks after they brought me home from the hospital. The dog had been her baby and Mum used to carry him around in her handbag like a celebrity accessory. It didn't take long before Putzi and I became very close. We moved from suburbia to the country when I was in grade two, which opened a whole new world to explore. The close-knit relationships I had known with neighbourhood children were replaced with school bullies who tormented me. For years I would come home every day crying, often with scrapes on my knees from being pushed to the ground. I would ask my mother if ugly girls would grow up pretty. The same question every time.

A deep sorrow grew in my heart at being subjected to such cruelty and unkindness. Animals became my salvation as they offered such unconditional love. I could connect with them telepathically. I could sense when their presence was near or what they needed. I felt completely at home in nature with my only fears being of snakes and, later, blood. We lived on large acreage surrounded by wild woodland with a creek running through our property. I would leave straight after breakfast and come home for dinner. No one would know where I was or even bother coming to check. I would follow animal tracks, build forts, climb trees and create dams to divert water to play in calm pools. I always felt safe and knew I wasn't alone.

I would play with a Native American Indian spirit who taught me many things. He looked after me. I've since developed a closer bond with him and have learned that Running Bear is one of my guides. He has been with me from birth and will be with me when I die. I have shut him out in the past and feel humbled that he's still at my side, loving and guiding me unconditionally. Encouraging me to step more fully into the truth of who I am.

My very best friend was my German Shepherd Maxi, who went everywhere with me. I was never alone with Maxi at my side and Running Bear with me in spirit. I would curl up next to her amongst the wildflowers while my little fingers would comb through her black and tan hair. Our relationship was pure love. She knew my heart and soul and I loved her more than life itself. I would have died a thousand deaths for that dog.

One night our family was awoken to the sound of carnal howling and scratching. My father went downstairs to investigate with me and my mother close behind. The strange sounds were coming from the semi-enclosed front entrance, which was constructed of stone with a high ceiling. My father turned on the outside light and peered out the window. There was blood sprayed everywhere and Maxi was the one making the painful sounds. My mother became hysterical and immediately phoned the vet who couldn't drive out and needed to be picked up. My father had to take my mother with him because she had lost the plot. I sat in the family room with Maxi, trying to soothe her. She had been shot three times and there was blood everywhere. My nightgown stuck to my skin like in a sick horror movie. The rest is a blur. The vet was unable to remove the bullets, including one shot between the eyes that fragmented in her nasal cavity. We were blessed to have Maxi with us for a number of years after. At the end she had to be put to sleep when the fragments in her head started moving causing her great pain and distress. I hated my father for making that decision. It's because of Maxi I'm still alive. She saved both my brother's and my life from a serial killer.

Like I've mentioned before, we lived in the country with no neighbours visibly in sight. Our house was located at the end of a long driveway with very few windows orientated towards the top of the driveway. My younger brother and I were waiting for the big yellow bus to take us to school. It seemed like too much time had passed with no sign of the bus when a navy blue station wagon pulled up. An old man leaned over the vinyl bench seat and rolled down his passenger window. He told us we were late for school and that we'd get into trouble if we didn't hurry up and get there. He offered to drive us. I told him we don't speak to strangers. He opened the passenger door and grabbed my baby brother and started to pull him into the station wagon. Meanwhile, Maxi was causing such a fuss inside the house that my mother thought she needed to use the toilet so she let her outside. She ran up the driveway and jumped into the car between the old man and my brother with the hairs on her back standing up on end while baring her teeth and growling. I started to run down the driveway when I realized my brother was frozen still with fear. I ran back and grabbed his arm so he'd run down the driveway with me. Halfway down I called for Maxi who immediately followed. I heard the motor of the car roar behind us. I saw my mother reversing the Volkswagen Camper van out of the garage. I managed to open the sliding door and all three of us jumped into the camper as the wagon swerved to miss hitting my mother's vehicle, tearing up the lawn to escape. My heart was pounding through my chest. I knew what the old man wanted to do to us and it sent chills through every fibre of my being. The police came to our school and questioned us.

My mother slept with a fire poker under her pillow after that as my father was often away working. When I was about 19 years old I opened the newspaper and screamed as an icy chill crawled over my skin. There on the front cover was the exact same man who tried to abduct us. The police struggled to convict him for decades as they believed he was responsible for over thirty children's deaths. He died of a heart attack before justice could be served. It wasn't time for neither my brother nor I to cross the veil. For most of my childhood I preferred to play without my younger brother as I felt I was expected to look after him. He was the golden child, a boy, which in my eyes was the better sex to be if you could choose. I didn't want to resent my brother as I really did love him even though we were treated differently the older we got. The closer I came to puberty the more sexist and domineering my father became towards me. Soon my brother started exhibiting the same attitude towards me, which was equally crushing. My mother had no power in changing the situation and I judged her for her weakness.

I could feel the distinction being made between the two of us by our father as he would often say one thing and do another. I knew when my father was lying as I was sensitive and psychic. I could read my father and he didn't want to acknowledge that. The anger and frustration towards me built within him. I would never back down as the warrior within me could see through him and challenged the hypocrisy he represented. As far as I was concerned he'd have to beat me into submission before I would back down from what I believed to be true.

When I was in grade six it was decided that our family was going to move back east to Ontario, leaving behind my beloved mountains of the west. I was devastated as I associated so many dark memories with living in Burlington. The school year had already started and we moved to Oakville, close to the Lakeshore. It was a total shock to my carefree nature-loving way of life. The houses were so close together. There was tension between my parents. I was a tomboy who loved dirt biking, not pea coats and penny loafers.

The downward spiral of depression enveloped me yet again. I didn't know how to be accepted or fit in. I was alone without emotional support. I wanted to die. I was desperately grieving the loss of my home and my friends. My parents weren't interested in how I was coping so I disconnected even more.

At night I would lock myself in my room and listen to John Waite's song "I Ain't Missing You" or Cyndi Lauper's "Time After Time" and Paul Young's "Every Time You Go Away", over and over again. The grief and depression built as my soul became numb. I just wanted to make the pain go away. I couldn't exist like this anymore. No one understood me or even cared as far as I was concerned. I was living in hell and I couldn't see a single way out. I felt like there was no hope, with my soul becoming heavier and heavier.

I started to sense a shadowy presence in my room at night. It would speak to me in a seductive tone, almost entrancing me with its words. It seemed to understand my pain and the darkness within my being. Slowly, over a couple of months this entity grew stronger, feeding on my pain; manipulating my thoughts with its own perverse desire to take over my body. I was unaware of its intentions then; however, as I write it becomes clearer to me now. I was being tormented at school and just wanted eternal sleep. Finally the day arrived. I went up to my room, lit a candle and turned on my music. I became entranced by the atmosphere, looking at how the light danced off the edge of the razor blade. I could feel the excitement building at the idea of escaping this torture. The shadow being lulling me like a baby, encouraging me to cut slowly. I didn't feel a thing as I watched each droplet of blood spill from my body. I carved patterns into my left arm from my elbow to my finger tips. I played X's and O's on my flesh.

When I was done I walked downstairs in an altered state to get a drink of water. My mother grabbed my arm in anger to tell me off for drawing on myself with a red marker when she realized it was my own blood. She started screaming at me, throwing things across the room in terror. I hid between the wall and the couch while my mother went into the kitchen and smashed dishes onto the floor. I rocked back and forth in fetal position humming a soft tune to myself.

"Wait till your father gets home!" screamed my mother. "For what?" I thought. "So he can crush me some more. Why can't I even get dying right? Why the fuck am I here? Why isn't there a God? I want to sleep forever because life is too painful. Please take me, please take me now. I promise I'll be good a girl. Just don't let me feel sad anymore."

My thoughts were swimming inside my head. And just like that, it was all swept under the carpet. My parents took me out shopping for a new outfit from Reitman's clothing store to make me feel better. Unfortunately, the kids at school saw the scabs on my arm and told the teacher. Every Tuesday I was taken out of class for counselling at school. The students put two and two together, which gave them a whole new twisted lot of ammunition to bully me with. I was told I was too stupid to kill myself and maybe I should sharpen my razor better for next time. My younger brother chimed in. The next time I took pills and was sent to school even though I was so sick, they didn't work either. We returned to our home in British Columbia before the school year was out. Being back in the Okanagan saved my soul and brought sanity back to my life. I was eleven years old.

Life was good again. Dad wasn't home that much and we lived in paradise. I spent the majority of my time outdoors either swimming, dirt biking, boating, exploring and skiing. I got along with most of the kids from school and my confidence grew as I blossomed into a teenager. I really enjoyed playing hard and found that I often hung out with the guys.

I still found that I was having spiritual experiences like premonitions that actually came true. This freaked me out a bit. With the age of sixteen came the sweet freedom of driving legally on the road in my sky blue Meyers Manx type dune buggy. It had an 1800cc dual carb VW engine with a short wheel base and three separate hand brakes. It ROCKED and sounded so good! I had steel wings of petrol grunt to fly with. I was on top of the world and life felt like it couldn't get any better, until my folks announced they were moving back to Ontario. I refused to move with them as I had been accepted into an amazing program called Earth Quest, an outdoor-based program for year eleven students. I had been accepted the previous year and had forfeited my place with my classmates when my parents bought a house in White Rock, British Columbia. They ended up selling before we ever lived there. I wasn't prepared to miss this opportunity again as there were limited places and it was my passion. Plus I had my first true love.

I put an ad in a local paper and found a basement apartment to rent when the course started in autumn. When summer arrived my brother and I drove across Canada towing my dune buggy behind filled with all of my mother's plants and the dog. It took us four days along the Trans-Canada Highway. My parents' new home was a diamond in the rough below the Bruce Trail escarpment. It needed a lot of work which was something my father was really good at.

I got a full-time job at Harvey's fast food joint to save up for my course, apartment and flight back to Vernon. I worked as many hours as I could and helped around the property when I wasn't working. It was insane how run-down the place was, and it was crawling with snakes. I'd shoot a couple a day with an air gun pistol. I hated stepping on them!

September rolled around and I left my family completely confident with my decision at the age of seventeen. I had saved every penny and paid my own way. I was looking forward to my independence and freedom. My apartment was cosy, Earth Quest was awesome and I scored a job at Silver Star Mountain as a ski instructor, providing me with a free season's ski pass.

Life felt pretty good; however, my boyfriend was having an extremely difficult time as his parents were going through a nasty divorce. They had only gotten married because his mother had accidentally fallen pregnant. There was no love between his folks and his mother was a petite freak. His father was really cool though and I was very fond of him.

As with many kids our age, we enjoyed experimenting with drugs as it was a great form of escapism which we did all the time. Shortly after Christmas I became pregnant. My boyfriend wanted me to abort the baby, given our lifestyle and his family history. I couldn't imagine making that choice. I knew the baby and I weren't wanted so I left the mountains for the last time, to face the wrath of my father. He was furious and demanded that I get rid of the baby. He made every waking minute as miserable as he possibly could. I got two jobs and worked ten hours a day, six days a week to pay my way.

At one point my mother and brother flew to Ireland to visit family for a month. My best friend was coming out for a month to visit and I was so excited. There was a two-day window where I was left alone with my father. He tried to bully me into having a termination at five months gestation. I refused. I told him if he laid one hand on me I would take one of his guns out of the cabinet and blow his fucking brains out. He backed off slightly, acting nice when Jenny arrived. It was so healing spending time together. She even sewed me a bunch of baby clothes. She was the only one I allowed to touch my belly as I hated being pregnant. Her friendship, love and support meant the world to me. It was hard for her too because she was adopted and trying to find her birth mother so we were both going through a journey that paralleled on some levels. Her visit ended shortly after my family flew home and the little bit of joy she brought left with her. It didn't help that I was constantly having nightmares of government type agents dressed in black constantly chasing me, trying to kill an abandoned baby I had found. It was like being in the Matrix with me often fighting three or more of these astral beings. After a while I gave up trying to just defend myself and started to fight back with the intent to kill. Yet they anticipated my every move, with me always narrowly escaping with the baby in tow.

Two weeks before my due date I went into McMaster University Hospital as my instincts told me something was wrong. My baby wasn't moving. I was immediately put on a fetal heart monitor where they found a faint pulse. They shook me hard to wake the baby up, with no response. I was told I was being admitted as the baby was in distress and had to be birthed within ten hours. I wasn't prepared for this even though I had a private labour support person I had done classes with who was going to be there for the birth. I didn't have my overnight bag, Gatorade or my focal point. I pleaded with them to let me go and promised I'd come back as I needed to process what was happening. I was given a gown and admitted into a birthing suite.

My cervix was inspected and showed no signs of being ready as it hadn't thinned or effaced. A few minutes later another nurse came and told me she was going to break my waters to get things going. At the tender age of eighteen I was feeling very nervous and shy. I felt violated as the process was extremely painful. The fluids gushed down my thighs and soaked the bed. I thought I was going to vomit and pass out. It was like I was in this echo or a surreal bubble. I think my guides were trying to lift me above the trauma of what I was experiencing. My mother arrived and started acting like a chicken with its head cut off. I asked her to leave as I couldn't cope with her energy. My labour support person was with another client who happened to be two weeks overdue, and I was two weeks early. I was on my own and open for full viewing as groups of medical students in training were paraded through my suite without my permission. Talk about birth rape!

I was in a lot of pain as I had fractured my coccyx during my first trimester of pregnancy and that's how I found out I was pregnant. I had been given Pitocin to speed up labour and the contractions were fierce, with little reprieve between. I wanted an epidural and my support person arrived just in time and was allowed to stay as she was a registered nurse. Unfortunately I had a lot of calcium deposits built up between my vertebrae and they ended up using a rubber hammer on four different spots before the needle would go in.

I birthed in silence. At 4:05AM my 6.1lbs baby girl was born blue with the cord around her neck four and a half times. She didn't pink up with oxygen and was as white as a sheet of paper. She didn't make a sound. Her Apgar score was two. While they were seeing to her, the reality of having just given birth and the responsibility of this new life came crashing down on me. I asked the nurse if I could brush my teeth before I went to my daughter. I needed to do something grounding. My support person quickly brought her to me and gently but firmly told me to kiss my baby before she was whisked away to the Neonatal Intensive Care unit. I named her Alissa.

I drove to the hospital twice a day every day so I could express my milk and freeze it for her. It was so intense seeing the room where all these tiny babies where plugged into machines to survive. The room constantly changing, with no comments about what happened to the wee soul who had been there a couple of hours ago. I was overwhelmed and was tearing up outside the unit in the hallway when a female East Indian doctor stopped me and asked why I was crying. She suggested that I should consider funeral arrangements for my daughter. I lost it and I didn't care about respecting my elder in that moment.

"You fucking can't tell me if my baby is going to make it through the night and you have the nerve to ask me why I'm crying. Just because I'm young doesn't mean I don't care. I didn't fight this hard to bring this baby into this world to lose her now!"

I realized I needed to harness this energy and channel it towards Alissa in a positive way so she could fight too. I could finally see a link that connected us which ignited my drive to truly become her mother as I hadn't made the connection during my entire pregnancy. My life had purpose because I had something to live for that needed and solely depended on me. I started to think about the future from a new perspective and embraced living my life as opposed to just existing in it.

There were times when I really struggled, though, as I was grieving the loss of my freedom of youth. But I stopped letting my situation define me. My dear friend Jenny gave me the book, "Simple Abundance" for my birthday, which sparked an inward journey of healing. I found when I focused on the positive things in my life more opportunities flowed my way. I started to see how the Universal fabric that connects us responds to every vibration we put out, devoid of judgement given the law of attraction. I set goals for myself and started believing in my potential to achieve them.

Little did I know what the next twenty years would hold as I went inward facing the dark night of the soul. Today, I am rebirthing myself into my divine soul purpose as a Psychic Medium. I am so blessed to have the loving support of my beautiful husband Mark and our two amazing children Phoenix and Malachi. I'm smiling to myself because today is Alissa's 23rd birthday and I've just finished my chapter. Alissa brought me the gift of change, a catalyst for personal growth and healing. I am so proud of the woman, wife and mother she has become.

* * *

*Franziska is a Psychic Medium certified by internationally recognized Psychic Medium, Lisa Williams. She had the honour of sharing the stage with her mentor doing a Platform Demonstration in Melbourne on August 23, 2013. She is also a qualified Permaculture Designer who values the subtle influences of Biodynamics. An eternal hippy at heart, she married her Aussie backpacking hubby on stage at the 1999 Woodstock Concert in Rome New York. Franziska is a Spiritual Healer, Spirit Artist, mother of three, nanny Franny of two and spruiker of sustainability & environmental awareness. For more information visit www.franziskaboon.com.*

# Ten Years in the Desert
## Life Beyond Divorce
### by Lori Bateman

*"Sometimes your only available transportation is a leap of faith"*
~ Margaret Shepard

It was late October, just before winter began, when I stood in the rec room of our rented house nestled in the northern Ontario town of Haliburton. I stared blankly at my husband across the room. He was angry and yelling because he wanted to set up a trust fund for our six-month-old son and he didn't think that I could be trusted with the money. As I listened to his rationalizations, I distinctly remember a tingling sensation on the back of my neck that trickled down my spine. When I look back at the many times in my life when I felt that same sensation, it usually came just before an event and that I was meant to pay attention. I learned to recognize it as my intuition that was hinting in an oh-so-subtle way, that change was coming and that I would be required to take a leap of faith. In this case, the leap of faith involved leaving my marriage. It was perhaps the biggest leap I have ever taken and perhaps the most life affirming move because it was in the years that followed, when I was on my own, that my journey back to being in relationships began.

In the last couple of years of my marriage, I had become an angry, resentful woman who felt lost and unrecognizable to the person I knew myself to be. The years of bad decisions, unemployment, bill collectors, moving, mistrust and financial irresponsibility on both our parts had taken its toll to the point where I wanted out.. And it was not an easy decision. I tossed and turned for two years to arrive at the moment when it was time to move on and knew that if I didn't, I was doomed to live the same life over and over again. Deciding to leave was terrifying because of the uncertainty and the unknown of how I would look after my two young boys, aged two and five, yet I knew I had reached a defining moment when my fear was surpassed by my willingness to move forward without knowing how it would all go.

*"And the day came when the risk to remain tight inside the bud was more painful than the risk it took to blossom."* Anais Nin

What followed were a few very difficult years that were compounded by the death of my parents within months of each other, my oldest son's autism diagnosis and learning to live on my own through many breakdowns. It was also a very reflective time that profoundly altered my life and led me to where I am today. I firmly believe now that we all need to spend some time on our own, that it is a service to ourselves and our own growth to be independent and to learn who we are inside of life's circumstances. Surviving on my own with my boys was the biggest challenge of my life and it gave me an inner strength that I wouldn't have learned otherwise. Was it tough? Absolutely.

In my case it was especially hard because I was mourning my parents while maintaining the daily routine of raising my boys. Independent of the other, my dad went first following a brain operation that he didn't fully recover from; four months to the day later, my mother died of liver failure from having had a transplant seven years earlier. It was everything I could do to get through the day, to get home and get to bed so I could cry and grieve on my own time in my own space. I was so sad and felt so lost without my mother. It was such a shock to me that the woman who I loved and depended on wasn't there anymore. I felt like I had the wind knocked out of me. Fortunately and as a stroke of divine intervention, I received a bereavement counseling package through my insurance at work and, since I had two close family deaths within a year, I was awarded a longer bereavement time. Every moment was crucial support as I worked through such a deep and painful sense of loss.

Losing my parents was even more traumatic as I faced my new life as a single mother and then as an orphan. I really did feel completely alone. Even though my brother was close, he was living his own life and was grieving in his own way. He had to come to terms with being on his own in a different way and without children of his own. I was blessed to have a few good friends who carried me through that time, who would check in on me, take me to movies and let me cry through the whole thing or listen endlessly to my sadness. My boys were too little to understand what happened and in many ways I was so happy to have them in my life at the time because they became my reason for getting up every day. I had to feed my children.

Since grieving is such a deeply personal experience and is different for each us, I was grateful to be on my own and not in a relationship. Even though it was an incredibly lonely time, where I feared I would get swallowed up by the pain, I was relieved to not have to explain my silence or moments of sadness that would wash over me at unpredictable times. Through my counseling I learned to allow my feelings to come up and acknowledge them, instead of denying them. It was a very freeing process to actually go into the raw, scary dark emotions and to learn that I wouldn't die myself if I experienced them. I also saw that my worst fear of losing my mother had come true. It happened and I survived. Looking back and even at the time, I felt an inner peace with being able to express myself freely without having to explain myself to a partner. Because I really went into the emotion of what I was feeling, I really think that my healing time was shortened, not that there is a rush or a time frame, but for me, I realized that I had moved on in a healthy way, by acknowledging what I was experiencing and by giving it space.

I miss my parents terribly at times and even though I am in constant dialogue with them in spirit, it is of course not the same as having them here. There is, however, a sense of peace that I have with having really grieved them. That process led me to forgive them in a way that put our past in the past so it no longer affects me when I talk about that time of my life. For many years I blamed them for my inadequacies and insecurities. I judged them for a decision they made back in 1963 when I was four and they were young married immigrants from Scotland, wanting to divorce. For our safety and to be sure we would be well looked after, they decided to send my one-year-old brother and me to live with our aunt and uncle in Michigan. Since we were very young and didn't know them, they were total strangers to us. Later, as an adult, I blamed my parents and called them irresponsible for not telling me that I was going there. It was a terrifying experience for me as a child to one day be living with my parents and the next to be living with strangers and not know why. Of course I thought it had something to do with me. For years I blamed them for my feelings of not being good enough. When they were alive, I learned the whole story and still blamed them for a long time. It defined me in many ways and gave me something to be angry about as if it somehow legitimized my experience. My former husband often said that I was angry and just wanted something to be angry about. Part of wanting to be on my own was to address that part of myself because I recognized it also, but never really knew how to deal with it. At some point later in my life, well after my parents had passed, it no longer made sense to be angry at them; they were dead, it seemed pointless. Forgiving them for their decision that they made out of love for wanting us safe took a long time for me to accept. I had to realize that their decision to send us to live with our aunt and uncle was the best they knew in that moment and that even though I would have done it differently had I been in the same situation, it didn't mean that it was wrong. It also took me a while to learn that it was okay for me to be angry and scared as I was as a child but to carry those feelings into my adulthood and keep blaming my parents for something that happened so long ago was actually a waste of my energy. I saw that I was carrying around an experience that no longer had any relevance to my current life and that the old feelings I associated with had softened also. At some point I saw how much effort it took to stay angry and resentful, and decided it wasn't worth it.

Learning to be responsible for the way I respond to circumstances or events was something I learned over the years when I was on my own and it seemed as though there were endless opportunities to learn this lesson. One especially tough time was when my son was about six, just after he had been diagnosed with Autism (which was later updated to Aspergers). Those early years were very challenging as I learned to handle his behavior and support him with predictable routines and safe environments. A big part of learning to manage autistic characteristics is to understand how important it is for the person to have predictable schedules and routines and when something is out of sync it usually leads to a meltdown that can last anywhere from five minutes to two hours. Because meltdowns would affect a whole evening and definitely would influence an event, I did everything to anticipate a possible situation that could throw him off. It was like trying to hold off the rain because rain was perceived as a threat. I was very reactive in those days, by getting angry or frustrated. I would yell back or cry when I didn't know what to do. My excuse for the way I reacted was that I was in over my head dealing with a child who needed help, but who I didn't know how to help. I had support from behavioral counselors thankfully, but even after an evening of discussing different strategies they would go home and I would be left to apply what I learned to all kinds of different outbursts and situations. It was overwhelming and exhausting. AND I never gave up. My reaction to the way my son reacted was not always graceful and when he would have a meltdown or tantrum I would sometimes be right along there with him because I was so stressed. One defining moment came to me when we both collapsed on the stairs in our home after a particularly exhausting struggle that involved hysterics and tantrums and aggressive behavior that he couldn't control or didn't have the tools for at the time. I realized that I had to do something about my stress and the way it was affecting me. To get a different result, I had to do something differently, so I asked God, the Universe to help me find a better way to manage it all.

The answer that appeared within days or weeks was a form of chiropractic called Network Spinal Analysis that literally stopped the meltdowns, aggressive behavior and restored my son to a peaceful child whose nervous system calmed down enough for him to become less reactive. For me, the anger left my body little by little with each session and I too became less reactive and calmer. Dr. Anthony Posa, to whom I am eternally grateful, was sent from God as far as I'm concerned. It was also one of those times when I received a nudge from the Universe and I took a leap of faith. I've always been interested in holistic treatments and more of a natural lifestyle, and being on my own allowed me to follow my inner guidance and to explore many different modalities and practices that may have seemed a little off the wall to most people. However, when I have followed my gut, it has usually led me to a positive solution. The NSA sessions were life-altering for me and my boys as each of us experienced a new sense of calmness that allowed our bodies to soften and our emotions to be less reactive. For my son with Aspergers, it meant less aggression in his body which enabled him to listen to instruction instead of going into fight mode. This made a huge difference for our family dynamic since meltdowns meant that my entire focus went to restoring peace while my younger son sat on the sidelines feeling left out. NSA was really the beginning of a new way of being for all of us.

One of my favourite things to do when I was single was to discover new interests and do things that I enjoyed. It was also a big part of my healing when I was grieving my parents. I discovered that I loved to ride my bicycle down by the lakeshore in downtown Toronto, or around Lake Drive on Lake Simcoe, where my mum and her husband's family had a cottage when I was growing up. A friend from work gave me a bike rack for my car which was a huge gift because I used it a lot, and took my bike everywhere. I would wake up early on a Saturday or Sunday morning, pack my journal and a snack in my backpack and off I would go to ride for hours. On the mornings when the boys were returning from their dad's, I would go early so I could get home in time to greet them. I would go to movies, often on my own if a friend wasn't available, and I enjoyed taking writing courses on the one night of the week I had to myself.

I also took up rollerblading after being at a party one night where I met a cute younger man, six years my junior, who had an extra pair and asked me if I wanted to go "blading." "Sure!" I replied," how hard could it be? I love to skate so why not! " It turned out to be an amazing fun sport that I love and have a natural ability for. It also led to a nice little romance with the young man. By the time he showed up, I had been on my own for a couple of years and I was beginning to heal from my parents. I was really enjoying being single and since I had my hands full with working and raising my boys, I didn't really think of romance or relationships, so it was quite a fun surprise to suddenly be interested in a man again. AND he was hugely different from my husband which is probably why I liked him. He turned out to be such a gift to my life at a time when it all felt very hard. During the week I was totally consumed with the daily stress and routine of being mom and on the weekends when my boys were with their dad, I would escape into another world with my friend. We would rollerblade by the lake, have relaxing picnics in his living room and passionate sex on his water bed! We had no expectations or commitments to one another which allowed me to enjoy our time together and for my fun side to emerge. It felt like I hadn't really had a great time in years and it was so refreshing to be appreciated without any expectation. He liked me for who I was and since he didn't have children, we were both happy to have a frivolous short-term relationship. Inside this perfect fling, my heart opened and my sadness gradually diminished. It was a pure escape from my difficult life as a single mom.

After about a year of casual sex and occasional get-togethers, I grew less and less interested. There was never a chance for our relationship to develop into anything more, so I found myself enjoying it less and less. About a year after we stopped seeing each other, I met another man who really turned my world upside down and not in a good way! I went on a blind date and ended up falling hard and fast and  thought he had it all going on. He was interesting, a great communicator, was keenly interested in me and he showed a huge interest in my boys. (Big points!) He didn't rollerblade but he did dance and bike ride and he had great taste in music. Unfortunately he was a closet alcoholic. I say closet because it wasn't obvious to me. After we split up I could see the signs but because I had never experienced being around an alcoholic, I didn't realize that the three or four glasses he drank to my one were a problem. When we went for dinner, he was quick to order a bottle of wine and, before I was on my second glass, he was on the second bottle. In private, as it turns out, when I wasn't with him, he drank enough to fill about two or three small garbage bins (which I saw on occasion in his laneway beside his house, and didn't put two and two together until after the fact). Our relationship ended abruptly when I turned up at his house one night to surprise him. The man who flung open the door had dark sunken eyes that bore into me like a crazed animal as I watched him bounce off the wall and stumble over himself and into the

kitchen at the end of the hall. I knew I was dealing with a completely different person than the one I was dating. I was terrified and kept my back to
the wall as I inched along the hall back to the front door. The whole time
he shouted strange insults at me about how I interrupted his little party.

The relationship may have ended but what actually happened was more
of a personal awakening. A good friend talked me down when I was in-
consolable, telling me he was a "psychic vampire" and that I was best off
to find out about him early in the relationship. I agreed through my tears
but I was heartbroken. I really enjoyed our time together and I really liked
the way he treated me. He sent me flowers at work, took me out for nice
dinners, spent time with me and my boys, took me for weekend getaways
and bought me little gifts. What was not to like? What really got me was
how much I had been fooled and that I had actually fallen for someone
who was so "troubled" and the opposite of anyone I wanted to be with. I
went on a crusade to learn about alcoholics…their behaviours and characteristics, which led me to learn about codependency. I devoured Melody
Beattie's book, "Codependent No More" practically in one sitting, and a
whole new way of seeing myself and my relationships started to emerge.
I saw that I was codependent, which meant wanting to take on other people's problems and make them my own, or to take on other's drama and
make it more important than myself. I saw that, apart from the alcohol, I
had attracted a man who was not dissimilar to my former husband. This
revelation sent me on a whole new journey to change the patterns that I
saw in myself which had always led me to attract men who were either
abusive, controlling, angry or dominating.

It was four years before I ventured into another relationship. I really was
afraid of repeating the same pattern and attracting the same kind of person.
I didn't have a barometer to measure against so couldn't be certain, so I
stayed away from men completely. I began to do courses and attend workshops and, in 2005, I did a program that changed my life in many ways.
As I was sitting there on the Saturday afternoon, I was hit by an emotional
brick, hurling its way across the room, when I realized that the long distance relationship that I had most recently attracted, for the most part
looked like it was much different from the others. I felt somewhat safe venturing into new territory for this man was spiritually evolved, successful,
worldly, kind, generous and he didn't have any obvious addictions! The
brick that hit me, however, was to show me how needy I was and that I
was actually doing a dance to please him to ensure that he liked me.
"What??!!" I thought I had learned my lessons with men! You mean I'm

not fixed yet!! Well, I spent the rest of that relationship attempting to be noticed and jumping through hoops to get his attention. As it turns out, he liked me but he just wasn't into me in a way that I fantasized about. And of course this fed into my "I'm not good enough" profile that I painted of myself when I was young. I still felt there was more work to be done because I knew in some way that I had something to do with who I was attracting into my life.

In the meantime, I spent a lot of time with my boys and really gave them my full attention as often as possible. In the summers we rode our bikes through the many paths around our house, we swam in nearby lakes and pools, had tobogganing parties in the winter, went skating on the local pond. We went to movies, played board games, learned simple games on the computer (way before Facebook and YouTube!) We had sleepovers with friends, cottages or camping trips in the summer. I really enjoyed my time with them and felt like a tight little unit. With all the personal development I was doing, my relationship with my ex began to shift also. After a few tumultuous years while we established custody arrangements and when there was a lot of anger and hostility, we eventually got to a point where we agreed to get along for the sake of our boys. They had been going back and forth the whole time between our homes and what was really great was that we got to a point where we were able to take short vacations together. I knew we had evolved when we agreed to take the boys to Ottawa one summer about four or five years after we separated. We each had a room with a door between us so they could go back and forth between our rooms. Once my younger son began racing motocross, much of our family time was spent together on weekends at the tracks where he raced. There was a lot of driving and shuffling him around and we also did a couple of trips to the US together. I was able to go on these trips because I wasn't yet in a relationship with anyone new and neither was my ex. I was clear about it being my choice to go and that I was there for my boys and to make it easier for their dad, since long distance trips could be stressful for only one parent.

During the years on my own, I got to know myself in a way that I wouldn't have if I had been married. I was able to spend time getting to know what I liked, what excited me and what I valued. It also meant that I took responsibility for my own happiness when I realized that it didn't come from another person or circumstance. When it was tough and I was on my knees begging for change, I saw that I was part of the solution and that if I altered the way I responded or reacted then that would make a difference. I

43

learned to be resourceful and to figure out problems without losing my cool and realized that there is indeed a solution to every problem. I gave up drama when I saw that I played a role and that by disengaging, I would no longer be involved in the dance. I made it my mission to be the best mom I could be for my boys which meant being honest with myself when I was the one having the tantrum! I changed my story from being the victim of an unhappy childhood and blaming my parents for the way I turned out, to forgiving them and letting go of the past which no longer has anything to do with the present. I redecorated my room and surrounded myself with inspirational pictures, books and mementos that I collected on my travels. I found out that I like my own company and that I am completely at ease with being alone.

I developed a spiritual connection to God and the divine source within, which I believe is what got me through the most challenging times. When I developed faith and trust in a power that is much greater than me, I learned to trust life and what it could deliver. I took risks because, after all, I had already taken the biggest one of my life, and not only did I survive, I surpassed my expectation of what I initially thought was possible all those years ago, when I was tossing and turning. If it weren't for being single, I would never have gone down a different path, to one of self-discovery and of choosing a different course. The experience of being single actually led me back to being in a relationship. Even though I was quite happy being on my own, I did wonder if I would ever be in a relationship again, and the thing that was most important to me was that I not repeat my past. I wanted to feel like I had evolved enough to choose a new story, a new person and one who was more aligned with my current set of values rather than just settling on someone for the sake of not being alone.

The transition into a relationship was seamless by the time I met my current partner. I think this happened for a few reasons. I was ready, I had done a lot of inner work and let go of many of the old patterns and I embraced a new possibility to be in a totally new and different relationship. My metaphor of spending ten years in the desert, exploring, discovering and excavating myself and my life was necessary for my soul's evolution to chart a different course. Had I stayed in my marriage, my life would have gone very differently and I was keenly aware of that. My intuitive nudge told me to move on in order to save myself. Those ten years I consider an enormous gift that gave me a totally new opportunity for my life. My new partner appreciated that I was my own person, that I was comfortable in my own skin and that I was independent and could fend for myself. I was not dependent on him, nor did I "need" him. I chose to be with him.

My current relationship mirrors the changes I made in myself and is a reflection of the calm and at ease person I've become, who is light years away from the lost angry woman I was when I left my marriage. Our relationship is based on similar values, open communication and respect for each other as individuals. There is no drama, deception, judgment, arguments or tantrums. It is so different from my past experiences. We have created a new family unit with my sons, now aged 21 and 18 that is based on our values of open communication and respect for one another. Sure there have been difficulties and plenty of adjustments; however, for the most part we have a family that works.

My oldest son, who struggled with many of the Aspergers characteristics when he was young, has grown into an exemplary young man. I like to credit many of the "off the wall" treatments to his amazing growth and development and to acknowledge him for his willingness to participate and go along with almost everything I suggested. He is a stellar example of perseverance and a positive attitude that shines with everything he does and everyone he meets. His recent Film School graduation has connected him with his passion for screenwriting and directing and I have no doubt his name will be up in lights in our near future. My younger son is on hiatus from his motocross career that began when he was nine, to figure out his next steps. He has had some setbacks that I am confident will not deter his dream to continue to ride or be involved with the sport. I am so proud of both of my sons for everything we have been through together and I thank them for calling me forward to be the best version of myself that I can be.

And now it's my turn. My ten years in the desert laid a foundation for my next chapter which is doing what I am passionate about. With my past in the past, I am now free to create my future in a way that totally inspires me. Bring it on!

* * *

*Lori is a lifelong writer with a passion for journaling. Having developed the unique Open Heart Journals process, she is happiest facilitating workshops and online programs that teach how to write powerful and touching journals of acknowledgement to your loved ones. Lori is the author of the soon to be published "Open Heart Journals -- Acknowledge the Ones You Love" companion book due out late 2013. Lori lives in Richmond Hill, Ontario with her partner and two young adult sons. For more information visit www.openheartjournals.com.*

# A Light in the Forest
by Wendy Monsinger

There was a little girl inside me. A little girl I never knew. She was a beautiful, blonde curly haired little girl but all the voices inside told her otherwise. She was shy and afraid and the agonizing hurt inside her made her believe she was powerless, worthless and alone. This little girl was "buried" for over 30 years and was unknown to the outside world. She tried hard to get the attention she desperately needed from her adult self who unknowingly covered her up. She felt so insignificant there was no way she could come out from her safe hiding. She cried but was never heard because of the thick walls and impenetrable coats of armour that the adult had built up around her. She was scared and had no glimpse of light in the dense, dark forest. She was a victim.

I was that little girl. I am the youngest of three children. I remember life being pretty normal; whatever normal means. My parents were together; we lived on the water, went swimming, boating, camping and did a couple of holidays. We always had pets – usually a cat and a dog. My dad worked and my mom stayed home and looked after us until I started school.

Since the age of four, it feels as though, if something is to happen, January is the month. January is a very difficult month for me to get through and, if it were up to me, I would just wipe it off the calendar entirely. Events that happened in January included my tobogganing accident and the death of several family members including my dad. Also when I was ten, my parents separated and, immediately after, I became a victim of childhood sexual abuse. This is the reason for my story.

That despairing and unforgettable day, I lost my father, my brother and my dog because I made the choice to live with my mother. The next-door neighbours separated at the same time and the couples ended up switching spouses. All six children were ten years old and up so the adults thought we were old enough to choose which parent we wanted to live with. One of my parents was going to be unhappy and I was going to be the reason for that, which made it the hardest decision I had ever made. I chose to stay with my mom because I was a girl and I knew my mom the best. My dad worked a lot so he wasn't home very much. My best friend lived next door so, besides staying with my mom, I got to live with my best friend! Little did I know what this decision was going to mean for me. Life changed in an instant and the darkness set in.

46

My friend and I had to share a bedroom, but we were happy to be together. There was a wood stove in the basement and her dad kept it burning for heat. The first night I heard him come down the stairs, open the woodstove and put some wood in. I thought he would just go back to bed but I was wrong. The basement was dark when he entered our room and approached my bed. I thought he was just being a dad and was checking on us. Well, he did, except the checking went beyond anything I could have ever imagined. My body was frozen in fear. What was I supposed to do? He touched me in places that no one had ever touched. "What's going on? Why was he doing this? Should I ask him? No, I can't let him know I'm awake." My mind took myself to another place so I didn't have to be in that room with him. After what felt like hours, he left my side. I could "come back" and breathe again.

When I got up in the morning, he acted like nothing happened. "Did I have a nightmare? Did last night really happen?" The questions in my head were endless. How could I tell my mom? I couldn't bear the thought of hurting her after she had just separated from my dad. I just couldn't. Besides, I doubted the night even took place and so, no one would believe me. Each night, I went to bed with the same fears. "Is this the night? Will he come in again? What can I do to stop it from happening?" Maybe if I sleep right against the wall, he won't be able to reach me. If I wear the right pyjamas, they will protect me.

Nothing, nothing at all changed the way those dark nights would go. It happened three or four nights a week for almost three years. Not only were those fearful nights happening but things happened throughout the day. He would make comments about my body, how I looked that day and about my clothing. Then he started coming into the bathroom when I was in there. It didn't matter what I was doing; he would come up with an excuse to be in there. If I was in the bath, he would ask if I wanted him to wash my hair or my back. I remember eating "Tums" almost every night like they were candy. I ate them because 'I liked them' but now, I wonder if it was my subconscious wanting to settle my stomach down.

I enjoyed school and had good grades but, from approximately grade four, I was the target of bullying. I wanted so much to be part of the group, but slowly I started to withdraw from the other kids and my grades started to decline. I would volunteer to be a monitor for the younger grades so I didn't have to go out at recess. It became challenging because I didn't want to go to school but I didn't want to go home either. Those terrifying nights were always looming in the back of my mind.

The darkness consumed my life. He portrayed himself to be a great family man so I felt I couldn't talk to anyone. Who on earth would believe a ten-year-old? He would certainly deny it if anyone questioned him. Without awareness, I started building up walls and putting on some pretty heavy armour. This was not something a young girl should have to do.

Just a few months before my thirteenth birthday we moved out of his house. You would think that it would have been the greatest day of my life but, honestly, I have no recollection of it whatsoever. One moment we lived with him and the next, we had our own place. Sadly, it didn't end there! We lived within walking distance and he would come over to our house and beg my mom to come back. Again, I wasn't safe. What was it about me? Why did he pick me? What did I do to make it okay? Is this normal? If he loved me, why would he want to hurt me like this?

For twenty five years, I buried this pain. I convinced myself that, if I didn't talk or think about it, it would go away or, better yet, that it didn't even take place. I couldn't let anyone see the wounds and scars and, after all these years, it was second nature for me to pretend life was good. I buried the turmoil so deep that I couldn't feel. Fear and panic was deep inside my body but I didn't know what the emotions were on the outside. My walls were built up very thick and I thought people would think I was "crazy". I even had my husband convinced that I wasn't affected by it.

On January 14, 2006, (the seventh anniversary of my dad's death), my life changed again with a phone call from the police ... here we go with January again. My heart stopped for a moment and I felt like I couldn't breathe. I was concerned they were calling about a family member as several live in the area they were calling from. I nervously answered the phone. The woman on the other end asked for me. She then said that she was informed that I may have some information about an incident that happened (and said "his" name). I couldn't believe my ears! It's been almost 25 years! I could not have waited wondering how this got started so was relieved that she came to my house that afternoon. The few hours that it took for her to arrive seemed like days. Thankfully she came to my house in her own car and was not in uniform.

My heart felt like it was beating outside my chest. She said that someone had come forward with allegations of abuse and asked if I had anything I wanted to share. My husband looked at me and said that it was up to me but that he would support me every step of the way. So without hesitation,

I said "yes". She asked a few general questions but then explained it was a requirement that my statement had to be taken at the station on video. Panic set in. I hated being on camera. We booked the following Saturday for me to attend the station and make my statement. Let me tell you, that was the longest week of my life! I hardly slept, I couldn't eat and it was all I had to make it through work without breaking down. I was not prepared for this. I still can't explain the fear I had inside me that week. I had no idea what I was going to say in my statement, let alone how I was going to tell my mom. After all these years, she had no idea that moving out of his house had ended nightly terror.

My list of fears was pretty large and most are still in existence today. I have a fear of the dark, being alone, looking in the mirror, having my picture taken, people seeing over my walls, someone breaking down my walls, undressing, my emotions, not being in control, letting go, of knowing exactly what was buried inside and, most of all, of someone knowing my true life story. As you can imagine, fears surfaced and they all seemed to arrive at the same time. I also have discovered many other fears (or what I can now call triggers). I don't like white older style vans, bunk beds, a certain "male name", a certain "factory name", particular touch, a couple of roads and a certain "look" of a house. I get anxious when people have conversations about abuse and, now because there is more awareness, there are always stories frontline in the news. There's no question that this is a positive thing but flashbacks happen faster than I could even imagine.

I had to tell my supervisor because I would need time off work to attend court. How can I do this? I had no idea how to start a conversation like that, let alone tell someone it was about ME! I was so afraid of my emotions that I couldn't risk the possibility of others seeing so I told her that I had something to share that would affect work but I couldn't talk there. We met the following night at her house and, to this day, have no idea what I said to her. I was trembling in fear of the unknown and I was also afraid of what her reaction would be. Only a couple of people knew what happened and this was the first time I was telling someone who hardly knew me. Afterwards, I had some relief as you would have thought that I gave her a script of what to say. She was amazing.

The next step; tell my mom. My mom was on vacation at the time and was to come home the following day. I couldn't have the police talking to her first but, even more, I had fears of hurting her and having her be disappointed in me for not coming to her at the time. To describe how I felt at that moment is almost impossible. I told her what happened when we lived with "him" and that the police would be calling to ask her questions. She didn't say much and she had a look of despair but I think she was just in shock. She asked me how many times it happened and I said "I don't know mom, too many to count". I told her that I had to go that coming weekend to make my statement.

Saturday arrived. I hardly slept the night before – my brain just wouldn't shut off. It was the longest forty minute drive my husband and I ever made. My entire body was numb with fear. After twenty five years, was I really going to "tell"? That little girl inside me didn't know which way to turn. The officer took us into a room, explained what was going to happen then asked my mom and husband to leave the room. She turned on the camera and started asking me questions. I don't know what I said but I know that little girl inside me could hardly talk. My adult self didn't have the knowledge at that time to hold her and tell her she was safe. She needed to know it was alright for her to tell the truth and that someone was listening. She and I couldn't wait for the questions to end but we did the best we could at the time. When the camera was turned off, my husband and mom came back into the room and I fell to pieces. It was over; I did it! WE did it! The officer thanked me for coming in, told me I did a good job and said that "he" would now be contacted for questioning.

We went home and, within an hour, the officer called me and advised that "he" had already been to the station and was arrested. I didn't know whether to be happy, nervous, relieved, or scared. Actually, I was terrified. Did I do the right thing? What was he going to do? Will he try to contact me? What will he say his story is?

When I agreed to come forward, I had the misperception that coming forward would resolve everything. This was it! I had been wanting this moment for twenty five years! I could get my life back and he would have to own up to what he did, but the tables really seemed to turn. I felt like my power and life where in his hands again (even though I know now that I had never taken my power away from him). After I made my statement, the officer said that she believed that he wasn't going to get a lawyer and was not going to fight the charges. I trusted this but she was wrong. From the first court date, he made all the decisions. He didn't show up with a lawyer so they gave him another date; then another and another. Time was at a standstill. How could the court system allow this to happen? Why should he be catered to? I had more anxiety than I ever thought possible.

There were months in between each date and I was not prepared for that. There were so many thoughts and emotions surfacing, I didn't know what to do. Our children were at ages where they knew something was going on but I wasn't ready to tell them yet. We just assured them that everyone was alright and that we had some meetings we needed to be at.

Finally, we had the date where he would make a plea. This was it. It would be the first time I had seen him in many years but I was ready.....so I thought! We walked into the court house and the instant my eye caught him I broke down. I did an abrupt turn and my feet were frozen and my brain said "no way, you can't do this". My whole body was shuddering and that poor little girl inside me had no idea what to do.

We had a room to ourselves but the thought of what lay ahead was incomprehensible. After sitting there for a while, my statement was given to me and it was the first time that I was able to read it over. There seemed to be several errors but remembering the absolute terror I had the day I made my statement, it was impossible to know what I did or didn't say. After a couple of hours, the day was adjourned with nothing accomplished.

He had the choice of whether or not it would be a trial by judge or jury. It was so challenging to believe in my heart that I had the power ... that I took it back the day I came forward. Sentencing day arrived and it was now just under two years from the charges being laid. It was about a week before Christmas. I sat in the courtroom and the judge started talking. She asked him how he pleads to the charges that were read. "GUILTY". Did you hear that? He said he was guilty! After all this time, he said the word. He was finally going to be sentenced and he would spend Christmas in jail but, before we knew it, the judge postponed sentencing. I now had to spend Christmas still worrying about this.

The awful month of January was approaching but all I could think about was ending this. We were back in court on January 11th, 2008. Through this whole ordeal, his wife sat beside him, supporting him all the way. I couldn't fathom the idea that she could sit and hear his plea, yet still be by his side. I wrote my victim impact statement and made the decision to read it aloud myself. Inside I doubted that I had the strength to do it but I wanted him to sit there and listen to me. I needed him to hear my voice, my emotions and hear how much I had suffered; not only during that time, but every single day since then.

The judge re-read the charges and again asked him what his plea was. "GUILTY". He was then allowed to make a statement so he turned on his tears, looked at me and started saying how sorry he was. He said he was sorry for what he did, that I was a good girl and it wasn't my fault. I didn't know what to feel but my heart didn't want to believe for one second that he was truly sorry. The charge was indecent assault and he was sentenced to only 6 months in jail, 2 years' probation and 10 years on the sex offender list.

Even though I didn't feel justice was served, it was over. Finally, after two years of this torture, it was over. Without thinking, I signed up for victim notifications which provided phone calls to let me know if he submits an appeal, applies for early release or if when he was released. About six weeks after sentencing I was notified that he applied for early parole. The parole board asked him a series of questions. One answer I will never forget was that it was my fault. MY FAULT? He also went on to say that he had found his Saviour and that he would have no problem reintegrating back into the community and return to work. I found this astounding. How on earth would there be no issues after being in jail and knowing the likelihood that all your friends, relatives and neighbours knew where you were and why? Even though I wasn't allowed to speak his wife was. She spoke about what a good man he was. Are you serious? What part of this do you not understand? What makes him a good man? The board made their decision right there. Early parole was denied.

On Mother's Day 2008, I was getting ready for brunch with my favorite women when the phone rang. It was an automated message notifying me that he had been released. What a way to start the day -- he inflicts me with a life sentence and gets out on good behaviour after serving only four months?

My adult self and my little inner child felt safe when he was in jail but now, he's out and lives only twenty five minutes away. Wounds were wide open and tidal waves of emotions would flood in, making the most negligible things trigger panic. My adult self still didn't have the understanding of how to embrace her inner child and ensure her that it was over and she was safe.

Something in my heart told me that I really needed some counselling but the thought of the same thing repeating scared me beyond measure. Many years prior to court I had seen a male psychiatrist but, after a year of appointments, I stopped attending after he said "Look at me, I was abused and I got over it."

With reluctance, I ended up getting a new referral from my doctor. "I can do this…..I need it". On the appointment day, I walked into the building and started down the hall. The only thought going through my mind was "I'm not crazy, I don't belong here". I would hear a little voice speak up and say "yes, you need to do this; you need to do this for you". My heart was pounding so hard, I couldn't feel anything else. The waiting room was filled with people and I felt like they were all staring at me knowing too well why I was there.

Finally, my name was called. I walked into the doctor's office and, just like before, he was sitting behind his desk. He asked me a few questions about myself and then asked what brought me there that day. I briefly described what I went through in my childhood and after about five minutes he looked at me and said "well, I don't think you're depressed so I don't think there is anything I can do for you." Did he have any idea what it took for me to walk through that door? I cried all the way home. I am finished. I cannot do this again. This is life and I have to figure it out on my own. I stood up to him and sent him to jail. What more could I want? I felt that there wasn't anything a counsellor could possibly tell me that I didn't already know.

I buried the pain so deep that I no longer knew how to function day to day. The emotions that were coming to the surface were unbelievably scary. I didn't even know what half of them were because I had never felt them before. "Someone please tell me what's going on!" I buried information, events, conversations and many other things. I would talk with friends and relatives and they would tell me about something that took place and it was like I was never there. Why don't I remember these things? Some of them were quite significant; like the day we moved out of his house. I should have remembered every detail of that day. I don't even remember packing. It was like time travel. I felt like there was no way those things happened with me present.

The next several months were excruciating. Each waking day brought new emotions and turmoil. You know, I truly felt that life was much easier when I buried everything. What have I done? I couldn't even make it through the day without crying. It was a whirlwind of emotions, confusion and doubt. Why did I put myself through this? Why do I want to relive these events? I should have just stayed silent in the small box that surrounded me.

It took me about six years and three years of counselling to really believe that I did the right thing and that being silent was much worse than talking. Yes, I did more counselling. I started with online counselling through the employee assistance program at work. This was a great first step for me because of all my fears and I couldn't have picked a better counsellor then the one I was assigned. Doing it online meant that I didn't have to see any-one face to face which was one of my greatest fears. I couldn't stand the thought of seeing the look on people's faces when I told them what I had been through and, as you know, I also feared disbelief. Writing to my coun-sellor was the perfect fit; I didn't have a specific appointment time so I could read what she wrote as well as write back to her when I was ready and it didn't matter what time of day or night it was. I really connected with her. She always started her "session" with a quote and it was directly related to what I was feeling or going through which gave me something to think about. Even though we didn't talk in person, I felt warmth and calm from her. She seemed to understand me and I would almost instantly be calmed by her words. This counselling was short-term so there came a time where she had to move me forward. She provided a couple of names of counsellors in my area and suggested that I contact one of them as she felt that I could use longer term guidance and support.

Even though this counsellor fit, sharing my story with another counsellor and the fear of hearing "get over it" was agonizing. Maybe it was the little girl inside me telling me she couldn't bear that pain again. The vicious cir-cle of balancing life and emotions was happening again. I had actually called a counsellor and she assured me that she felt very comfortable work-ing through my issues but I got scared and said I would work some dates out and call her back. After a few months, I got worse and worse. I would email a close friend of mine and let things out. She kept mentioning coun-selling but I would quickly dismiss it as I was terrified of making that call. I would break into a million pieces if I heard those words again and that would be it. After quite a few lengthy conversations, she got firm with me and told me to make the call. She offered to be there with me when I did and she would support me through the whole thing. She made me promise and put it in writing!

That was the best thing I ever did. I booked the appointment and forced myself to show up. Walking down the hall to the appointment, voices in my head kept telling me to "turn around", "you can't do this" and "what are you going to do if the same thing happens?" I just ignored them and kept walking. I was greeted at the door with a warm smile. We introduced ourselves and then sat down. The best part was that she wasn't sitting at a desk. It was like we were in her living room. She asked me how I was and I said "I'm fine" which was my usual response. But at that moment, something came over me. I followed it up with "Well, I guess I'm not fine, otherwise I wouldn't be sitting here, would I?"

She asked me to tell her about why I was there. I told her that I was a survivor of childhood sexual abuse and that, a few years prior, I laid charges, he was convicted and I was now dealing with the after affects. I continued to explain what happened but she said "let me just stop you there for a moment and acknowledge what you have been through". I couldn't believe what I had just heard! Someone who I didn't know wanted to acknowledge what I had been through? She then went on to recognize the courage that it took for me to show up that day. I thought I had won the lottery! Within minutes of being there, I knew I was in the right spot. I had found the one. I could have sat there and talked to her for days, and although I walked out of her office in tears, I also had a smile underneath all of that. I finally knew what it was like to make a connection and trust that I did the right thing. Maybe I not only needed a true connection, I needed a female counsellor.

Throughout my life, I was fortunate not to have gone down the road of addictions in the true sense of the word, but I am addicted to putting on heavy armour and burying everything so no one would know what I had been through. I have been diagnosed with depression, been on medication and have had to take time off work. I didn't want anyone looking at me, talking about me or worrying about me. I looked after everyone else and stayed in control because I hated attention and I thought they would figure me out; and I wouldn't know what to do.

I consider myself fortunate to have had the support of my family and friends. I have an amazing husband who has stood by me since I was sixteen. We have now been married for 21 years and, like all marriages, life has thrown things at us, but we have had even more with me being a survivor of childhood sexual abuse. I was running my life with great routine but, until I started working through it, I discovered that I wasn't "living" at all. I protected myself with control and order and I couldn't let anything get in the way of that. I took on everything possible so I didn't have time to think. I couldn't stop being busy for the fear of reality setting in. As long as I didn't stop, I could forget those years existed.

I have learned some valuable life teachings. Even though "he" didn't get the sentence I thought he deserved and that he said he had no issues returning home and to work, he is human and I have to trust that there is no way that even one night in jail did not affect him. He knows what he did and I may not be around to see it, but one day, true justice will be served as the universe sees fit.

If you haven't "connected" with your counselor, don't be afraid of moving on. Even if it takes seeing four or five counsellors, keep your chin up – it's worth every ounce of energy you have. I never thought I would be in counselling for three years, but I suppose to try and heal over 26 years, it takes a little while. It was very hard work and with that came a lot of memories and emotions. With all the years of burying things so far down, I had forgotten a lot them. There will be many, many times that those voices tell you to stop because it is so difficult and unbelievably painful but I can promise you that going through all of that is much easier than burying it. You come out a new person with more light than darkness.

Be courageous and be vulnerable. Share your story with someone you trust and then share it again. It is extremely painful, but when you open your heart and share what's underneath all that armour, the pain eases and each step gets a little calmer. You will learn from each person you tell. They will either be exactly the person you thought they were or they will be someone completely different. We always want to make the right choice due to personal fears but should we happen to choose the wrong person, then we walk away with a new understanding. That person will teach us more about trust and will have shown their true self to us. At times, you may feel as though the path in the forest is dark and is growing over before you have a chance to walk on it but there is always light waiting for you on the other side. When you open your heart and talk, your little girl will thank you, love you, forgive you and you will get to know her. The universe is constantly providing opportunities for us to learn and grow; we just have to believe – believe that we are worthy. I am not sure that healing will ever be complete but it gives me something to look forward to everyday. I am 43 years old and I feel like my life has just begun – for real this time and life couldn't get any better than that!

There's this little girl inside me. A little girl I now know. She is beautiful and I love her. She knows that she has the power, is worthy and is no longer alone. This little girl has crept her way out of hiding after 33 difficult years and is getting to know the outside world. She finally has the attention she desperately needed from her adult self and she no longer feels insignificant. Her cries are heard and her adult self has her arms wrapped around her. She still gets scared and has more growing to do but she is now following the light in the dark forest. She is a survivor -- I am a survivor!

\* \* \*

*I want to dedicate this chapter to my husband and soul mate Mike for your endless patience, love, support and for believing in me more than I believed in myself; my two sons, Kollin and Dylan, for your support, patience and countless hugs, kisses and "I love you's" – I am so proud to be your mom; my mom Mary Jane, for your love, support and belief in me - you are a role model and my greatest hero; my sister Sherry and step-sister Carrie Ann for your strength and support; my brother Randy for your hugs and even though you never said a lot, I know you were supporting me; my like-a-mom friend Bonnie for your love, support, belief in me and gently pushing me beyond my fears; my best-friend-for-life Karen, for your love, trust and support; my Aunt Lenore for your love and always being there for me; to my amazing counsellors Mimi and Kristina for your patience, support, encouragement, guidance and homework assignments; and to all my other family and friends - your love, support and encouragement mean the world to me.*

*Also, to all the young girls out there who are going through or have already been through the same thing – believe in yourself, trust that little girl inside you and know that you are worthy. You are beautiful, deserving of everything that life has to offer and trust that when the time is perfect for you, the Universe will provide it to you.*

*I thank all of you who have shared this journey with me – even though at times I felt very alone, I know I was surrounded by all of you (in person and in spirit) and I couldn't have done it without all of you by my side. You are my world and I am so grateful.*

*With much love, respect, admiration and appreciation!*
*Warm hugs, Wendy*

\* \* \*

*Wendy has been married for 21 years and is a mother of two boys, ages 17 and 20. She has a Social Service Worker diploma, a certificate in Supervisory Skills, is a Caseworker with the County of Simcoe and also is Chief Steward of CUPE Local 5820. She has always had a passion for writing and is happy to now make it part of her life. She loves helping people and by sharing her story, she hopes to inspire others and put some flame to someone's light so the darkness may fade. Wendy resides in Barrie, Ontario.*

# I Can Do Plaid
## by Victoria Kaye

*'I do not date much. I do not do the online or offline thing. I have an imagination and, unfortunately, want reality to mimic fiction. I believe Hobbes is real and Calvin would be the ideal kid. I do not look my chronological age so, therefore, refuse to act it, and remain at what age people think I am. So I need a guy to understand that, and if his daughter looks older than me, well, we have a small problem... However, if you look like Richard Gere, circa 2003-2005 at the latest, or Roger Sterling from Mad Men, I MAY bend a few of my own rules. Must be able to laugh a lot, and humour is in your heart - silly but not stupid, and definitely not gross or mean. Also important, you must be able to dance ... I refuse to ever be a wall-flower again!'*

The above is the opening paragraph in my profile in an online dating service. I've never done anything like this before, and I am proud of myself as, for once, I am comfortable and confident with what I am looking for, even though it may seem 'crazy' to most.

I showed this to two friends of mine for their 'constructive' criticism. One, who is having a great time with online dating, suggests it's too restricting, and that "…you're not going to get any!" The other feels it is truly going to filter prospects. Reality - in the first four weeks I was viewed over 1,000 times and only a handful of prospects replied and, from that handful, only one has made it to coffee.

I honestly believe in the saying "One in a Thousand" – comfortable with these odds as I honestly now believe and embrace it … even if they make for lonely odds.

I haven't had many relationships in my life. I joke and state that I've been in love 3½ times – and the last ½ wasn't really love, as I reflect, but more of a reason to remove myself from a situation. I have been fortunate, usually able to remove myself BEFORE a situation can arise. The sad part is, I also removed myself from letting situations possibly happen.

Relationship is an interesting word. You can have relations with people, whether family or social, but it doesn't necessarily mean you have a relationship. There needs to be a correlation, an interpersonal connection, a successful co-mingling or entanglement of sorts. I find it amazing how, as

I now reflect back, I've never achieved successful co-mingling. I think it has something to do with "The Box."

Life is like a box… not the box of chocolates that Forrest Gump references, perfectly compartmentalized and wedged into little openings. Sure, at first you never know what you're going to get but, after a while, you know EXACTLY what you do and don't want. I've never been the type to order the same box of chocolates. I don't like routine; your sense of adventure dissipates as your mind becomes stagnant. I want life to be a new box, every day, even if that is not realistic.

And then there is that "other" box … the one you are either inside or outside. If you haven't figured it out as yet, I'm one of those "outside" of the box … three fields left of left field, as I said in my 20s. But somewhere in my late 30s and early 40s, I wanted to belong, to fit in, and thought I could learn to be happy "inside" the box.

Remember the Looney Toons cartoon where a chameleon leaps merrily from coloured background to coloured background, matching the colour as he passes in front, but not really paying attention to what the backgrounds are - and when a plaid background comes up, he stops in mid leap and promptly has a nervous breakdown?

I can do plaid.

But being able to do plaid doesn't mean I can do "inside" the box. Life, I am learning, is not like baseball where some play infield and others play outfield. No matter where the ball goes, someone is ready to catch it as everyone is part of the team and, collectively, the successes are celebrated as a team, even though many are individual in nature. Life SHOULD be like baseball, full of tactics and strategy and at times boring, but boy, when there is a play in motion, it can be extremely exciting. Sadly, life is not like baseball.

I have always been different, but the world, no matter how diversified, is not ready for different. Even now, as I'm on the cusp of entering into a new phase of life, although spiritually I am six years old and visually appear in my middle thirties, my chronological age of 49 has me assessing my past and trying to figure out why I am now so discerning, not only when it comes to potential online dating, but any relationship, whether with family, friends or in business.

As I look through old photo albums and see the girl I was in my twenties, I wonder what has changed. But to understand that, you have to go back to the beginning and, conveniently for me, it truly started at birth.

I am of Armenian heritage, born in Israel but not Jewish. Though not a Kardashian, I still have princess tendencies, birth rights as I put it. We emigrated to Canada when I was seven months old. Though we moved to the new world, the values of the old world lingered and, as a baby learns to grasp for their first set of keys, it was evident I was destined to reside in left field as I reached for everything with my left hand. No matter how hard everyone tried, I was going to be the first 'south paw' on both sides of my family.

This never was a problem until we moved back to Israel when I turned six and my sister was four years old. My father was homesick, but relocating us from North American culture made me ill. Though we were enrolled in a private British school, having been born in Israel, I was forced to take a Hebrew class that was government run and outside of the school's regular jurisdiction. My sister, Canadian born, was exempt from this and I do not understand why my parents never argued the fact that I too should have been considered Canadian and not forced to learn a language I knew nothing of.

The language wasn't the main issue, the problem was being hit with a ruler each day and repeatedly told the devil possessed my body as I was forced to place my pencil in a hand that was as foreign to my experience as the language I was being force fed. No matter how much I tried to voice my discomfort, no one in authority was able to intervene and, instead of protecting me, became part of the coalition to exorcise the demon within and remove not only the writing utensil from my left hand, but remove me from my right state of mind by preventing me from using my left hand entirely – even when eating!

I still wonder why my parents never defended my "uniqueness" and found it easier to let me believe I was a direct descendant of Satan. I have no idea how I remained sane in the insanity of the moment. Seriously, who deems right is right when it was blatantly not correct?

Needless to say, I experienced my first academic failure as I probably am the only six-year-old to ever fail First Grade Hebrew and, as I graduated to Grade 2, I was repeating Grade 1 Foreign Language. You could just imagine how thrilled I was when my parents announced we were moving back to Canada at mid-term.

But then something similar happened in Grade Six, when I was twelve, and the teacher asked where everyone was born during a lesson. You can just imagine how popular the girl born in Israel was to an 87% Jewish populated class. Then how quickly your fifteen minutes of fame can come to an abrupt halt when someone notices you are wearing a cross and asks, "How can you be born in Israel and not be Jewish?" In hindsight, I should have thought of something else other than making the correlation, "Everyone born in Pakistan ..."

When I was thrown in the mud that recess, I should have realized not everyone necessarily has the same sense of humour. A lesson I kept being reminded of as the bullying continued well into Junior and High School, until I was seventeen. Then I was able to change schools, using semester vs. term as the logic to move from the school that was literally a football field from home to one that was 30 minutes and two bus transfers away.

You know the saying, "You can run but you can't hide." Well, though I honestly believed I was in the clear to being "moi" – along came a family friend, visiting from Israel, saying, "I remember you; you were a cry baby and cried every day!" You can just imagine how unattractive I was when I spewed out years of frustration and tried to explain how you too would cry if you were hit with a ruler every day! I think it was the first time I heard, "You know, she's really pretty, but she's a little crazy, isn't she?!?"

Would it have been really hard for him to just say, "I'm sorry. I too was six then and never realized you were being hit. Now that I know, would you like to grab a soda and talk about it?" Same with the bullies back in Grade Six. They could have easily said, "The world is an amazing place as multiculturalism truly has no borders! After all, Keanu Reeves was born in Lebanon but is not Lebanese. He's just American/Native mixed and born on an army base where his father was stationed." Instead, society hides its ignorance by masking it and inflicting pain on an innocent without understanding the scar it may cause.

Fast forward. Now it's the early 80s and, at age 18, it's time to get my first picture ID for Canadian Citizenship. Imagine my surprise at the immigration centre as I learned there was a discrepancy because my landing card stated that I was born in Palestine. After a week, it was discovered that when I was seven months old and we arrived by QE2 at the port in Montreal, the immigration official assumed because my parents' passports identified them as being born in Palestine that automatically I too was born in Palestine, although it had become Israel in 1948 when my father and mother were aged six and four respectively.

Ironically, I never developed a prejudice against Judaism. I learned how to use my birth rights as a bone of contention to Canadian Jews as I was a product of their motherland and they weren't.

This ability to think "outside of the box" wasn't a popular trait. You quickly learn to withdraw from society as your imagination becomes your best friend and confidant. You don't see the world from the 'normal' perspective, and you truly understand the term 'creative thinker'. Somewhere along the way, the "obvious" and the "ridiculous" get blurred and your ability to make or keep friends is affected by what you consider an ability, but they consider a disability.

Fast forward to age 26. I went to Washington with a group of friends from Detroit. Instead of driving from Toronto, I decided to take a plane with a layover, as previous adventures by train or bus missed connections and, this time, I wanted to make sure nothing could go wrong. So I got to Detroit on the last flight, to continue to Washington the following morning, allowing us to try on bridesmaid dresses. I refrain from stating that I looked like a Vegas floozy or a two-bit hooker in my aquamarine sequin cocktail dress, but it was the bride's decision and, though I hated it, at least she thought I looked good.

We had a great time in Washington. But when we returned, we missed our scheduled flight, thus causing me to miss my connection that evening to Toronto. Instead of remaining at the airport with me, as I thought they would, they left me alone, at night, in Detroit. I was able to sort myself out and found a motel, but was put into a ground level room. It is advisable to NEVER put a lone female on the ground floor! I stayed up all night, with the TV and lights all on, and was at the airport very early the next morning. Instead of going home, I went straight to work, luggage and all. When I got home that evening, I called my friends to report that I was safe and sound.

However, instead of celebrating my bravery, they were quick to disown me as a friend. According to them, I was a pathological liar and they no longer wanted to be my friends. You see, when we were in Washington, we rented a Pontiac Sunbird and I thought there was a fault in the vehicle as the emergency brake would kick on regularly while I was driving and we would smell burning rubber. I wanted to report it to the car rental company when we got to the airport but, as we were rushed, missing our flight, and I was starting to worry about my connecting flight in Detroit, I never addressed it with Avis.

Actually there was nothing wrong with the vehicle, but they had watched me engage the emergency brake as I put the vehicle into gear and thought I was "acting" bewildered when I would say the car "did it again" as we started smelling burnt rubber. No one had spoken up at the time.

For the next three days, I was re-analyzing, reassessing and reliving the Washington weekend, trying to figure out my behaviour, and if I should seriously seek professional assistance. You can just imagine my relief when I went to start my Dodge Turismo to go out with friends, stepped on my clutch to use the stick shift, and realized that the emergency brake on the rental car had been EXACTLY where my clutch was. Surprisingly, I didn't run into the house to call my ex-friends to explain ... instead, I found joy in the fact that I was out of the bridal party and wouldn't be wearing aquamarine sequins. This may be the real reason why I hate weddings and avoid being a bridesmaid. It's not because of the often unflattering bridal party attire, but I believe those who stand up with you on your special day should be there because of your personal love for them, and you want them to share in your happiness. If your presence is solely based on contributing to a visual presentation, how much truth is there in that union?

I honestly think it was at that time my down deep inside fear of the word "relationship" started. Anyone with whom I'd had a close relationship/friendship up to that time had thrown me "under the bus" in today's vernacular. Why has no one defended me in situations where I was not in control? If you can't depend on your parents, teachers, peers or friends to 'watch your back' and protect you when you can't protect yourself, how can you expect them to accept you when you finally do protect yourself? Granted, my self protection had been the act of reverting within and hiding the scared little girl rather than summoning personal energy and confidence to rescue myself from uncomfortable situations.

There are so many examples in my life that have caused my overproductive imagination to engage and drive my behaviour. I find it amazing how quickly society would sooner label it as a deep psychological disorder than accept it as something different. Over the years, I have found myself in not-so-safe situations and unhealthy circumstances that, for most, would and have ended in compromising moments. Conveniently, for my own sanity, I have learned to walk away from them.

Depression, or finding yourself alone or distant from society, is not something that necessarily comes from an unhappy situation. As a defense mechanism, I escape into my own world and, though I consider it my safe place, it can be dangerous to have an imagination that is stronger than reality, although it is my sole protector. The many situations I have experienced due to misunderstanding peers have left me socially unable to develop personal intimacy, though I pine for it privately.

I should learn to stand up for my beliefs. But how can I stand up and defend what's right when, in reality, my position in the situation or point of view of the circumstance is not something considered worthy of defending? In any of the situations I explain above, can you honestly provide me a strategy I could have played that would have kept me in the game? Life truly is not a baseball game, especially for the player who is standing three fields left of left field, and all alone.

True, I don't look back … I realize I'm the one that walks away into the sunset, not because I've turned my back on the situation, but because I'm truly 'done' with it. I have been searching for an answer for most of my life, but I hate it when people tell me I need to settle and accept the situation as it is. Bullshit.

I don't have a lot of friends, a lot of acquaintances, but not a lot of true friends. My circle-of-friends consists mostly of people I haven't met yet. My new best friends are on Facebook, and I keep the total below 100. Every time it creeps close, I start purging. Amazing how people don't notice when you un-friend them. Says a lot about today's social network when the number of friends you have is what is important vs. their quality. I removed the display of the number of friends I have; people don't need to know that. But I do make it clear whenever I purge. It's my way of telling those that remain to be aware that I have no problem cleaning house.

To most people, these actions may translate as 'bravado' or a sick sense of humour, but these are the tools in my survival kit. I am a forward thinker and, over the years, I've learned to look 5 steps ahead, and am ready for what a situation or life has to throw my way. It's my one-two punch out of an ugly situation and, if people want to label it as 'crazy' or some division of mental health, please, I'm flattered – at least there is safe comfort in my aloneness.

Recently I was told that I'm considered manic depressive, hypomaniac more than bipolar. I am a little OCD; I think it comes with my ADD; I'm a creative person; it comes with the territory! Although I can be 'up' for 90% of the time, I also need 10% down time, and often society doesn't afford me this simple luxury. Bouncing off walls is hard work but it's amazing how many people are quick to gravitate to the Energizer bunny. However, when it's time to change or recharge the batteries, the bunny finds himself alone to take care of things. Then, when he's ready, he moves to the beat of his own drum, into the sunset, searching for the next parade to join and call home.

I have always danced alone, to the beat of my own drum, not because I'm a lone wolf, but I've never had the opportunity to collaborate. Even when I was married, we had our own bedrooms and spaces. I really don't know what being a couple or being part of a family in real life is like. I want my future reality to be what I see and like in the movies. I don't care about the harsh real world – it can be softened with rose-tinted glasses – I honestly believe this is what is lacking in conventional real life. Treat your life like a story book – why not!?!?!

I have been told I have an 'openness' about me, a childlike innocence and a bit of sensuality that people seem to gravitate to. The problem has been, when I don't do what they expect me to, or think how they think I'm suppose to think, the tables turn and I'm automatically in the wrong.

I find myself reflecting to both Marilyn Monroe and Princess Diana as, if still alive, both probably could relate to being lost in a society that has done them wrong. Tragically, their celebrity status didn't allow them to gracefully run away and hide as I can but, just like them, it is tragic to be alone.

I fantasize a supportive partner, someone to be the keeper of the key, letting me safely reside in the pretty room with padded walls that I call the confines of my imagination, letting me bounce around, causing no harm to either myself or others. I don't need to be scolded or told what I do is wrong or unacceptable, but need someone with the patience to go with the fumbles and falls, and help fix the problems instead of ignoring them. I am a great problem solver but often cannot see the blatant obvious. This may be because my personal journeys in life have taught me to look forward to the finish line and, though there are a few obstacles along the way, I consider them to be minor while others consider them huge hurdles. I find it amazing that I can do what anyone asks of me without effort, yet few have been able to do it for me. I'm not strong enough to keep doing it for myself.

I think this is why I am most comfortable as a journalist, the consummate storyteller. I can spin around truths and romance them to death and, though I need fact as my foundation, I can easily find humour in the saddest of its moments. With a solid foundation, I have no fear to soar and create the most compelling story ever told, to pique the curiosity and touch the heart of the reader. I've been pining for a similar solid foundation and story structure all my life - for my own story.

My overproductive imagination is my saving grace, and probably the only thing I possess that needs to be protected. Without it, I don't think I could ever survive what life throws at me.

Maybe my online personal profile is finally me, cementing the footings I have been looking for all my life. Now that the structural element has a sound foundation, maybe, just maybe, the architecture is in place, and I can finally come out of hiding, or stop running away.

* * *

*Victoria is a marketing/public relations/event planner/editorial journalist. Eclectic and chameleon-like in nature, Victoria is at home when wearing many hats as she is also co-partner in SpinalWrap.ca and ShowTimeChocolate.com, where she uses her unique style in writing and communications, bringing a refreshing new approach to the areas of well-being through balance.*

*It is very "Victoria-esque" that, during the writing of this book, she would become the Edtior-in-Chief on Enrich Magazine, a regional lifestyle magazine in her new adopted city of Brampton, Ontario.*

# Women Warriors
## and the Art of Having Balls
### by Kate Dillon

My friends and acquaintances call me a strong and brave woman and someone who they wouldn't like to take on in a battle, but one they would prefer to have holding their back and blind side. I haven't always been that strong woman; I had to grow into her. I like to think that I have grown a fabulous set of female balls over the last forty-six years and I've been quite proud of them at various times and none more so than when I've had to exercise them and won. But it isn't about winning, it's about my own sense of justice, reclaiming my power or the principle of not allowing others to do harm. I keep my set of balls nicely polished and exercise them regularly to maintain a healthy balance in my life. If nothing else, a woman should always carry her set at all times, along with red Chanel lipstick. But enough about my survival tools for now.

As a teacher I have seen how easy it is to become damaged by the messages we receive from significant others from a very young age, and I have experienced firsthand how this affects us for the rest of our lives. It becomes part of our DNA, it permeates our thinking, our perception and our beliefs. I recognize this in others simply because I had observed it in myself through my own journey, battling against these beliefs my whole life. Expectations of me, of my future and success in life was rock bottom from significant adults and teachers all through my childhood and youth, so I grew up with a fast deflating self-esteem, anger, little self-worth and a few daydreams to keep me going.

Just last year I completed a Masters Degree in Education, not an easy task and one of the hardest commitments I ever had to endure. Everyone says it's a difficult task, but when you are a high school drop out with little education under your belt and, albeit late attained, it becomes a mammoth endeavour. School and learning never came easy to me and by the time I left school at fifteen I had a long and excellent rap sheet of failings. The expectations for myself and from others was to be a check-out chick or factory fodder and that would exceed most people's expectations of my potential. My family didn't place much emphasis on career for us girls and I was a proven failure with my head in the Aquarian clouds most of the time, less than favourable report cards and much to my own disgust little sense came out of my mouth.

At the critical age of thirteen my family broke down, my mother engaged in a meltdown after years of domestic violence, and neglected and abandoned us three younger girls. My younger sister and I ended up in a Ward of State home for children for nine months. At the court day when we were assigned to be the government's responsibility, I recall my grandmother and other significant adults being present, but no one claimed us or attempted to keep us out of the state home. Rejection and abandonment was to forever play a part in all of my relationships throughout my life.

A healthy sense of worth and self-confidence was completely missing and my self-identity was as one who was stupid, worthless, incompetent, shy, inferior, ugly and with a major attitude problem that later surfaced, when mixed with alcohol, into social aggression and many stupid mistakes in my youth. A large part of me believed all of this about myself and I was fulfilling others' expectations of me beautifully, and why not? I simply couldn't see a promising future for me, but somewhere in my makeup there was always a burning desire to achieve a successful life, prove that I was actually in receipt of some genetically encoded intellect and that I had a birthright to live a happy and loving life. But for the life of me, I had not a clue how this was ever going to happen for me.

I left school at fifteen with a historically poor report card and started working full-time. Job after job came and went, hard work leading nowhere; significant loves and a marriage also came and went, a son was born too and after ten years of post-school aimlessness I finally found my motivation for making a better life and changing what I now see as my victim thinking into one which aimed for empowerment. This was the first instance where I sat up and took notice of who and where I was and what I wanted, more so what I wanted to provide for my child in the way of self-confidence and inner strength. As a mother I also saw the opportunity for me to repeat the behaviours others had shown to me and how easily I could damage my child's bright spark if only I chose to fulfil cyclic thought forms. Knowing full well I had this power was frightening; how easy it could have been to allow my own issues to block my child's potential, crush his self-esteem and destroy his opportunities in life.

As a now single parent I found myself more determined than ever to not go under and drown in life's stresses, but it was a difficult battle to keep gulping for air; at least that's how I felt. I was always struggling and battling, not only life and survival in the world but with my own thought forms and low self-worth. I have spent a good deal of my life feeling inferior to others and lacking confidence in my abilities and self-trust with most of whatever I did in life. I grew up in a family where there was conflicting messages about self-worth; my father had always taught us resilience and to be strong, a hard worker, not to suffer fools, and gave us an excellent moral compass, yet on the other hand my parents were non-affectionate, unsupportive and over-critical of all that I seemed to do. I rarely received encouragement or praise; I guess they didn't know how to give it. I ended up marrying a critical man too, who put me down and made me feel unworthy. To put it simply, I didn't know who I was and if I was anything it was nothing of substance; I was a nobody who felt that no real love was given to me and I felt rejection from all angles.

Up until my early thirties I mostly behaved like an introvert socially, I rarely engaged in conversation about topics and would clam up verbally if others were outspoken. I didn't feel that I had anything to contribute or the knowledge needed to carry on an intelligent discussion. Mostly I said nothing, but I observed and I angrily festered inside at others' egos requiring them to know it all and place their views on others, not allowing others, including me, to have their say, albeit clumsily. I noticed that people have a need to have power over others either verbally or by their behaviours, and I began to stand up for myself and others. Everyone treated me like this and lorded over me; I hated it, it incensed me, but part of me allowed it, because I believed everyone else was superior. I was letting myself act small and allowed others to treat me the same way. I felt invisible, I was invisible, I made myself invisible.

On the other hand, I had taken some control of my life over the previous ten years and had proven myself to be an excellent preschool teacher who had a lot to give others. I had a passion for literacy, exploration of creativity and science, and also a compassion and understanding of people that afforded me deep connections. Apart from being a great mum and teacher that is all that I had in my life; relationships with men who were of any substance seemed to avoid me and a big part of me loved my independence, but I was lonely and I never stopped hoping that one day I would find that man who would compliment me in the ways I desired.

I continued to throw myself into work into my late thirties and when my son turned twelve he decided that it would be fair for his Dad to have a turn at our son living with him. I was devastated, my son was my life, he is what kept me together, he was the only thing that made me get up in the mornings and keep trying and keep aiming for something better. I simply had no other reason for life; I had nothing else to live for really. He was the only reason I continued to strive and be strong. I did concede after many frank conversations because he was a mature young boy and knew what he wanted, so who was I to deny him a family life with his father and his new family? It seemed selfish of me to force him not to go simply because of my pain of losing him. A close friend of mine put our relationship into perspective for me when she said that it doesn't matter where my son lives because the relationship we have is so strong and close that it will never change. That was medicine to my soul but I spent the next five or so years mourning my perceived loss as full-time parent and it felt like a death to me. Here I was again, lost in life and alone. I sunk into depression, relinquished daily disciplines and routines and was angry most of the time; I became an angry insane recluse of sorts. I felt like the failure I always knew I had been and had been treated as, and this sense of unworthiness and rejection of myself by myself slapped me in the face. I had contemplated opting out of this world on a few occasions but something inside of me and my fear of what my son would go through kept these thoughts as just that. If it wasn't for his existence I wouldn't exist today either, I know that as sure as I breathe.

By thirty-nine I had accidently landed a job training international students in child care. I had dreamt of a job like this and finally it had fallen into my lap. It seemed that this job was what I had been waiting for without realizing it, and I found my professional niche. The job was all I had and I worked hard at it and built up a healthy sense of self-worth as students started thanking me for my knowledge and for teaching them properly. I still hold strong friendships with some of my first students who felt that I had not only taught them and set them up for their careers but also because they saw me as a mentor, a role I didn't see myself as holding, considering my own personal and educational background. In fact I was a reluctant mentor, I couldn't help myself but did help others when I could, but I rejected the mentor role as I felt underqualified in life and still pretty messed up as a human. I still struggled with self-esteem issues and, although I found that I had a plethora of knowledge that I didn't realize I had, I still felt quite stupid, a by-product of my youth which had never gone and still influenced how I saw myself and what I thought I was capable of even into my forties. I really had a limited view on possibilities for me in life, and a fear of stepping up into top level roles. I have always seen myself as a rebel and that was the reason for not wanting to move into top jobs, but it was really a deep-seated fear of my perceived inabilities and incompetence. This fear of and perception of being stupid had at times consumed me and in my early forties I was compelled to take on a Masters Degree in Education. Compelled, because it was an intuitive-based overwhelming desire, certainly not a rational choice based on my background, but more of an inspired push from the universe. I had never completed a degree before, just part thereof and a few Advanced Diplomas to speak of, but I had a hunger for higher learning and a desire to prove to myself that I had the intellect to take this on, and test out some of my own theories about education and leadership in the workplace. I had lots of those in my head but not the academic knowledge or articulation to really think them through to a conclusion. I was fortunate to be given the chance to enter the program by a very understanding Dean of the university I applied to, who had a blind faith in me and my story and I was granted permission to enrol, quite unheard of these days when you don't have a full degree under your belt. As I was all set to go and enrolled we got news from our father that he was diagnosed with lung cancer. He lived six hours north and our relationship had been up and down since I was a kid, he was an alcoholic and lived on a farm property with his partner whom seem to be always trying her best to put me down. Dad had moved in with her to get us released from the home so that he could show that he was in steady living conditions and they stayed together for thirty years, they had always had feelings for each other prior to this time and the situation met everyone's needs. Being a young teen at that time and having gone through what I had, I was fairly shy and withdrawn, she had brought up four boys and, when I got first my period living at her house, she told me to use wrapped up toilet paper instead of buying me sanitary products. She really didn't have a clue of how to bring up girls and particularly painfully shy and troubled ones like myself.

She, as well as my father, liked a drink so weekends were often spent sitting in a beer garden at the local pub waiting for them to have their social drinks. Dad had always drank and before he and my mother separated he had been a violent drunk. We girls would cry out for him to stop beating our mother, and for her to stop goading him. I knew that she often set him off with her nagging and goading, but knew also that it was no excuse for belting a woman. We watched as he punched and kicked her, and if we were unlucky we would cop the strap for anything that addled him while angry. Although he had a raging Irish temper and not the best childhood himself, he had been a wonderful father before everything turned sour. He was tough and could be very violent but he had such wonderful qualities, incredible knowledge and skills that you couldn't help but admire. In spite of everything I was proud of my dad; he had such potential, wasted for

71

the most part but still there. It's easy to judge a man's whole character when he is violent towards women and write him off completely based on that fact alone. But I knew my dad holistically and I knew who he was behind that ugliness.

When he was diagnosed with cancer my eldest sister and I were up at their place every chance we got. We helped him make sense of the treatment and we emotionally supported him. I think he was surprised that I actually loved him enough to be there for him. Mortality is a funny thing, how it causes you to put everything aside. Forgiveness just occurred and I saw in him not only the tough man's man trying to hold it together but also the sensitive little boy inside, that innocent being that we have inside of us. His partner went downhill with her own health issues at the same time and I really don't know how dad handled not only his health issues but her's too. She went from having some age-related health issues to wetting herself at the kitchen table, as well a form of dementia which took her to a childlike state and an eventual complete body shut down. I was very angry with her because at first I felt that she didn't cope with all of our attention being on my father and not on her and her behaviour appeared like an attention seeking brat. I think the shock of losing my father set her into a downward spiral and she died within six months. I rolled a joint for my father that night, not a role I would normally take on. He didn't smoke marijuana much and I certainly didn't, but it felt like the right thing to do at the time and it was available through my step-brother. It was a moment of knowing and maturity to move past the moral compass with this act of compassion.

I was getting right into my Masters at the same time and if I had deferred I wouldn't get the chance again to do it, so I kept plugging away at it. My dad was so proud of me, as was my son and my friends for taking it on, but the timing couldn't have been worse. We moved dad down from the farm to my sister's place so we could look after him during his remainder of the treatment, but the chemo had done its work well and truly and he was fast becoming a skeleton. He lasted a year longer than his initial prognosis and that year he stayed at my sister's was to be our time to reconnect as father and daughter. It was a wonderful time for us both; I hadn't seen so much of him for over thirty years and he finally got to know me in a real sense. I had always felt invisible and never good enough in my father's eyes. He commented on my strength and laughed at my humour and we shared. I read Australian bush poetry, including his favourite, Banjo Patterson's The Man from Snowy River, in his last few weeks as he lay barely coherent but I saw the pride in his eyes and the love as I read, at times taking long moments to control my emotions. I regretted that so much time had been wasted over the years in anger, resentment, hurt and pride. It wasn't until this time of my father's imminent death and afterwards that I realized how surprised he was at the love I gave him during his greatest time of need and of how much he loved me. The other thing I realized is how life can deal such hard blows and it is how we deal with them that can turn our path into a growth or a downward spiral; that inner strength of whether we handle things or whether we let them control or handle us.

It makes me so sad whenever I think of him, of his potential and where he ended up in life, the choices he made and didn't make, his drinking habit and how that smothered opportunities and also alienated most of his daughters for a good part of his life. I see that in myself sometimes and where I have allowed life to get the better of me and allowed my own view of myself keep me from rising above it. I've had times of deep and dark depression, self-hatred, alcohol abuse and periods of rage and anger which mostly turned inward, but there's also been that deep pressure lever that would limit the depth to which I would sink, and I would find myself swimming to the surface again, getting my shit together.

During my study with the masters degree I wanted to give up many times and I saw within myself my father's lost potential and the lack of self-belief. I also saw the young girl and woman who saw herself as a failure and unable to accomplish anything of value. Studying at this level took me into those moments frequently, but it was such an uncomfortable space to be in that it spurred me on even when I felt physical pain in doing so. I couldn't stand to bear the painful burden of such a mammoth failure upon my shoulders when I had fought so hard against it all of my life.

The beliefs of failure, and having a lack of intelligence also permeated my idea of how I thought I looked. Not only was I an unintelligent failure but I didn't even have good looks to fall back on. I had always believed that I was a plain looking girl and my relationships with men reflected my belief of myself, the rejection I experienced in relationships, the lack of affection, interest and compliments that came my way helped cement my self-perception. This idea that I was ugly and plain looking made me even more shy, and a lack of confidence prevailed all through the years well into my thirties. I would shrink if a man came up to talk to me and if I did gain attention from the opposite sex I didn't believe that it was for any higher reason than fishing for a booty call. Occasionally I would follow the carrot

73

though and I would find myself in a relationship like all of my relationships, where rejection was on the menu and emotionally unavailable men eventually walked. I desperately wanted to be loved yet as I matured and aged the need stayed but I also became more comfortable in myself, or so I thought.

Choices of suitable beaus became less frequent as I became more fussy with the offerings and more accustomed with my singledom. Once when visiting my father up in the rural town where he lived we visited his local watering hole which consisted of local cattle farmers and regular country folk. The locals consisted of one particular catch who, with his cowboy hat, weathered face and exposed front gums stood a ways away from our table staring at me until venturing over in his country swagger and saying to me "well yer a fine little filly, are yer married"? I stupidly said no and he asked "Do yer wanna be?" I nearly choked and immediately in my mind I thought, this is it, this is what I have to choose from, this guy thinks he has a chance, he thinks I'm a filly and he's going to ride me! wow! I really must be plain looking or this guy has a huge set of balls. I didn't know whether to laugh or cry but I made a promise to myself to always wear my old wedding ring when visiting in the future.

Over nineteen years of being single for the most part and happily independent, I kept looking for love but none were ever right for me. I seemed to attract those who were emotionally unavailable and critical, and they never lasted more than a few months. They say that like attracts like, and if that law of attraction plays a part then I attracted men who reflected what I thought about myself deep down, that I wasn't good enough, and so their behaviour enacted my beliefs. That's a good theory and although, throughout each relationship I blamed their lack of balls and inability to love, it possibly could have been a reflection of what I expected to receive. Although I seemed to attract dysfunctional men to me, I never repeated my mother's mistake of being with violent men. No man ever laid a hand on me and if they had, I wouldn't be free in society to write this story.

When I was nineteen I had a boyfriend who would risk his father's wrath and his friends' disapproval by being there for me. Back then I was in everyone's face and drank too much alcohol. He was my first love, sweet and pure and it wasn't long before I had sabotaged it. After we broke up I never saw him again, I moved to Sydney and met my first husband, and he ended up marrying my arch enemy. We lived separate lives for twenty seven years until very recently. Letting him go and destroying our relationship was always my biggest regret, but as luck or fate would have it, we have reconnected again after all of this time. Once we saw each other again it was like we had never been apart. The immense feelings of love and connection was overwhelming and a shock for us both. That was over six months ago and we are still together. It's not an easy relationship as we both have a lot of baggage from our separate pasts and triggers that have both of us reeling into defensive and self-protection mode, yet there is some kind of anchor keeping us from flying off in all different directions even when it seems all too difficult. And although it has its difficulties and fears, entwined within it and between us is a great love and mutual respect that I cannot even begin to fathom; it's like nothing I have ever felt or experienced and I can only liken its nature to being something on a soul level, as though it existed even before we did. Where this will take us I cannot predict, all I can do is try to let go of my past pains, try not to let my history get in my own way and keep an open heart and let time, intuition and conscious choices do the rest.

I'm forty-six now, and over the years I have tried my best to reflect, grow and find myself. I've taken paths that have enlightened me somewhat, or proven to be not for me. I have explored my humanness in all its beautiful glory and ugly facets, and I am still driven to grow and succeed in all aspects of life. My career is steady and starting to grow again in different directions, including having been asked to write my story for this book. Writing is something I've always wanted to do and have dabbled with over the years and here I find myself trying to condense my life in just a few pages for you to judge somewhat. Is my story good enough, dramatic enough, tragic enough for you to be drawn in and feel some empathy, recognition and perhaps take my lessons and use them to benefit or motivate yourself? I do hope so. I would like to think that pain and challenges for ourselves and from others' experiences are to be learnt from and used as a springboard for better things to come. The only thing that stops us from being what we want to be and having what we want in life is us. If I've learned something from knowing myself and recognizing how I've dealt with life it is that we are truly in absolute control to turn life around, to walk away, to prove others and ourselves wrong, to make new choices and to empower ourselves.

As women we have our own share of strength, often forgotten but drawn upon when required. We grow up with the insane yet accepted mindset of being needed to be looked after and protected. Yet it is this mindset that we often prove to ourselves to be a false reality as any woman who has had to take on the role of independent survivor, breadwinner and main role model for their children will know. For anyone, man or woman going out into the world to survive, bloom, grow as an individual and succeed on your own merits and through your own battles ... it is a warrior's journey yet harvests incredible resilience and rewards. There are, however, two pieces of equipment required for any woman warrior and that is to always nurture your set of balls and keep them exercised, and most importantly always always keep your red Chanel lipstick at the ready.

* * *

*Kate is an Early Childhood and Business Trainer in Adult Education in Australia. She holds Advanced Diplomas in Children's Services, Business, Adult Education and a Masters Degree in Education (Leadership & Management). With a chequered career and personal life history she endeavours to enrich others' lives with her accumulation of experience and lifes' lessons into her teaching and everyday interactions. She is a lover of writing empowering childrens' books, organic gardening, food, hiking, with a passion for promoting others' potential and social justice.*

# Turning Lemons into Lemonade
## by Elizabethe Vick

Janet, a counsellor that I know, used to tell me all the time, "Elizabethe, you know how to turn lemons into lemonade." When I asked what she meant by that, she said, "You are always a person that I see as able to make something positive out of any situation that has been thrown your way. You can see the beauty and this affects the outcome. You are a very positive person." What a great way to look at life.

So, in my pyjamas, I humbly take a deep breath, sip my herbal tea and with gratitude I start to begin writing about my journey...

You know that you are on an incredible journey when circumstances beyond your control start with your birth.

Being born the second in a set of premature twin girls, I was given the name Lisa while my twin sister was given the name Elizabethe. A visit from my aunt would prove to be life-changing, even at days old!

With my aunt's first glance at us, she turned to my parents and said, "Elizabethe should be named Lisa and Lisa should be named Elizabethe." "Why?" My parents questioned. "Well, Elizabethe looks like her mom's side, and Lisa looks like our side," replied my aunt. So, with this observation, fate had stepped in and our names were legally changed. I don't know how you can tell the difference between a set of twins—especially newborns.

Marriage came quickly for my mom and dad, because as they say, there was an "egg in the nest".

My mom and dad both worked to support the family of two boys and three girls. My mom has always maintained that she was attracted to my dad because of the similarity to a certain famous singer of the time, Elvis! Looking at the high school pictures of my dad, I can see a slight resemblance. I think it was the hair!

Alcohol was part of my dad's downfall. It would take control of my father and my mother would be at the receiving end of his brutal force. As my dad aged, the alcohol slowed down but did not disappear. Through all of this, my parents remained together, and are still together after fifty years.

This brings me to the next and most influential trauma that I have encountered in my life. It has to be spoken about to get a deeper understanding of my journey. I became an incest survivor when I was sexually molested by family members. I found that the more that I have spoken about it, the more other survivors have come out of the woodwork. This is a subject that is hard to talk about not only privately but publicly.

I found myself in compromising situations from a tender age. Is this the way of giving love to someone you adored? At this age, I thought that what was done to me was the norm. As I look back I see relatives taking advantage of an innocent child.

On top of this, how can "loving" parents side with one of the perpetrators? My parents asked me why I didn't tell them when I was younger. I told them I had blocked it out all these years. Could this be why I had issues being intimate with my husband? My abuser is an old man and will not survive the incarceration. He will be dead soon and it won't matter after that. He lived for a few more years. I never did get my answer.

It takes a lot to make a child stop loving their parents, but when they do, it takes even more for them to forgive. When I won't forgive and can't let go of the past, I am binding myself to the past. When I am stuck in the past, I cannot live in the present time and create my glorious future.

I was a young career woman, when I met a man who would change my life. He was handsome and very charismatic. I had fallen head over heels for him. Not only did I find out he was living with someone, but I found out I was pregnant. He went with me to the doctors to discuss aborting the baby. I was informed by the doctor that this procedure could not happen as I was too far along. The father of the baby was not happy with this. I did not want anyone at work to know about the situation, so I quit.

I could no longer hide the belly or the baby that was growing inside me. The time had come to tell my family. My dad shocked me by telling me he had a feeling that I was pregnant. My dad and my brother paid a visit to the father. The baby's father did **not** want to be a part of this life.

The night came when I would deliver my child. I asked my younger sister to be in the delivery room with me. She was so excited and cried many tears as her niece was born. As a final gesture to my sister, I named my precious bundle of joy after her. This gesture would eventually become a tribute to her.

As a newborn, her father and I had agreed he would offer support payments. To this day, I have not received any payments for her. I am fine with that and I think it is better. Recently my daughter married her knight in shining armour.

I worked two jobs to give my baby girl a great upbringing. We shared a lot of memories, until the time would come when we would meet the perfect father and husband for us.

I was climbing up the corporate ladder when I met the man of my dreams. It was hard to resist his charm and good looks. He had no issue with seeing someone that had a child that was not his. We would even go on family dates. He was completely different than the ones I had dated in the past. Within no time we were engaged. Some of the family members were telling us not to rush in. You haven't had enough time with each other yet to see if it will work out. I didn't listen to them and the rest, as they say, is history.

My time with this man has been nothing short of astonishing. We recently celebrated our twenty-fifth anniversary. Shortly after our marriage, my husband wanted to legally adopt my daughter. This was not an issue as the father had gladly given up all his parental rights. She was now part of him. They have such a special bond together.

Life was great until I was involved in a car accident. As I sat at an intersection waiting to turn, I was broadsided by a van. Within a millisecond, life had changed. I had impacted the front windshield with my forehead. The only visible trauma was the bruise on my forehead. For the next four years, I would suffer from severe headaches. My eyesight was affected so much that I was told by my physician not to drive or I would lose my license. To top it off, my jaw line was affected to the point where I needed surgery. There are permanent surgical steel pins and plates in my chin and jaw joints.

Over time, I was able to regain my full potential eyesight. The best thing of all was I was able to drive. You never know how grateful you are for something until it is taken away. You learn to appreciate all that you have.

More children were what was waiting around the corner. Who would have thought that carrying a child would help with the healing process of a body? The doctors found out that the increase in hormones helped my body heal faster from the accident. I was excited about mending as well as being pregnant. My unborn child was so excited about coming into this world that it wanted to come three months early. I was put on bed rest to stop the contractions. Still, arriving early, we welcomed a little bundle of joy, a son. Shortly after his birth, we welcomed another son.

My next job was very stressful. I was in charge of payables and receivables. The atmosphere was more chaotic than calm. I was not aware of how stressful the job was on me at the time. I found out later that the girl I had replaced left for stress reasons. Within a short time, I began to have symptoms that were unfamiliar to me. I had sweating, headaches and most importantly chest pains. Could these be symptoms of heart issues?

One day on my lunch, I went to a walk-in clinic. I never returned back to work. The stress had taken such a toll on me that I was given nitro-glycerine as I blanked out. I was rushed to the hospital. Several different tests were given. Tests were inconclusive to any heart issues but what really astonished the doctors was the lack of speaking that I had.

The stress was so great that it took away my ability to speak. The doctors would hold up items for me to identify. Funny thing is, though, I knew what the items were but somehow my communication skills did not allow me to be vocal. Words would not come out. I was released to go home. The doctor's conclusion was.... too much stress. Diagnosis was rest. I was told not to worry about my voice, that it would return in a few days. Needless to say, the voice did not come back as predicted. What was happening to me? How could I lose the ability to speak?

As I looked in the mirror, I didn't see me. I felt as though the person in the mirror was in a movie. My face had become very thin from the loss of weight. My eyes, which are the path to my soul, showed no life.

Communication with my family was through handwritten notes. It was very detrimental to my family to see me in this state.

There were numerous visits to physicians and specialists. Tests were done to see what had happened. A conclusion was found from a specialist. He had seen alot, but of course not to the extreme that I had. What was his conclusion? Stress that I was under caused a breakdown in my brain. Somehow, the "wires" in my brain that control my speech had shorted out. To make matters worse, they were reconnecting at their own pace and to another spot on the "mother board". They were redirecting themselves and would heal in their own time.

"How can I live my life without my voice? I have always taken it for granted and now that it is gone. I want it back!" It would take me nearly eight months to get my voice back.

Part of my therapy was to see a speech therapist. I shortly began to notice the difference. As my speech was coming back, there was a difference with my tone. My words would come out slurry as if I had had too many drinks. Think of what it is like when you hear someone who is intoxicated. This is the part that affected a lot of people as well as my family. Everyone was supportive and patient as I struggled to get my words across. This was great news for me as it meant that, if I persevered, my voice could come back.

Don't forget, I told you earlier that I am stubborn and determined. This was so true at this time of my life. Throughout this whole ordeal was the loving support of my little sister. She was my "taxi" to a lot of the appointments with the doctors. I had no idea that this bonding time would be one of our lasts before she became my angel.

As well as speech lessons, I was asked if I would like to take up yoga as a part of my therapy as well. Every week in the basement of the hospital was a relaxation class. It was available for patients. Not all hospitals offer this. I was willing to give it a shot. We were taught to relax and release the tensions in the body. How exuberant it felt! I loved doing yoga. I would look forward to each class. I began to feel better with myself and with my voice. When we were in the yoga class, a lot of focus was on the breath. At first it was hard to focus on the breath. As my breathing became deeper, I noticed a significant change in my voice. I could talk more easily and not sound like a drunk! Could this be what I needed to help me with my final therapy?

Stress is now considered one of the foremost contributors to our modern chronic ailments. Stress is a major factor in causing heart disease, cancer and other chronic and acute diseases in the body. How do we end up with stress in our life? How does it get such a hold on us that it creates havoc on our bodies? I know only too well what this word stress did to my life. I had the stress effect once and I vowed that I would not let it get a grip on me again.

I began to "ask" for caretakers and healers to help me. Lo and behold, I was somehow connected to them. As it has been said before; no matter what the problem is, the main issue is to work on loving yourself. There is no magic wand or potion that dissolves all the past. It would be great if life was like that. It took me a very long time to develop a peaceful loving relationship with myself.

I was so intrigued with what yoga had done for me that I wanted to learn more about it. I wanted to find out if there was a way in which I could teach this to others. I began searching and taking the classes that I had found around my area.

I began teaching yoga to my neighbours. The neighbours were so appreciative of what I was doing for them. I found that, as I taught classes, my voice was **not** an issue. My speech not only sounded better, but it was also calmer. I was so happy with how my life was going.

As I was searching the websites, I noticed a yoga studio that was looking for volunteers. Could this be something that I could handle? I definitely didn't want to have another breakdown. I took a deep breath and made the call. I was asked to come to the studio. As I entered the studio, I was not alone as others had applied as well. I needed to stay strong and focus on my breath if I wanted this to transpire. I was offered the volunteer position. The "job" was to keep the studio cleaned in exchange for participating in classes.

As time went on, I was given an opportunity of a lifetime from the owner of the studio. As my hours of volunteering accumulated, I was asked if I wanted to be a certified yoga instructor. This was more than I could imagine. They say that when the student is ready, the teacher will appear. Well, I guess I was ready!

As I worked towards certification, I was aware of my breath. No matter how far I have travelled on my healing journey, this is my strength.

A friend of mine and her children know all too well about the breath. One of the groups I was fortunate enough to teach was a group of teenagers. We would work on the breath as well as yoga postures. At the time, I didn't know that what I taught would be lifesaving for them.

One night as the girls and their mother were driving home, they were hit by another vehicle. Their car lay upside down, but the girls did not panic. They remembered the breathing that was taught to them in class. As they lay upside down, they did their breathing and showed their mom how to do it. I was truly speechless when the girls came up to tell me what they did. The mom has come to me to help with more breathing techniques.

This is just one example of the benefits of the breath. Breath awareness is the simplest way to break through all the veils of illusion. You cannot fake the breath. When we are relaxed, we breathe more slowly, deeply and into the well of the diaphragm. As stress and tension accelerate, our breath becomes more rapid, shallow and stays in the upper chest area. When I feel I am in an uncomfortable position, I know to focus on my breath.

Just when I felt that I had everything under control, I got a call from my brother-in-law. My younger beloved sister had been rushed to the hospital. My gut told me that this was not a good situation.

As my husband and daughter entered the hospital, I was met by my brother-in-law. He informed me that my sister had a heart attack. He then informed me that she did not make it. I WANT TO SEE HER! As I entered the room the coroner had just finished his report. I asked him what happened. "Your sister had a massive coronary and we tried everything we could for the last hour. I am sorry."

With those words spoken, I walked over to the lifeless body, still warm to the touch. She looked like she was sleeping. I just wanted to wake her up. I gently held her hand and kissed it gingerly. I kept telling her how much I loved her. To see a body that does not move to the touch is something that will forever be etched in my mind. Rigamortis was starting to set in as I stayed with her throughout the visitation. How could this have happened? I was devastated.

She had just been at the doctors weeks ago and had a physical completed. There was nothing outstanding that would indicate an issue with this. Okay, she drank and she smoked, but she should not have died at such an early age. My goodness, my parents still smoke and drink.

It is hard to deal with such a loss when you are not prepared. Patients who have terminal illnesss get the opportunity to say goodbye to their loved ones. When a life is taken away suddenly, you don't get that reward.

As preparations were being made for her funeral, I found myself doing more yoga. I would even do yoga in the middle of the night on the lawn.

It was my stress release and I swallowed it whole. Yes, yoga! Without hesitation my body was already telling me what I should be doing to decompress. I would do some of my postures but more importantly, I would focus on the breath. Without knowing it, my body was getting me to calm down, and reassessing what was important to me and that was...ME.

I wrote a letter to myself with all my feelings about her and the situation and all others that had happened. This gave me an outlet for my feelings. There were tears and there was joy. LIFE ISN'T FAIR! When I wrote all that needed to be said, I disposed of it. There was a release of emotions and then....calmness. If you are still grieving after a few years, you are wallowing in it. You need to forgive and release the loved one. If only we could understand that our so-called problems are just opportunities for us to grow and to change.

According to the paramedic, her heart was already beginning to die from the back of the heart to the front. I had the privilege of speaking to the paramedic months later about her death. I always wondered if she was in pain and if she asked for her family. The paramedic was able to fill the in the blanks for me. He told me that she was not in any pain and that she did not ask for her family. She was scared about what was happening, but she didn't think it was life-threatening.

I talked to the Heart and Stroke Foundation looking for answers about heart disease. What I found out was astonishing. More and more women are at risk of dying from heart disease than men. Every seven minutes someone in Canada dies from heart disease. It is the number one cause of death even more than cancer! WHY? Women put such a burden on themselves. Women put everyone in the family before themselves. Taxi driver, chef, wife, employee are a few job titles we hold on a daily basis.

Men feel chest symptoms and know that something traumatic is happening. They will get treatment right away. Women can feel it in the jaw, stomach or upper back. Women will go for days as if nothing is wrong. For both sexes, time is critical for survival. The sooner you can get the heart treated, the less damage there will be.

This is what I found out with my sister. She had stomach pains. Why would you think there was anything wrong? She had these feelings before. This would be detrimental to her life. A tragedy can turn out to be for our greatest good. We have to approach it in ways from which we can grow.

*SISTER: you are special and our relationship was strong and true, so when I count my blessings, I always think of you, my guardian angel...* Always in my heart.

What could I do that would benefit others? I could raise money for heart defibrillators! So, this is what I did. Since her death, I have organized fundraisers for that reason. The last event that I held featured a very special guest speaker. He is well aware of what heart and stroke issues are. He has been a stroke survivor and is the Canadian spokesman for Heart and Stroke. Not only did he volunteer to speak at my event but he also donated hockey memorabilia of his famous son. His name is Walter Gretzky! I was truly blessed to have him as part of my event.

The awareness of taking care of me was all too real after my sister's death. I go every year and get a heart checkup done. This past year was no exception. Part of my physical was a mammogram. A lump was found on my breast. Surgery was scheduled to remove it. The lump was the size of a golf ball, loaded with puss and blood and luckily was non-cancerous.

I woke up in the recovery room with uncontrollable shaking. My whole body was thrashing from side to side. I heard the doctor say that he has never seen this is the five years that he has been at the hospital. More blankets were layered on top of me. This did not help. Finally, a shot was given to calm me down. This worked.

As I woke up the next morning, I could not move. I felt as if I was paralyzed from the waist down. What was wrong? I could not get out of bed. So, what did I do? I did my yoga poses in bed. I found out that I had pulled all the muscles in my lower back. My legs felt like two tons of steel and were sinking with every move.

When I had my followup appointment with the surgeon, I found out some interesting news. I had a reaction to the anaesthetic that was given to me in the hospital. I was given a note to keep in my wallet. I was not allowed to have this drug anymore. It was Propofol! This is the same drug that was given to Michael Jackson!

Life continued on for a few years until the universe intervened in my path again. One of my tasks in my latest job was to make natural peanut butter. I would place peanuts at the top of the machine and the grinder would crush the peanuts into peanut butter. I finished making the batch and started to clean the machine, when I heard a "click". When I pulled my left index finger out, it had been cut off to the first knuckle. The machine was off and somehow a peanut was jarred until it was freed. Unfortunately the finger could not be attached as it was too mangled. As I still continue and heal, I realize again that I am not in control of my life; the universe is. How many lessons does one need before they get it? I do not hold any remorse for my job which I have left. I realize that the universe was sending a message to follow my path. Ironically this accident happened eight days before the anniversary of my sister's passing. I no longer ask what am I to do, I wait to be shown. The universe has its own schedule and I have to listen to the higher power, to align with the divine.

No one is capable of making me upset without my consent. Before, I gave my control away too frequently. I could throw up my hands in horror. I could call my life a mess, but would that not be giving into the past? We know that the past is done and over. I cannot change it now, nor would I want to. It is what has made me. How foolish would I be if I thought I could change the past?

I am paying attention to my inner feelings. I have moved on and forgiven everyone and everything that has happened in my life. I will not play the victim's role. I will not let my personal power be taken away again. I have taken responsibility for the changes in my life. The best gift I can give myself is the gift of me. I am on a voyage of self-discovery and I love it! I want you to be able to see that life is not just about the negative but also about the positive.

My husband and my children have learned valuable lessons of life from me. I am honoured to see that they are not afraid to go after what they want in life. They are creating their own paths and not afraid to do it. I am simply amazed at what they have accomplished and are willing to let go of to get their dreams.

Yoga and meditation are part of my passion. It is for this reason that I keep my "eyes and ears" open for the next road on my path. I can't wait to see what happens next... but I will have to be patient. I will offer yoga and meditation to those who have had trauma in their life.

I have been happily married to my soul mate for over twenty-five years. I am the proud mother of three extraordinary children and one very intelligent dog.

I am humbled to teach at various studios and organizations. Along with offering reflexology and Thai yoga massage, I am also a reiki master and a reiki teacher. I will continue to raise money to purchase, maintain and educate for heart defibrillators.

I will continue to train for triathlons and for tough mudder events; bringing awareness for women's heart issues.

I will continue to sew handmade mediation cushions as a tribute to my beloved sister.                                                        www.celove.org

My new motto is "mudder on a mission". Helping hands that help humanity                                           www.mudderonamission.ca

* * *

*Elizabethe approaches all of life through the heart of service. She believes that we can speak through our authentic voice and genuine caring. Elizabethe offers practical tools that empower her students to become conscious participants in their own healing and growth in order to embrace a meaningful and purposeful life. Her vision is to shed what no longer serves, to focus on the journey within and with an open and loving heart. Her hope is that students take away something that they can integrate and project into their everyday living and the lives of others. She lives in Brantford, Ontario.*

# Sisterhood
## by Jan Porter

*"One woman is a tiny divine spark in a timeless sisterhood tapestry collective; all of us are Wild Women."*

Imagine finding out that your DNA tests indicate that you are a descendent from a long line of powerful wise loving ancient sisterhoods, healers, mystics, saints, peaceful warriors and visionaries. Actually, you are of this lineage and have this amazing resource within your cellular memory.

Many years ago, the adage that 'Happiness is Sacred' became one treasured mantra. I have walked many, many miles in my own journey and now the fortitude of post menopause (chuckle as you may), brings a very different objective sense of discerning grace, faith, passion and confidence. I have sincerely grown to accept and appreciate what I once considered as my flaws, quirks, cyclical issues and mistakes. Most importantly, I have long accepted the majority of dramas and misunderstandings as aspects of Life 101 gift lessons. The older I grow, the more I know I am blessed with family and soul women friends who may not belong to the enlightened millionaires club, but we are treasured beyond measure. With Mom in spirit world now, there is not a day that goes by that I do not feel, sense, see and hear her loving comfort and guidance which gives depth extension to this comfort knowing. Having a loved one in spirit exponentially brings you to profound experiences in knowing divine unconditional love. There for the allowing, is a doorway to a higher consciousness above religion, science and philosophy which surpasses any prior comprehension. There is no mistaking her loving presence, the touch of her hand or hug and distinct voice and for this, I am profoundly grateful. Along with acknowledging and growing in awareness of her presence, there are guides, masters and angels who also continue to grow in deeper communion.

At this juncture in life, without doubt, it is all of my soul loved ones and friends along life's path who exemplify what I would consider 'angels'. At this time of sharing with you, a summer has passed without a lawnmower, yet a neighbour seeking no financial remuneration or gratitude otherwise has consistently tended to my lawn care. Ah, it is the simple gifts in life that remind us of all the good in people and the world around us and today there are simply too many to articulate here.

So, rather than talking with you and share expounding on heartaches that I have unwittingly received and dished out, I would rather hope that my loved ones and readers consider this contribution of words coming from a passionate higher love from heart and soul, thus ripple our individual healing journeys into collective wholeness. Oh and please, if any of the terms or words offends your religious or non-secular sensibilities do not get your knickers in a twist; simply replace the offending word with one you are comfortable with. This contribution is not intended to be a religious exercise or new age regurgitation; it is simply a love offering. What I do know for certain is that healing of self and loving of self is the sacred key to happiness which ripples outward positively affecting life and those around us; through our past and ancestral lineage, now and for future generations.

I thank all of those angel friends who have come and gone along the way. Now, I can honestly say that this includes those that I considered more nemesis at the time, for all offer a gift in various capacities. The learning continues and, while it is an annoying fact, those most challenging of relations and situations are those experiences that offer the most profound teachings, if we aim to not sink too far into the emotional effects and allow the higher insights to come forth into conscious awareness. Some insights are the big a-ha's that transcend challenges and time, and we can blossom more in love while others remain mysterious riddles awaiting soul and spirit freedom. Though many have fallen out of contact, I know our bond is timeless and that as we cross paths again, we simply pick up where we left off.

Those intimately personal hurts such as being molested and date raped lose their punch when we consider that the issue is pervasively historical and global; one in four means we are not alone, nor have we ever been. Offenders can be forgiven in time when understanding that they too are wounded souls and, in some cases, simply predators wired differently. Losing babies also loses its grief pang when we understand that those little spirits continue on, the profound love bond exists beyond physical body. Regrets are few, yet those that linger are my own hurt words blurted out of a moment of fear, erroneous expectations and misunderstandings. While hurtful words or thoughts once delivered cannot be erased with an apology, I have prayed for forgiveness. I would hope that my children and loved ones take only what they appreciate and forgive me the rest of my bumbling nonsense.

Life is strangely circular, in that we have many opportunities to learn and grow from our life patterns, concepts and experiences. This I find a truth where most of us, particularly in our latter menopausal years, notice a common theme of life lessons. Major life events and transitions may haunt us from time to time yet, exposed to the light of day, they do offer the opportunity to re-evaluate what is ours and what simply does not belong to us, and who we thought we were as opposed to who we really are. This awareness offers opportunity to heal on deeper levels, thus bringing new perspectives, freedom and growth. At my age, I find that humour, especially with my own foibles, is the best anecdote to carrying old garbage which serves no good to self or others. I have, though, long been fascinated as to why some people can go through the most horrendous of traumatic events, quickly brush it off and move on, while others take a lifetime to recover or, in some cases, never seem to quite make it in this lifetime. We are all unsung heroes and heroines just for giving this earthly existence a go, most often blind to the bigger picture.

I thank God/Goddess/Creator that no one asked me to write this section prior to menopause. That aged re-wiring throws a passionate curve ball into tolerance; we post-menopausal crones lose tolerance for insincerity, longing for harmony, passionate love, laughter and fulfillment. While I am not so crazy about those pesky crone hairs, achy bones or sagging skin, I do love this chapter of life. Vantage points change constantly for the better. I seem to care less and less of what others think of me, my past or their perception of who I am and what I ought to be doing; a piece of soul and psyche freedom. I also now see through much of my own personal garbage and my faith has grown from an intellectual philosophy of world religions and thoughts to an experiential love that begins with self. It has been said by saints and masters and new age gurus alike; 'You have the right to be happy, simply because you exist'. I recall as a child church religious icon gazing and wondering why I was exempt from their acceptance and those haloed rapturous experiences. I did not realize until adulthood that I had actually been on a mission of sorts; the first chapter of life lived in naive pursuit of running away from assuming some odd notion of blame, shame and sin as a result of childhood sexual molestation and numerous date rapes. Oh I have lost babies, loving partners, good jobs and wonderful women friendships for any number of reasons. One thing is for certain, we cannot run far enough away from what dwells within. Sooner or later we all have to face our shadow haunting boogies and monster in the closet ghosts that leak drama into our days. Time is a great healer and, more importantly, it is in realizing what a grand waste of energy it is to hold onto regrets and misunderstandings that we find relief, fulfillment and happiness. I had made it an adult quest to find out what constitutes happiness, fulfillment and good healthy loving relationships and why, for so many of us, it evades much of life. I discovered that happiness is simply self-love in hand with an attitude of gratitude turned habitual way of interacting with life that grows into a natural state of being.

Old stories of childhood, adolescent and young adulthood hurts, traumas, trials and tribulations ought not to be reiterated from pain; my stories are too common. How can I go back and speak of anguish when I strive to disallow those hurts to be the summation of who I have become and who I am growing into? I have been back a thousand times, searching for insights and because life is a journey I ask, I am done with it yet? All of life is circular or, rather, life lessons come around again and again, yet each time those old bugaboos resurface, and it is in the sharing with women that I see that I have grown. The original crippling effects have long lost impact; in fact most of it seems like some else's story or a crappy B movie I once watched. Now those old difficulties serve to carry insight into human nature, tolerance and compassion.

It does, however, blow my mind that statistics have remained a constant estimated one in four are survivors of sexual trauma. These numbers are staggering! This has been a continuous massive ripple effect that affects all of us, including the pain and harm within the psyche of offenders. From a broader perspective, sexual assault has been a shadow aspect of civilization since time recorded, often used as a war tactic to kick out a culture's stability at its pillars; women, children and the vulnerable. This is a social and global issue. So if you feel alone and are a survivor, take small comfort in knowing that you are in company with millions and there are many more who do care.

Why on earth is sexual assault still a social issue in our global society? How on earth have we become so disconnected and isolated from believing in a loving higher power, our own innate goodness and each other? It boggles my mind. I wish for and envision that I may live long enough to see the issue as ancient history in this lifetime and that any residual harmful effects are not carried through into my children's generations yet to be. I wish for a rekindling sense of sisterhoods, brotherhoods and community.

Some thirty years ago a wise spiritual man halted my perfectly valid drama rant with: 'there is much freedom found in simply taking a moment to notice that ninety eight percent of what you felt about someone imposing harm upon you does not belong to you. Stop, close your eyes for a moment and bring to mind a hurtful exchange and ask yourself, how much of this is really mine?' I was first stunned and annoyed, yet as I began to play with the notion, I could ascertain what were my own hindering beliefs. This is a work in progress. I hail from a generation of dutiful childhood and adult roles and mindsets. As dutiful caregivers, we often tolerate or engage in unhealthy exchanges simply because we have not been taught or allowed otherwise. We must understand that we have much to teach our children of self-worth and navigating life intuitively. The Buddhist adage holds true; that if we taught children how to meditate, and harvest innate intuition, the world would transform in one generation. For sensitive people, we unconsciously pick up and absorb the erroneous thoughts and feelings from offenders that mix and mingle with those of family, friends, community or the cultural religious beliefs around us.

It is an odd conundrum that adversity and harsh realities make one question the benevolence of a loving higher power, yet in dark nights, that is exactly what we look for, pray for, yearn for and search for. It does not matter how you perceive that higher power or if you are an Atheist; in quantum physics we now know for certain that there is a quantifiable and powerful law of the universe that miraculously works when prefaced with the sincere emotions of love.

Without doubt, crisis brings an opportunity for a different kind of wholeness and healing; a process of coming to know who you really are, the authentic and natural you. You are divine just as you are. This natural state of being feels like a familiar homecoming, where we naturally relax and go more with the flow that is followed by the knowing that we are doing the best that we can do with what we have.

Unfortunately, when traumatic sexual events occur, they are often uniquely challenging experiences to recover from for many reasons. They are not simply external events, such as being in a car accident where something outside of your physical body has been damaged and can tangibly be repaired. It is a deeply intimate experience in nature, where an unwanted intrusion has touched and actually penetrated the most private parts of our bodies and our soul; it feels dark and very much 'internal'. Putting the event(s) and concepts of self into the perspective of the Universal Law of Love, which is higher than the Law of Attraction, offers us the opportunity to consider perceived misunderstandings and beliefs in order to grow more into loving ourselves and into our higher spiritual authentic nature.

Love is the way out; love of self. We are all vastly more than the roles we assume at birth within family, community, life patterns and experiences. We are so much more than a summation of what those around us expect or want us to be. Yes, I believe that the old adage is true; we are spiritual beings, having a human experience. We are all aspects of God and our spirits live on infinitely. Healing occurs when we remember this, with heart and soul; who we really are: something good and powerful, Creator, Goddess, Allah, God, or whatever feels comfortable in perception.

If you were my daughter, sister, granddaughter, or simply a soul sister or male companion sitting here with me, aside my desk over a cup of tea, I would, on behalf of the higher powers that be, share with you how they see you; a magnificent being of loving light with unique skills, attributes and capabilities to contribute to the world. We all have a phenomenal capacity to love and to be loved, just as we are. You were meant to be here in this lifetime. You were born of good and wonderful gifts and shall always be so; a gift from God so to speak. No hurtful word or experience can ever take away the wonder of your soul and spirit in the eyes of the divine. In honouring this higher truth of who you are, all good things naturally flow from this sacred state of being.

I also have long ditched my martyr fix-all inclinations and come to understand that not all of us have come into this earth life to be fixed or to align with anyone else's ideal of what constitutes a good person, soul or fulfilled life. Love your life as it is and know that current difficulties and challenges will pass. Know that change is constant; nothing stays exactly the same forever. These are the higher perspectives so stay focused on your own journey by paying attention to what feels good and what does not. Hand over what does not feel good to God, Goddess, Creator, the Angels or your higher soul mind for care, solutions, insights and inspiration.

Your physical, emotional, and mental bodies are finely tuned and aligned with your soul's path for a higher good. The natural inner guidance system that lies within you always has and always will be there for the tuning in and listening. Explore how it works within you, count on it, trust it and allow it to be your priority focal point. You will find this direction when you are mind calm and especially when you are doing activities that you love to do. It is the awareness sensation and direction within your own heart and soul. In assisting others and constantly offering gratitude for all good things that flow through you, you naturally attract more because you are in that divine flow of life.

Life is a gift. Your life is a gift. Consider that your life is imbued with angelic magnificence of oneness with the all that is. This higher love power in motion begins within your own soul and radiates outward into the world to awaken, lighten and inspire others. Stay aware of how much lighter, brighter and freer this notion feels. Choose this pathway always. Meditate, pray, do activities that you love to do, learn and share, and growth into the happy sacred state of being is assured.

Your Guides and Angels can and want to assist you with all aspects of your life. Your happiness and life is their primary mission. You are, have always been and will always be surrounded by a group of spirit world guides. Allow their assistance and love to naturally flow through you. All things in life operate within the realms of Spiritual and Natural Laws that are foundationed in a higher unconditional love than human comprehension. These higher laws, your own soul and Spirit Guides all conspire to align you with all that is good and joyful. Always allow your childlike wonder, joy, gratitude, love and laughter to serve as your own soul's tool kit for life's most difficult challenges.

You are here at this crossroad in life, because your soul is calling you to grow, to love yourself, to follow the path of doing what you love to do; activities that give you joy and inspiration. Every life experience, challenge and joy has brought you to this point; even the most challenging situations have opportunities, gifts, lessons and insights. You are stronger than you know and give yourself credit for, and there are kindred soul friendships awaiting your shared tears, love, wisdom, laughter and support.

The journey to wholeness is essentially the process of stepping out of those stuck record thoughts and feelings, sharing both tears and wisdom and shifting those wounds into wisdom. This is the art of inspired transformation. Your happiness is sacred. Your body, mind, feelings and contributions to the world are your own sacred space. Without doubt, the pathway to wholeness is in boldly walking through those shared soul-healing journey that bring authentic empowerment, growth and fulfillment.

Remember, above all else, that you have a natural inner guidance system within you that is set for a fulfilled life and happiness. In fact, that inner compass is finely tuned and aligned with your soul's path and higher good. It always has been within your heart and soul. Count on it, and when you find yourself off kilter and out of sorts, eat a good meal, rest and aim to make a shift in activities and thoughts by seeking this inner direction. Like tuning into a radio station, as you quiet and calm down, during relaxing enjoyable activities and when caring for others, you will feel a deep letting go and contended sigh. To build that power and flow, add gratitude; in giving thanks for all good things that do flow through your life, you naturally attract more good. It takes practice staying in a good attitude space and balanced.

Your own unique life path and journey to wholeness is primarily a solo process and it is one that we all must take. You are not the first to travel those dark times and challenges and not the last. In sharing your life, interests, skills, abilities and love, you do make a wonderful difference. While it is good to have quiet alone time to sort through a problem, there are many who make it their life vocation to assist you through your process, whether via professional education or alternative healing modalities or simply the friend who has been there and done that. So take some time out in honour of yourself and allow those doors of assistance to open.

Transformation most often occurs during and following life's most defining moments, which are profound opportunities sending out beacons guiding and calling you to a whole new chapter in life. While stress at the beginning of a transformation process can seem long and painfully up and down, know that the journey is really about the incremental breakthroughs of self-discovery. Your soul is navigating you through life's experiences, and supports are there for the allowing. In hindsight, it was not in confronting my abusers that has set my soul free; it has been in confronting my own beliefs and misconceptions. It has been in finding and honouring my own authentic, quirky self that has led me to my divine connection and communion with the all that is good and loving.

So please, if sexual assault is a part of your history or someone you care about is struggling, understand that stigmas surrounding sexual abuse are unique compared to other forms of assault. Societal judgments and outdated religious morals concerning sexual modes of conduct and behaviours are often deeply ingrained. Our core psyche is deeply personal and often reacts to abuse as a profound invasion of personal sacred space within our physical, mental, emotional and spiritual bodies. Adding injury to injury, negative judgmental words float around in our minds and negative assumptions filter through our sensing mind via spoken words, body language and insinuations of others, as well as from old standing belief systems and programming of the victim's own perceptions. Commonly terse erroneous judgments such as; bad, slut, sinner and 'dirty' can pervade and plague a survivor's psyche for years or a lifetime, and can in turn further perpetuate unwarranted guilt, shame, unworthiness and crisis. Long term ingrained harmful internal thoughts and beliefs eventually manifest outwardly as life crisis, physical problems, emotional - mental illness, disease and addictions. At minimum, running anxiety can be experienced for a lifetime when left unchecked. The most horrific experiences and after-effects can dissipate when inner wisdom, love and care of self is allowed and viewed from a higher perspective. Sometimes the most beautiful things grow in the most inhospitable of environments.

While we cannot yet single-handedly change people and the world around us to completely ensure our ideal life for all, we can consciously choose to live to our own highest potential and make self-care and self-love our priority, which in turn positively affects our lives and others in unimaginable ways. As we grow, we find a new sense of joy and community as we take our past hurts and assist others with the sole aim to empower, assist and inspire teach those who are more vulnerable. As we pay it forward in support and empowerment, we in turn grow stronger, wiser, more confident, and capable of bringing our unique gifts to the world.

Today's all too common complicating twist is found with those who perpetuate a misinterpretation or misunderstanding of the new age spiritual Law of Attraction. Herein lies an erroneous assumption of personal responsibility where everything that happens to an individual is a direct result of the law of attraction or karma. The 'shit happens because you attracted it' or somehow deserved it adage is too simple a retort and does little to alleviate and can dangerously perpetuate pain. When the onus is thrust back onto the survivor for having attracted the incident(s) in the first place, it does profound disservice and damage to an individual's already bruised psyche. The higher truth in this law, the wisdom and insights that set one's soul free is found by viewing the experience from a profoundly higher perspective than pain, shame, fear and inner torment. Survivors must have validation of innate self-worth, strength and hopeful fortitude of the future. Know that there is a higher Spiritual Law operating at all times, that supersedes all governing Spiritual and Physical Laws of the Universe, including the law of attraction. This is the Law of Love. Healing begins when soul and psyche are allowed to permeate love within and without.

On a simpler note, the older we grow, the more we come to know that it simply takes too much energy to play roles that run contrary to who we really authentically are as innately good. This does not mean that we completely do not care what others think of us; it is simply that we grow to become comfortable in our own skin and soul, vulnerabilities, quirks and all. As we begin to accept, and then love ourselves just as we are, the world around us adjusts in kind and, as a result, goals and dreams naturally manifest.

So let go and uplift!

A higher truth is that we come from love and return to love. It is difficult to comprehend any kind of love while in the throes of trauma. Yet within the crisis mind state lay opportunities for profound positive change and growth. Our soul naturally searches for insight to make sense of the world around us, and yearns for peace and love. A small amount of hope is all that is needed to navigate to a loving, harmonious and balanced reality. Love is our most natural state of being. Anytime you feel outright bad, know that you have simply disconnected with this higher and natural state of being. In simply aiming for love and harmony, we naturally gravitate back onto the path of living life to it is fullest. This is what the saints, mystics, philosophers and spiritual wise ones referred to as Divine Love. Science is just beginning to tangibly measure and work with this powerful energy.

It has been said many times in many ways that we came into this lifetime with free will, that we have the capacity to consider options and make choices. Herein lies the glitch of personal responsibility for making new choices; to reconsider and adjust our sails when certain reactions continue and do harm to self or others. When you allow yourself to rid your inner shadows of guilt, negative self-judgments, shame, regrets and the fears, and shift into doing the things that you love to do, you naturally evolve, and grow out of those old harmful patterns.

Be good to yourself and grow at your own pace. Remember always that love is the way out; love of self and love of your life as it is.

You are a divine spark in a timeless sisterhood and brotherhood tapestry collective; you are wonderful and loved, and can make a positive difference in the world, just as you are.

The following is a short healing prayer that I find helpful:
*Om, Mother, Father, God, Creator, Guides, Ancestors, Angels and Archangels, we ask for your divine presence to be with us now and forward. We also ask that*

97

*you radiate harmonious waves of divine healing flow through all who have hurt and are hurting, in unconditional love throughout life. We thank you for being with us in our lives and ask for your assistance in growing happier and more ful-filled, thus making the world a better place for all. We ask that you enhance our relationships, work and activities in alignment with our highest potential and good for this lifetime. Please assist us in allowing the divine flow to comfortably and naturally raise our spirits to bring an abundance of insights, comfort, information, health, well-being, laughter, friendship, inner peace and spiritual growth. Watch over us, walk with us, inspire us and nurture us. May your spirit of peace, love, wholeness and miracles always be consciously known to us today and in all ways. For this and all that give, we thank you. As is above, so is below and so it is.*

And I personally wish you loving comfort, laughter, warmth of good friendships and to always see the beauty in the world. I wish you faith, hope, grace, acceptance, confidence, insight and courage.
Blessings on your journey!

\* \* \*

*Jan is a published author, member of The Writer's Union of Canada and workshop facilitator residing in beautiful rural Belmont Lake, Ontario. Her personal joy comes from assisting others to live in joyful fulfillment and to pursue their aspi-rations in soul path alignment through non-secular writing, one-on-one, groups, and events. For more information visit www.inspiredsoulworks.com.*

# The Dragonfly
## by Moragh Lippert

I "come to" on the couch in the living room. What am I doing here? What time of day is it? My stomach is gripped with fear and apprehension as I try to figure out what is happening. I'm afraid to. A familiar feeling of dread spreads throughout my gut.

My brain is foggy and my head aches. Thinking is not a function that works well in a head that feels like a bucket of sticky sludge. My body is sore from the one position collapse I did hours ago. I realize I'm naked, except for my trench coat. "Why am I not dressed?" I ask myself. I tentatively venture further inquiry "What am I doing passed out on the couch in the middle of a work day? Where are the kids? Are they ok?"

I look at the half-finished rye and gingerale on the coffee table with a mixture of abhorrence and longing. I'm too tired to reach out for it and too afraid any physical movement will set in motion the reality of what I've done. Or not done. Of who I've hurt. Of the next self-degrading and destructive action I've taken. I know with movement I will fully realize the deep and destructive shame of my actions. With dread, I glance at the VCR clock. Its 3:06 p.m. What day is it? Are the kids at school? I think to myself I'd better get dressed before they get home and see me like this. But first I need to down the remaining drink on the table to give me the courage to get off the couch……

This memory waves across my consciousness as I sit in meditation at a seven day silent retreat. The meditation is to practise Metta. In Vipassana meditation, Metta is a practice of the cultivation of Loving Kindness. It uses phrases of good wishes toward oneself. Then the meditator sends the same wishes to a loved one and others; eventually to all sentient Beings. As I started to say the phrases to myself, I had spontaneously visited this harsh reality of my past - 28 years ago. As I sit in the meditation hall with my teachers at the front, surrounded by thirty or so fellow meditators, I feel the strength and support to stay with the memory and see where it takes me.

The memory is of the day that was my "spiritual, emotional, mental and physical bottom". Perhaps the worst day of my drinking "career". Not knowing exactly why this was happening, I allowed myself to return to the past.

That day, I had awoken as usual with a massive hangover. I was a daily drinker at that point, consuming most of a twenty-sixer of rye whiskey. I was eating minimally. Perhaps half a sandwich and a few bites of dinner. With experimentation, I had found the foods that worked for me; the foods that I could keep down despite the almost constant state of nausea and diarrhea. The night before I had picked at the dinner I had managed to make the children (probably Kraft Dinner). That morning I would not even consider a coffee. Despite liking it, I had given it up months ago as the smell of it made me sick. That morning I was very thirsty and chose orange juice…..with a splash of vodka. I chose a "hair of the dog" to help me function. I knew it would stop the shaking that I did not want my children to see. That *I* did not want to see.

Like most of my drinking episodes, I blacked out shortly after starting. I was awake but could not remember my actions. The rest of that day carries only intermittent memories. I recall rushing my children ages 10 and 7 out the door so I could finish getting ready for work. Earlier, upon rising, I had thrown on my trench coat because it was in easy access as I had poured my morning cocktail. It did not seem odd or ridiculous to me that I was walking around in a trench coat instead of a house coat. It did not seem odd to me that I was helping myself to vodka first thing in the morning. Rational thought is not the strength of someone whose brain is constantly addled with alcohol, obsessed with alcohol or experiencing the effects of alcohol.

After the children were shuttled out the door, I did not make it upstairs to dress but chose to stay in easy access to my booze. I called in sick and continued to drink until I passed out on the couch. My one objective was to get absolutely, uncompromisingly drunk and kill all feelings. To kill the shame, guilt and pain that haunted me. I wanted to numb my suffering from grief, self-hatred and doubt, unfulfilled dreams, remorse, abandonment, abuse and betrayal.

I was a "functional drunk", one who, on the surface, has a normal life. I was a drunk who managed to keep home, car, family and job. In my case, my children were looked after in terms of food, clothing and shelter, but I was just going through the motions. I was very emotionally distant. I had minimal emotional resources to give to them or me.

So that day in the Metta meditation I relived that memory. What I felt in my heart was not the customary guilt and shame. There was a shift in my perspective and, miraculously, a huge wave of compassion and love arose for the drunk on the couch. What emerged was something I had never felt before for the alcoholic Moragh. I felt her pain, denial and sickness, and sent her Loving Kindness. The *Present Moragh* reached out to the *Past Moragh* with Metta. Somehow, I am certain that the energy of love and compassion that transcended time affected the *Past Moragh*. Although that was not the last day of drinking, it was the beginning of the end of the drinking; a beginning of seeing the truth. It was a moment of grace, a miracle. It was a transformation from self-hate to self-love. In the meditation hall I cried silently as I realized the significance of this deep transition. This transformation would not have been possible had it not been for years of healing work. Before I discuss the healing I pause to ask myself for the millionth time, "Why did I drink?" A number of possibilities and thoughts unfold as they often do when I contemplate this question. Was this genetic? My father was a self-admitted and chronic alcoholic. He was a highly successful doctor and heart surgeon but never-the-less, an alcoholic and probably addicted to pharmaceuticals.

Was it from my childhood? I was the fourth and, as I was told by my father, and "unwanted" child. I had two A-type parents who did not know what to do with their angry toddler. As a toddler I craved attention and my way get it was to cry and have temper tantrums. As a result, I was locked in the basement with the lights out to silence me.

Was I a drunk because I was abused physically and sexually as a child? Was it because I was abandoned at 14 with the death of my Mother and then by my Father who remarried six months later? Was I a drunk simply because I was just a lush and did not know when to stop? Was it self fulfilling prophecy?Back then I believed what my Father said."Moragh, everything you do, you overdo".

The blessing is that I don't need to know the answer to these questions. As I learned at the inpatient Alcohol and Addiction Program that I entered in February 1991, and later during hundreds of meetings of Alcoholics Anonymous (AA), it does not really matter. As I learned in the treatment centre, it is a combination of conditions that arise into full blown alcoholism and addiction. The most freeing fact I learned in the hospital is that alcoholism is most definitely a disease; a biochemical malfunction that most often leads to a physical and emotional dependence on a mind altering substance. I learned that it is a physiological quirk that turns a drink into a highly addictive substance and triggers obsession. Another anecdotal fact, it seems that the majority of folks in recovery were sexually abused as children. Whatever the reason(s), I am an alcoholic and addict. But that's not all I am.

On the day I lay on the couch I did not consciously believe I had a problem with alcohol. I had a problem with life, and drinking was the solution. On that day at the climax of the illness I was a wreck on all levels. I was devastated physically, spiritually and emotionally. I was soon to be diagnosed with severe depression and social anxiety disorder as well as alcoholism. At that time, I hated myself so much that I wished almost constantly to die. I tried to take my life. I had so much self-loathing that I could not look in the mirror. When I did, I saw a reflection of my insides and spiritual state and it scared and disgusted me. My colour ranged between yellow and grey. I had huge circles under my eyes. I was malnourished and very underweight but puffy and bloated. Putting makeup on for work was a struggle. That meant looking in the mirror. That meant I had to look into my eyes. I could not bear to. I could not bear to see a soul so sick and pathetic. I hated myself.

I know now that I suffered not only from a disease of spiritual, emotional and psychic devastation. The physical devastation from seventeen years of daily drinking included chronic malnutrition and biochemical imbalances. It affected my digestion system the most and resulted in major deficiencies of vitamins, minerals, amino acids and essential fatty acids. These deficiencies caused further havoc. It was a vicious cycle.

Further, like 94% of active alcoholics, I was riddled with candidiasis. Alcohol is almost pure sugar and feeds candida albicans bacteria which trigger cravings. Systemic candida (candidiasis) causes damage and nutritional deficiencies. It devastated my digestive system causing an inability to absorb nutrients and the development of Leaky Gut Syndrome. It further contributed to food sensitivities and seasonal allergies. Candida had taken up residence in my brain and caused unclear, irrational, confused thinking and poor memory.

Mentally I was also in total victim mindset. I took no responsibility for my life situation. I had everyone and everything to blame for the negative and traumatic circumstances.

I was a chasm of emptiness that I sought to fill with something, anything outside of myself. I drank to fill the unending internal void. I drank to compensate for a deep and utter longing to belong and be loved. Ironically, I was a lone drinker so the drinking only made me feel lonelier, more the victim, increasingly anxious and depressed and more separated from my community and family.

So how did I heal? What was the turnaround? What woke me up?

No one thing fixed me. It took time and it is a process of transformation that still evolves. I believe today that sobering up and turning one's life around can be done with more ease and grace than the path I travelled. But my path was the route I chose and it molded who I am today.

In the treatment centre, I started to eat, sleep, exercise and take care of myself. I saw fine psychiatrists and counsellors and participated in one on one and group sessions. I was introduced to and benefited tremendously from regular attendance at Alcoholics Anonymous (AA). I was encouraged to meditate for stress relief and journal to help me process the myriad of emotions that I had kept repressed for so long. I was told in the treatment centre that 25% of us would be sober in one year; 11% sober after three years. The odds did not look good for me.

And I turned out to be part of the majority. Within one week after leaving the centre I was drinking again. I "fell off the wagon" at least a dozen more times before I ultimately surrendered to the disease when I took my last drink on 31st July 1992.

On that day I was on a family vacation and went for a walk with my twelve- year-old son. He had seen much of my struggle to get sober and, like the rest of the family, had supported and loved me along the way. I know how hard he, his sister and their father took it every time I failed and drank.

On that day in July 1992, I had not had a drink for 30 days. I felt good that day and had no stress. I was not upset or bothered about anything. There was no particular reason for me to drink. So why I picked up a wine cooler I have no idea. I remember seeing the coolers in the convenience store refrigerator and thinking "I love Quebec where you can pick up booze in a convenience store on a Sunday" and proceeded to purchase a wine cooler and a juice and candy bar for my son.

We sat on a bench in the warm July sun and enjoyed a gorgeous view of the St. Lawrence. We cracked open our drinks and took the first swallow.

As the familiar burning started in my stomach, my son opened his chocolate bar and began chewing. While munching, he picked up my cooler and proceeded to read the ingredients. Is that normal behaviour for the average twelve-year-old? That behaviour is a clear indication that substance abuse is a *family disease*. My son looked at me and I dreaded the look in his eyes. There was so much pain, anxiety and fear as he said "Mummy, did you know there's alcohol in this?"

I felt like I had been stabbed in the heart. I REALLY saw and felt for the first time the massive impact that my drinking had on my child. I felt his fear...fear that his mother was lost to him again. Fear of a vast chasm of unpredictability, uncertainty, imbalance and dis-ease entering his life again with my taking that drink. I saw the pain cut to his heart and could not bear to inflict that upon him again. So, intuitively I said "Oh yes it does and I don't want *that anymore*" and promptly threw the bottle in the garbage bin. I saw and felt his relief. This was a huge spiritual awakening. It represented a complete surrender of my disease to my Higher Power. I finally realized that I was an alcoholic and could not safely drink alcohol.

Was that day, 21 years ago, the beginning of a true and lengthy sobriety? Unfortunately not. My body had been so damaged by hard drinking and malnutrition that I had numerous health issues that were very painful. I was prescribed Tylenol with codeine for the pain and ordered to take "as directed". For a while I followed directions but soon I began to realize the buzz I had felt from alcohol could also be obtained from codeine. I became a codeine addict.

After using codeine sporatically for about eight years, I realized I was on a downward spiral. I woke up to the fact that I was an addict. I became willing to become responsible for my addiction and committed to get well. I applied the same principles to the addiction that I had to the alcoholism. I went for outpatient care with an addiction counsellor and again took the AA 12 Steps to heal my life.

Why did I become an addict after committing so strongly on that July day in 1992 to be sober? Why did I again and again fall off the wagon and rely on something outside of me to change the way I felt? I used pharmaceuticals as I did alcohol: to elevate my mood, fill the void, provide confidence and seek oblivion from feeling.

Many addicts/alcoholics can safely take pharmaceuticals as directed. However, I had not done all the healing that would make it safe for me to consume narcotics. My body was still in a state of nutritional deficiencies and candida overload. I still experienced cravings. Further, emotionally and spiritually, although I was working a program and continuing with the 12 Step work, I had not done the necessary deep spiritual healing. Given these deficits, it is no surprise that I became addicted.

 I know today that even though I was "doing the right things" I was not truly healing at the deepest level. I was following a program for sobriety and continued to go to 12 Step meetings. I continued to work with my AA sponsor. Every time I slipped I was welcomed back again and again to the meetings and the arms of my sponsor. I was supported with love and wisdom but I failed to truly thrive. Why?

I believe addiction is a sickness of the Spirit. Yes it is also a physiological, mental and emotional illness that involves an obsession to kill feeling using external substances. At the heart of the issue, it is a deep and endless vacuum of Love and failure to connect with the Divine (Spirit, God or Higher Self). Experts in addiction like David Hawkins speak of the urge of addicts and alcoholics to feel at one with God. Hawkins describes how addicts use their drug of choice again and again to escape from pain and obtain euphoria. It's a huge irony that alcohol is called spirit! The sad thing is that the rare and fleeting Divine Connection causes the addict to continue to use and drink with a never-ending hope to feel it again. It is the definition of insanity: doing the same thing over and over again with the same result.

So how did I stop the addiction to a substance outside of myself and heal? I finally realized on 12 April 2002 that the answer was not outside of me but within. This realization did not come with a massive jolt of lightening but rather arose from the conditions that unfolded in my life and the willingness to consider a radically different perspective. It was gradual transformation and insight. *The answer is within me. I am a part of God. I am connected to The Source of All. I choose to let go of the self hate and embrace the magnificence of my True Nature.*

This was not a realization in an ego-bound way. It was a true realization of my worth as an individual and integral part of the Universe. A part of the Divine. I was like a drop of water in the ocean. Unique as a water droplet but also part of the grand and beautiful sea. I realized that the willingness to consider that I'm a child of God and a piece of the Universe would allow me to fully heal. And I need not take a drink or pill. To start, I needed to be willing to change my perspective with trust, faith and hope.

Was it easy to trust and see my True Authentic Self? Does the perspective of me as a Divine Being, of a human being having a spiritual experience stay with me always? Not at all. I can honestly say that when I see my reflection in the mirror today, I can say I love me. But I still have feelings of self-hatred, doubt and victimization. But the more I believe and trust and take responsibility for co-creation in my life, the less I experience doubt and fear. I know that the intentions I set today are tomorrow's reality.

Addicts have a number of "isms" that need healing. These manifest in various ways. Mine include compulsion, depression and anxiety. They also include negative self-image, lack of confidence, fear and a need to control others and situations. Addiction has come in other forms too including: relationships, body image, shopping, caffeine, nicotine and sugar. Addictive foods are common place in society: sugar, fast food, artificial additives and refined carbohydrates. In my practice as a Registered Holistic Nutritionist (RHN) I see rampant food addiction. However, there is hope, and by healing body, mind and spirit we can transform our suffering to healing.

When love, compassion and a willingness to realize our Divinity arise, we start to rely less on addiction and begin to heal. For me it took hard work. It took a lot of self-discovery, self-awareness, counselling and tears to reach a place where I could trust my Divine Wisdom and begin to feel peace within. It was a metamorphosis that started long ago and no doubt will continue for my life. Gwen, my dear friend, spiritual mentor and AA sponsor and I had a very special twenty-one year relationship before she died. I am very grateful to her for her wisdom and love that helped me transition from hate to love. When she was dying I reminded her of our mutual promise to reach out after death. Long ago she had promised to come to me as Queen Anne's lace and I promised to come in the form of a Dragonfly. Dragonfly was always significant to us because it represents the huge transformation required to change my self-perspective. As Wayne Dyer says "When you change the way you look at things, the things you look at change." With Gwen's help and encouragement I started to seek and trust my own wisdom instead of always relying on something outside of me. She was an integral part of this transformation. Every time I see Queen Anne's lace, I feel a huge amount of love and appreciation for Gwen. Every time I see a dragonfly I realize the huge change that Gwen and others helped me realize.

Self-acceptance is part of this metamorphosis. It is about being REALLY honest about who we are while refusing to feel recrimination and self-loathing. It is about facing our actions and accepting them while releasing self judgement. After acceptance comes forgiveness. And forgiveness has to start with oneself.

The finest explanation of forgiveness I have heard is by Jack Kornfield, a much loved and well-respected teacher of mindfulness meditation. He says that true forgiveness is "no longer wanting to change the past". I heard those words from Jack one day as I drove. It was at a time of my life that was almost as painful as losing my mother to ovarian cancer at age 14. It was almost as painful as the abandonment and betrayal I felt six months later when my father married a much younger woman. At age seventeen I called her a "gold digging whore" and was told to leave the family home.

As I drove and heard Jack Kornfield's explanation of forgiveness, a similar pain was ripping me apart. It had started a number of months before when my seemingly wonderful marriage to a loving and supportive man exploded. In one instance I realized with irrefutable evidence that my husband was having an affair. I had naively believed we would live happily ever after and was secure in the marriage. So the devastation of betrayal was mentally, spiritually, emotionally and physically shattering. The foundation of my life fell from under me. I was in grief, shock and extreme anger.

And yet, I wanted to feel at peace with it. I wanted to let go of the anger and move forward in my life. I wanted to accept that the man I had loved so blindly had chosen another. I wanted to close that chapter in my life. So when I heard the wise words of Jack Kornfield I realized that yes, "I have a willingness to not want to change the past". I was able allow forgiveness to edge in. But like a healing alcoholic/addict, I had to forgive myself first. Forgive myself for not seeing the truth of the marriage and the duplicitous nature of the man.

Forgiveness has been an integral part of my healing as an addict/alcoholic. It is part of the transformative process to heal from the "isms" that drove me to drink and use. But before I could forgive I had to accept. Acceptance of the choices I had made as a struggling drunk. Acceptance of the damage I had done to my children, my husband and my family. Acceptance of the self-devastation. This acceptance was a true letting go of the blame and self-hatred. It was also a letting go of attachment to the victimhood in which I was so firmly ensconced. It was taking responsibility for my choices and actions. Then I could start to forgive me.

It was also an acceptance of the actions done to me. My father's marriage early after my mother's death. The child abuse. The sexual abuse. The infidelity in the marriage. It was not an endorsement of these things but an acceptance that, for some reason, they did happen. All of these things happened and contributed to who I am today: strong, resilient and very human.

There is much resistance to acceptance. It is felt especially in the body. When there is lack of embodiment of facts, they can manifest as illness and stress. There is a wise saying "what you resist, persists" and I found that to be very true as I fought to let go. I literally fought with myself to allow acceptance to happen. Once it happened I forgave.

Why do we forgive? I used to think it was for the other person. After I was kicked out of the house an aunt said "never, ever forgive your father for what he has done". Others encouraged me to hang onto the resentment. However, my gut was constantly in knots when I considered the path of hanging onto the anger. I remember describing to a friend that it felt like "a cancer growing within and taking me over". Despite the flack I got from family and friends I felt a vast relief when I did forgive my father. A huge weight was lifted from my shoulders and my guts relaxed. I benefited from forgiveness.

Nurturing is another important factor in transformation and healing. In the months following the marriage "explosion", I received some wise advice from a dear friend. She said "You are not well...treat yourself like a sick person for at least one year. Love and nurture yourself. Love the inner wounded child who feels betrayed and abandoned." Although it was very hard, I paid attention to that advice. One of the things I did was to dig out a painting I had of me aged five. The painting had been stuck for decades in the basement (interesting I chose storage in the basement). I dusted it off and hung little Moragh on the wall. I saw her every day and promised to love, nurture and protect her. This radical love and self-acceptance helped me heal my inner child. Self-nurturing is hard but also one of the most rewarding gifts. It is highly transformative.

Nurturing comes in many forms and it is important that we find what works and do it! As long as it is healthy, loving and supportive, it should be done often. For me, it means long walks in nature. My daily walks along the Speed River accompanied by my two dogs, Pura Vida and Salsa have been highly restorative. Healing happens every time I give myself this gift. Mother Nature holds us and carries us whether we are conscious of it or not.

Meditation has also been an integral part of my healing. Addicts/alcoholics tend to live in their minds lost in the future or the past. An unhealthy collection of regret, grief, guilt, worry and disappointment keeps the addict in a whirling mind set of obsession and fear. It also keeps them from being in the Now and feeling present in the body.

While actively using and drinking, I was disconnected from body sensations. I had no wish to go there because it meant coming to terms with what I was feeling and coming to terms with the pain. Over many years, using the breath as an object in meditation, I was eventually able to spend time in my body and experience feelings I had denied all my life. Once I experienced them, they lost their sting. I now rely on my meditation practice for stress relief and to help me process my emotions.

A few years ago, I entered a mentorship program in Vipassana Meditation and am now a Meditation Teacher. Healing occurs as the meditator pays attention to their body and is encouraged to meet anything that arises with compassion and non-judgemental awareness. As described earlier, in the Metta practice the practitioner benefits (as do all of us) from the cultivation of Loving Kindness towards self and all beings. Meditation has been hugely beneficial in helping me stay in the present moment and be more able to handle stress, emotions and sensations with self-love and acceptance. I'm not sure how life would have been had I not been a meditator for a number of years when my marriage ended and life took such a shocking turn. I have no doubt that the meditation practice facilitated the ability to handle the shock and devastation.

I had emotional bottoms in sobriety but I never chose to drink or use. Even though I have twice been diagnosed as clinically depressed, I did not need to rely on the "solution" of the past. Instead, I addressed the physical disorders and nutritional deficiencies that manifested as mood disorders and depression. Working with a skilled Naturopath, I started deep healing through supplement therapy and holistic nutrition. The success of this has been an integral reason that I chose to became an RHN.

Why did I not drink during these troubling times? I believe it was thanks to the conditions in my life that had led me to a place of self-love rather than self-destruction. Many facets contributed to these conditions including addressing the physiological problems, love and support from my family, friends like Gwen and others, supportive co-workers and employers, AA and Al Anon and meditation and yoga. Most important has been nurturing my connection with the Divine and cultivating my innate wisdom.

The outcome of this work has been to embody the practice of self love and self respect. I have an excellent relationship with my children who, despite a very rocky childhood, are wonderful, well adjusted adults who love and respect me. I have a number of supportive friends who carried me when I was unable. I am at peace with my ex-husband and truly wish him well.

At age 55, I am in a relationship with a wonderful man who I love and respect. He has taught me it is safe to open my heart again and love. This relationship has allowed me to be vulnerable despite my fears. He has taught me much about myself and we challenge each other's attachments, beliefs and perspectives. We help each other grow. Most importantly (and new to me) I do not depend on him or anyone else to provide my happiness. I now know that joy come from within and "happiness is an inside job".

A recent event demonstrates the beauty of life today. I was present at the birth of my second grandchild. My daughter was birthing a sister for her first child, a boy born 7 years before. I was asked to be a coach again. I am so proud of my lovely, strong daughter who stayed present, without drugs through the excruciating pain. (She obviously does not get pain tolerance from me!) During both births, I stayed calm and focused and supported my daughter and her partner with love and compassion. They truly appreciated my presence. At no time during the birthing did I feel the need to escape for a drink to steady my nerves (and hands). Once the baby was born I did not need to rush out and pop some pills to help me handle the flood of feelings and emotions that accompany such an important life event. Instead, I walked calmly to the waiting room where I happily shared the joy of the event with my daughter's father, my present beau, my grandson, my son and the family of my daughter's partner. It is a miracle that I was welcomed into such an intimate and beautiful life event.

Such are rewards of taking the first step towards healing. Of being willing let go of hate and open to light and love. To move through the excruciating pain to practise radical compassion by accepting all that is without judgement. To engage love to help embrace and accept fear, anger, grief and self-condemnation. To be willing to let go of patterns, obsessions and thoughts that block the path to joy. Miracles await us when we are willing to see and feel who we really are.

My life today is proof of the miraculous transformation and healing that has occurred since that day on the couch. Life today is not perfect, but I have infinite blessings. Like a dragonfly, I have transitioned and grown and changed. The way I feel about me today is a massive shift from the energy of hate that filled me some twenty years ago. I love who I am and I recognize my Divinity.

* * *

*Moragh is a Registered Orthomolecular Health Practitioner, Registered Holisitc Nutritionist, Meditation Teacher and Reiki Master. Through her company, Guided Holistics, she specializes in addressing nutritional deficits and biochemical imbalances to help people heal from mental and emotional disorders such as depression, anxiety, fatique, alcoholism and other addictions. Moragh has been on a healing journey for many years and, as a recovering alcoholic, she uses experience, insight and deep compassion to help people heal. Moragh lives in Guelph, Ontario and is a mother, grandmother and community volunteer. She is passionate about nature, sustainable food, yoga and inspired writing. She lives in Guelph, Ontario. For more information visit www.guidedholistics.ca.*

# Full Circle
## by Sherie Cunningham

I'm about to be homeless and there's not much room in my car. I've been living on a small amount of spousal support along with the money I make from the jewelry I design and create. However, circumstances have changed for the woman I rent from and I have to be out by the end of the month. I am demoralized and feel defeated. I sold the last two pieces of my beautiful oak furniture for next to nothing. The rug is being pulled out from under me. The only choice at the moment was to take Mom up on her offer. I could sleep on her sofa until we figure something else out. I stored all my earthly belongings in her garage and the shed in the back of the house. To other people we appear to have a harmonious relationship. However, we have a past with numerous ups and downs, which includes fighting in public, screaming obscenities at each other and not seeing or speaking to each other for months at a time. Empathy is not her strong suit and giving in is not mine. I'm relying on all my worldly experience to make the right decision here. I turned around to get the whole picture of my "stuffed to the brim" car, no room to set a soda down; the maxed out mess mirroring my mind. Catching a glimpse of my haggard little self in the rear-view, and thinking its best to take her up on her offer … and be grateful. I am exhausted mentally and physically. I could not face one more thing, especially unpacking this car, unpacking my life.

I decided to drive down to the edge of the bay, parked and gazed out across the steel blue water. The sun began to set. The light was bouncing from the windows in the tall, city buildings; the reflection, almost blinding, bringing sparkle over the water. The city glistened with brilliant gold and orange tones. Tears were spilling from my eyes and down my cheeks. Is this where all the wisdom of my sixty-two years has brought me? A half-hearted thought, oh dear God, I can hardly wait to see what happens next. Demoralized and helpless I began to pray for the answers and the past unfolded before me.

\* \* \*

My first experience of the hard reality of life came when I was nearly four years old. Being in that moment, fear is lodged in my chest. I'm afraid and can't breathe. I'm a little girl taking care of my Mother. She has fallen to her knees, her head buried in her hands and quietly sobbing. She is quiet and doesn't speak. I reach down and softly pat her back to whisper, "Mommy, I love you". I quickly brush away my own tears as I don't want her to see me cry. I am a little girl taking care of my Mother. I'm holding a small bouquet of white daisies which is the representation of a life that ended before it began. My baby sister died during her birth. We came to leave flowers at her grave.

However, my first feelings of grief were quickly silenced. As an act of protecting my Mother, Daddy quickly cautioned me against talking about this with her. In other words, your Mother will get over this in time and talking about it will only make it worse for her. Judy Lyn was buried, my unresolved feelings and emotions are hidden and my sorrow is repressed. My natural instinct is telling me different. I am left with sadness and confusion as a result and I had my first lesson in suppressing my feelings. No one talked about feelings.

For seven years I had grown up sheltered, and over-protected by my Dad. On my eighth birthday my life turned and left me devastated and confused. Nothing would have prepared me for the change my life would take from that moment on.

It was a beautiful fall day, still warm from the infamous Santa Ana winds that blew every year. My friend Nancy and I sat impatiently, beneath the huge walnut tree at my small table in the back yard. Daddy was preparing his special pink ice cream sodas for us! Upon delivery Daddy flashed a half-cock-eyed, silly face at me, and gave me a wink, and hugged me, tighter than normal, I thought, then went back into the house.

Not much later I heard the car start. My first thought was "Daddy's getting ready to wash the car, as he always moved it over to the lawn. However, something was different. I could feel. I jumped up and raced in the back door. Thoughts were running through my head a mile a minute. All of the sudden I felt a panic set in that I couldn't explain. I ran quickly through the house and flew out the front, the screen door banging behind me. The driveway was empty. I bolted across the yard while screaming at him to stop. "Daddy, Daddy", I continued to yell, while running into the street. He was only three houses down; surely he could see me in the rear view mirror. He must have heard me; I thought the whole neighborhood could hear me. Standing in the middle of the street, tears were streaming down my face, and I fell to my knees. My heart was sinking into my chest with an ache I couldn't explain. I watched until his car turned the corner and he headed towards town. It was unusual to be left without a hug, a kiss and an explanation, especially telling me when my Mom would be back. Frantically searching the house, I entered my Mom and Dad's bedroom, and froze standing in front of their closet. The door was open and only a huge empty space was left where my Dad's clothes had hung! Even in my child's mind I knew that Daddy had moved out and left me … without saying goodbye. From that moment on my life was never the same. Everything drastically changed; I viewed Daddy leaving as Daddy leaving me.

Shortly after my Dad moved out my Mom began dating. The little 'me' was not prepared for the huge changes that were taking over my young life. My heart was breaking at the loss of my Dad.

The day started out innocently enough; we were only going for a car ride. It turned out that I was along for my Mother's first date. After being in the car for what seemed like an eternity, I fell asleep in the back seat. I woke up knowing I was not in my own bed. The sky was dark; I remember feeling cold and reaching for my sweater, still tired and sleepy. I was confused and trying to make sense of where I was. Suddenly it became clear to me; I was alone! I went into a state of panic. Trembling with fear I sat up, sweeping the hair out of my eyes. I pulled myself up and discovered the front seat of the car was empty. There was no one with me. I frantically began to search for any sign of my Mom. As far as my eyes could see, scanning in every direction, no one was around. The car was parked on a long abandoned road. Dead stillness engulfed my body, my being and the core of my soul. The sky was changing from a stark black into a soft pink glow. It was not twilight as I had thought; it was sunrise. Had we been there all night? Time stood still, tears filled my eyes and I was scared beyond my ability to cope with what was happening. I was left alone. Reality began to set in, my screams were uncontrollable and panic consumed me. I was crying so hard I couldn't breathe. Daylight cast a dim glow over the cold stillness of the desert, the sun creeping over the rim of the mountains. Feeling like a two-year-old child I pulled my knees up close to my chest. The silence was deafening. I clung to my sweater; it was familiar. My head dropped to my knees and I began to cry while singing the words to "Jesus Loves Me".

All of a sudden I could hear voices in the distance. I panicked and froze with fear. The voices were getting closer and sounded as though they could have been right beside the car. I was on the floorboard of the backseat, curled in a ball with my head buried in my sweater. I heard someone fumbling with the door handle; the passenger side opened. I heard my Mother's voice, and looked up in a panicked state of relief. I was clearly an emotional mess, filled with remnants of fear and panic and couldn't move. I imagined she would pull me close to her so I would feel protected with the assurance, "You're safe, I'm sorry you were scared, I'm here now". What I heard was annoyance in her voice as she scolded me. "For heaven's sake, I was just down the road and could see the car the whole time, now stop acting like a big baby." Mom's disapproval was mainly about my behaviour and how it made her look as a mother, not about the emotional needs of her child. My heart was breaking and I needed my Daddy.

And so the games began. The passing of the child between the parents. Everybody knew their rights. Mom mainly wanted her freedom to run around and Daddy just wanted to be right.

At the beginning of each school year, class pictures were taken as well as our individual photos. It was an exciting time as all the little girls couldn't wait to know which of the boys would ask us to exchange photos with them. My heart was set on having a picture of Chris Allen and he having mine. Of all the boys in school, he was the one you hoped to sit next to on the school bus. The day he carried my lunch box, I didn't doubt for a minute we'd be sweethearts until the end of time or at least until the end of the school year.

Daddy had remarried as soon as the divorce was final. I now had a stepmother; her name was Verda. Of course, with the divorce came child support and the beginning of visitation rights. It was supposed to be about me sharing equal time with my Mom and my Dad. As it turned out, the relationship between them turned into the "War of the Roses". My Mother's lifestyle was a network of dating, working full time and starting back to school to get her real estate license. Daddy's was that of being self-righteous and judgemental because my Mother's lifestyle was not that of a nun. Never mind the fact he had just broken up our family for a woman with whom he had been having an affair.

Daddy and Verda picked me up every other weekend on Friday, and brought me home on Sunday. Dad made sure to always be on time. Today was no different, except Mom was late getting home and just created new fuel to add to the fire. While sitting in the car, to break up the looming mist of Daddy being "pissed-off", I decided to share my new collection of school photos. He knew almost everyone, recognizing my friends from our little neighbourhood gang. Then I pulled out my pride and joy … the photo of Chris Allen. With the excitement and giddiness of a 3rd grader, I giggled as I showed him my favourite photo. His response was unexpected. He tossed the tiny photo back over the front seat at me. He was enraged and screamed at me "You're going to grow up to be a whore just like your damn mother." There was complete silence in the car. My playful excitement turned to tears in a flat minute. I picked up the photo and slid it back in my wallet without saying a word. I was hurt and embarrassed by his angry outburst. I just added shame to a whole new set of emotions of which I was now cognizant. I wasn't completely sure I knew what it meant but hearing his nasty tone I was sure it wasn't a compliment.

I began Jr. High School with a brand new attitude. I had just turned thirteen years old and started seeing life in a whole new way. I felt grown up, the centre of attention and I liked it.

The confusion of my childhood disappeared with the new power I experienced within myself. I was making new friends and the boys were paying attention to me. I was accepted for who I was and not where I came from.

Life was looking pretty good most of the time, and yet other times there was lingering fear that maybe nothing would change. My need for approval and attention was seated deep and yet never filled the empty spaces in my heart.

Mom worked hard and put in long hours which meant she was rarely home. I was alone a lot of the time. I quickly mastered the art of learning to entertain myself. The other side of the story meant I had a lot of freedom. Mostly, I could come and go as I pleased. In one respect this was a huge plus for the renegade me; I was never a big fan of the "being told what to do" thing! After Daddy moved out I adjusted to flying by the seat of my pants and making my own decisions. My choices weren't always in my best interest but life was fun and very entertaining. Mom held down her full-time job at the hardware store during the day, often worked evening hours as a waitress sometimes until 2 a.m., and began selling real estate on the weekends. My time with her was sparse.

In the midst of all the changes in my life the one standing out would be Mom's long-standing affair with her boss and broker. The repercussions that followed would be long-lasting in my life.

My best friend Nancy was spending the night. Mom had gotten in late and thank goodness we were off the phone by then, she made a bee-line for it the minute she got in the door. To say she was angry after the phone call wouldn't come close. The sudden burst of my bedroom door flying open was a strong indication of what was to come. She had been drinking and plainly had way too much, was on a mission and taking us with her. In one huge sweeping gesture of her arm she motioned us to get a move on, "Come on we're going for a ride, get in the car." Unbeknownst to us she just had a fierce fight with Ken, her married real estate broker with whom she was having the affair. We all flew out the door and down the stairs.

The next thing we knew we were rounding the corner on Ken's street. Mom pulled up to the house. Up and over the curb, while relentlessly laying on the horn; straight over the lawn while breaking and setting off every sprinkler that was in her path. Nancy and I looked at each other. Holy crap! The nose of the car was embedded into the house. Ken flew out of the house and his wife, Jan was right behind him. Angry did not describe the mood. Tempers flew and the screaming grew louder. Ken attempted to hold his wife and my mother apart. We sat in the front seat, the grill of the car firmly embedded in the wall of their bedroom. Water was skyrocketing from the broken sprinklers, covering the entire car and three adults. I use the term "adults" loosely. After Daddy left he warned me "I'm done trying to raise your mother, it's your turn now". I believed this qualified as one of those moments.

Age fourteen was a pivotal time in my life. I was rapidly turning into a certified "Wild Child". Mom was preoccupied with her career and her married boyfriend. I had plenty of freedom and time on my hands. I was in my element and there was no slowing me down.

Going steady with a cute senior who drove the hottest '57 Chevy in town was a definite highlight. However, the chances we took on our first date were not ideal. Five of us girls were going to the movies. Nancy's dad gave us a ride and dropped us off at the front of the theatre. In two short minutes the coast was clear. I ran across the street, jumped in Lee's car and off we went headed for the local drive-in theatre. Freedom rocked and I loved my first taste. The evening fulfilled my highest hopes. Whatever the consequences were to come, it would be worth it and I'd worry about it later. This was the highlight of my entire existence, so far.

I began to feel very timid. This was a brand new sensation for me. I could feel the anticipation welling up and racing through my body. The instant Lee pulled me closer my heart melted. He was an amazing kisser, soft and gentle. I began to sink into a mesmerized, weakened lump. All I knew was that I was safe and cared for. The attention was overwhelming for me. I never wanted it to end. Both of us lost track of the time and fell in to a panic as we noticed the ending credits for "Mutiny on the Bounty" were showing on the screen. At that moment, I should have been meeting the girls in front of the theatre. I was so screwed. We raced to the other side of town, turned the corner to the theatre and pulled in directly behind Nancy's dad, just in the nick of time. The girls were already climbing in the back seat. I jumped out of Lee's car and quickly ran into the middle of the group without skipping a beat or being noticed! As we pulled away I turned around, blew Lee a kiss out the window and off we went.

I wore Lee's senior jacket and class ring. We had been going steady for seven months.

Lee had stayed home from school sick. I had the brilliant idea to ditch school during my lunch break and run over to his house to see how he was feeling. I came up to his bedroom window and lightly tapped on it. He pulled back the curtain and motioned for me to go around to the back door. He let me in and then jumped back into bed. My intention had been to run by, say hello and scoot back to school before the lunch break was over. One innocent kiss goodbye had turned into much more than we expected. We heard a car pull into the drive. Lee's mother had come home for lunch. We both panicked. I grabbed my clothes and hid in the back of his closet. I sat as far back in the corner as I could get, I was scrunched up, clutching my knees close to my chest while feeling pretty vulnerable and completely humiliated. I held my breath when I heard his Mom come into the bedroom. Oh my God, she was standing at the end of the bed directly in front of the closet, quizzing him on how he was feeling by now. I shut my eyes and held my breath, listening to their conversation. While reaching over to feel his forehead she commented, "You're feeling a bit warm Lee, you might be running a fever". His only comment to her was "I'll feel better after some sleep Mom and back in school tomorrow". I heard the back door close, the car starting and backing out of the drive. Lee opened the closet door and peeked in. I was a pathetic mess; holding my breath, I didn't dare move. Here I sat in the corner of my boyfriend's closet clutching my clothes and clinging to whatever dignity I had left! He reached out for my hand, pulled me up and held me close. This momentous occasion did not fit any of my expectations of what my first sexual experience would be like. I didn't feel anymore grown up, I didn't feel anything. Lee pulled me close and whispered "Hey Campbell I love you". Tears began to run down my face. I said "I love you too, Selter". Lee said he would take me home, and we both got dressed.

The minute I got home I jumped in to the shower, stood under the warm water and let it slowly run down my body. I didn't feel grown up or complete in any way. I was numb; I didn't feel anything.

I hadn't eaten all day and was starving. I slipped on my comfy robe, wrapped a towel around my hair and headed for the kitchen. I opened the door to the fridge, it was bare ... again. No one had been to the market yet, no one ever went to the market. The only thing that sat on the shelf was the eight elegant, long-stem, crystal martini glasses filled with green jello I made the night before. I HATED green jello.

Mondays were never fun and I usually stayed in bed as long as possible before getting ready for school. However, this morning I was jolted out of a dead sleep by loud knocking at the front door. It was 6 a.m. on a school day. Mom answered the door and right away I knew it was not good. There was a policeman with a warrant for my mother's arrest in his hand. She came screaming through the house. "I'm being arrested and you're coming with me", demanding I get out of bed and get dressed now. Daddy had served on the police force for many years prior to their divorce, which meant we were all on a first name basis. The arresting officer was profusely apologetic for the whole situation. I went through every step of Mom's arrest, being handcuffed, fingerprinted and booked, complete with a photo and her long ponytail slung over her shoulder. When she was finally released, I was expelled from school and grounded for what seemed like forever. I had ditched school forty-five days in a row. Consequences meant nothing to me, I just did not care. I had fallen into "Desperately Seeking Sherie" mode and I just kept rollin' with the flow. I did what I wanted when I wanted.

During one of our infamous "Ditch Days", my car had been towed away while we were off playing at the beach. I parked on a side street out of view from our apartment and figured I'd be homefree. A group of us piled in to someone else's car and headed off to the coast. There was only one problem. Someone had attempted to throw their cigarette out the window and it ended up lodged in the back seat. After a fun day at the beach, we pulled up to find my car was gone. It had completely burnt to the ground and towed away. All that was left of my little Ford Falcon were the imprint of the ashes where it had sat.

This incident had fallen on the heels of my last attention-seeking moment. Included in my stunts during my forty-five day vacation from school was the day a few of us decided it would be fun to get some wine and go cruise the high school in a neighbouring town.

We managed to get back to our own home town safely enough. I did pretty well until that last stretch, when I attempted to park the car in my parking space at our apartment and mistook the gas pedal for the brakes. I rammed my little Falcon into the six-foot block wall. I hit my head and the next thing I knew I was in an ambulance and headed to the hospital. I did get my Mom's attention but not exactly the way I wanted it. The hospital had called to let her know I was in the emergency room. She was fit to be tied and extremely unhappy with me, but then what else was new?

On and on it went, one drama to the next. In spite of my proper Christian upbringing during the first seven years of my life, any sense of integrity or self-worth had clearly diminished. I continued to spiral out of control through the better part of my early adulthood. My choices were out of self-ishness, poor self-esteem and the overwhelming need for attention. The absence of parental supervision and guidance in my life was taking its toll. Justification continued to block the consistent, nagging little voice in the back of my mind. Hmmm, could that have been my conscience trying to break through? By the time I turned thirty-two I had been married four times and gone through numerous affairs. My self-esteem had all but vanished. It was time for me to take a hard look at where I was going and what I wanted my life to look like.

For the better part of my life, I'd been hell-bent in believing the "Prince" was going to ride in, swoop me up and lay the life of my dreams at my feet. As cliché as it sounds, I knew when I found "The One" the sky would light up, the heavens would part and surely I'd finally be happy, safe and secure. The results of that dream went down as unfulfilled expectations. I've spent the better part of my life looking for love in all the wrong places. Somewhere in my heart I believed I was not enough. When one man couldn't fill my soul, I moved on to the next. I never hesitated to change what was "over there". What I know for sure is … there is no "Bleeping Prince". So where does one begin to look for their lost soul?

First, I needed to acknowledge the mess I had made out of my life. It was important for me to look at the hard, honest facts. I needed to tell the truth to myself for the part I had played in creating this mess. It didn't need to include any more distress or suffering. Taking the path of the illusion and fantasy got me where I was. What I needed was the willingness to take responsibility for my past, the hurt and the pain I'd caused myself and so many others in my life. Only then did I have the freedom to let it all go.

In the beginning, when I first moved in with Mom we experienced several moments that led me to believe our relationship would always be a never ending, hopeless situation. We butted heads and ran in endless circles around our past and the heartache it created over the last fifty years. Life was tense and I felt like I was constantly walking on egg shells. I kept my mouth shut when I wanted to scream. We never brought it up or discussed it. Most of the time I stuffed all my feelings and the anger began to make me sick. Finally, I was diagnosed with Lupus. The stress had become overwhelming for me. Mom fell ill and, as it ended up, the tables were turned. She was now dependant on me. Because she unable to drive, we had to sell her car. I was running the house, taking care of the shopping and cooking our meals. I was in constant communication with her all of her doctors, scheduling appointments, and keeping track of her meds. I was responsible for her wellbeing.

\* \* \*

I am right back where it all began. It's clear to me now, I had to come home to heal my relationship with my Mother. I've released the illusion along with the fantasy that I created so many years ago; believing my childhood was the only time these bonds could of been formed. I'm a work in progress. I strive to live in the present and take every day as a new opportunity to experience the love between us.

In retrospect I can honestly say I wouldn't change anything about my life. Having been forced to grow up overnight brought me to a place of resilience and gave me the ability to climb out of distressing situations through the years, that would have otherwise torn me apart and taken me down.

The bottom line is there aren't any fairytale endings and Sherie Cunningham finally had to grow up.

There came a time when I had to forgive myself in order to "give myself peace".

Authentic power is something inside of us. You cannot lose it and no one can take it from you.

I always had the power. I always had it within.

* * *

*Sherie is accomplished in many ways. She is an active member of "The Writers Café", "The Write Practice" and "Poets and Writers" groups. When she takes a break from writing, you'll find her working on her own custom designed jewelry, taking long walks along San Diego Bay, or engrossed in photography. She has four children and three grandchildren ... so far. She has made her home in San Diego for forty-five years.*

# I Am Not Broken
by Lee Pryke

When I was asked to write my life story several years ago, I wondered what I had to say that would serve another, not realizing that putting the words onto paper was an important part of my own healing. I wondered what I would call the story and, when I thought about my not so happy experiences as being stuck in the mud, I remembered a time when I was a little girl and decided to make a pie for my mother out of playdough. Everything would have been fabulous had I not turned on the oven with the pies inside. They began to melt and the smell brought my mother running. The rest of the story was not one of joy and gratitude. All of a sudden I heard the words in my head - Mud Pies to Miracles. This would be my life story, taking the readers on a journey through six decades of remembering, releasing, and recovering from the experiences and lessons along the path. There were many stops and starts, up and downs and forward, to exactly where I am today. So many journeys and even now a bit painful for me as I peel back the layers like an onion. I was torn between letting go and pulling up my big girl panties, to knowing that deep within the dark corners of my soul there was hidden shrapnel from the battles of life, still untended and showing up in my physical world today. I am ready to take on these little mud pies better now than a few years ago when denial and laughter got me through, but never really cleared the debris.

This is the time for me to de-clutter on the inside and in doing so it is my desire that, through my own process of healing, somewhere around the world in the middle of the night, another will read my story and find their own healing with the understanding that we are never alone in our sadness or fear. We share a connection, and together can shine brightly as the dawn enters a new day and life can become more like a miracle than a mud pie. My story details may be unique to my life, but the feelings and emotions surrounding the events may feel very similar to yours.

When I was invited to write for this book, I was touched and honoured. This was an opportunity that came along at the perfect time, as everything does, and it was important for my wellbeing that I share a part of my life story on these pages. I asked my universal managers to guide me to a portion of the story that was important to share in these pages and that has brought me to this moment.

Some years ago, I read a few books written by Maya Angelou. Her struggles and empowering words helped me on my journey. She wrote, *"I've learned that no matter what happens, or how bad it seems today, life does go on, and it will be better tomorrow. I've learned that you can tell a lot about a person by the way he/she handles these three things: a rainy day, lost luggage, and tangled Christmas tree lights. I've learned that regardless of your relationship with your parents, you'll miss them when they're gone from your life. I've learned that making a "living" is not the same thing as making a "life." I've learned that life sometimes gives you a second chance. I've learned that you shouldn't go through life with a catcher's mitt on both hands; you need to be able to throw something back. I've learned that whenever I decide something with an open heart, I usually make the right decision. I've learned that even when I have pains, I don't have to be one. I've learned that every day you should reach out and touch someone. People love a warm hug, or just a friendly pat on the back. I've learned that I still have a lot to learn. I've learned that people will forget what you said, people will forget what you did, but people will never forget how you made them feel."*

These words give me the strength to throw some things back and open my heart to the process of healing by sharing my journey and understanding the miracles that come through life's lessons. I could go back to my childhood, teens or even my thirties, but I have been guided to open my heart to a time I packed in a box, thinking I had moved on from that place and survived. Indeed I have survived; however, the process of writing has me asking myself if I have truly looked at all the parts of this experience enough or has this been responsible for creating other events in my life through the years that followed.

Our beginnings do have an effect on our decisions and how we manage the results later in life. As I matured there was much forgiving and soul searching to do. Throughout the decades of my life one question came to mind. *"Why did I choose the parents I did?"* I understand that everything happens for a reason and that would come clear to me years later.

Before I begin to unravel this particular incident, let me share with you a little about my family. My father came from England at the age of four and was the oldest of four siblings. He could only finish grade eight as he had to go to work to support the family. I don't know firsthand how his parents raised him, I can only imagine by how he lived his life. He was a quiet man and most days dealt with his pain in the comfort of a bottle of beer or whiskey. I do know that he was angry and hurt and, after too many bottles of beer, that anger showed up on the bruises and broken bones my mother wore for many years, until my father stopped drinking.

124

SHARING: *our stories, our selves, our success*

The most incredible moment came only six years ago when my father transitioned. In his own struggles to survive he had values that I see coming through me now. If he didn't have the cash he didn't make the purchase and sometimes as a teen I thought he was a miser. Well that miser managed to leave his wife a millionaire and more than able to care for herself and her family. It didn't take away the pain and hurt, but I realized that this quiet man in his own way was doing the best he could to provide for his family in the only way he knew how, by working hard and managing his money. It cleared up many things for me and I was able to forgive him for so many of the broken years.

My mother was from an Irish family, the youngest of six brothers and one sister. Her father died when she was very young of TB as she watched him bleed out until he took his last breath. Her mother remarried soon after, and I am sure there are volumes of her feeling neglected and unloved. Being married to my father, her life was about survival and left little time to nurture her own children. I have an older sister who tried her best to protect me from my mother's anger and rage. My brother came along ten years after me and we are kindred spirits on the same path of discovery. We shared many bottles of Scotch in the earlier days and now praise each other's sobriety, growth and expansion. I was the middle child with a voice, and believed my mother's 'nagging' was the reason my father drank and was abusive to her. My mother would take her frustration out on me with a strong hand. I thought it was because I took my father's side but as I matured I could see similar traits in me to my mother. She was a very talented woman, a self-taught seamstress who played honky-tonk piano and always tried to laugh through the pain. She was a bit of a wildflower for many years before the beatings wore her down. She was indeed a survivor. In her own way I believe she was trying to break me of my outspoken nature so I would not repeat her mistakes. In many ways I did break the mold but the scars traveled through time and space inside my soul and empty heart.

I am grateful for the times when the fog cleared and mom and dad got along; in fact when they loved it was beautiful, and those moments may have been what got us through the rough patches. Living in a love hate situation, where emotions were intense on both sides, can be very confusing for a young mind and definitely not the best scenario for learning to deal with life lessons -- and there were many to follow. I learned from a very young age how to survive and negotiate my way out of situations. What I did not learn was what it felt like to be loved or how to feel good about my own decisions. My anger turned to rebellion and it seemed that any time a life lesson presented itself, I took the long road in and out looking for the easy way and finding the toughest challenges as I dug myself deeper into the middle of the mud pies.

My family never taught us how to avoid troubling situations as they seemed to thrive in the drama of pain and anguish. When things were good there was laughter and fun, and then the battles would begin again. I became the little girl who would try anything for a laugh or attention. I was like a clown hiding the pain behind the mask of a smile and it wouldn't be till much later in life that I could actually remove the mask and trust myself and the decisions I made. Funny thing is, one of my collections is pictures and statues of Perot Clowns with big tears on their cheeks.

There were many events to follow that brought tears down my cheeks, and those moments would eventually build the strength I have today. When I read this quote it began to help me heal years later. *'Stop trying to fix yourself; you're not broken! You are perfectly imperfect and powerful beyond measure.'* - Steve Maraboli

It was imprinted at a very early age that I would never amount to anything, and that may have be part of why I didn't always choose people in my life that led me on a path of glory and why I made a lot of not so great choices. In my biography, I detail the decades of my choices and the results that followed in sequence, however for this story I was guided to write about one situation and although I am still not completely aware of why, I know my Universal Managers are guiding me and I trust their reasons.

So here we go back in time to 1999 and the end of my fourth decade. It is winter and a few weeks before the holiday season. I am living on my own after a breakup of a seven-year relationship. This was the first and only relationship (and there were many as I never really got the couple thing figured out) where I didn't do the walking. That, in and of itself, was a tough time for me. Throughout my life I tried to see a train wreck in the making, I would derail the train before it happened so I could walk away with less bruises and maintain my dignity. Yes, that is another chapter!

I was still visiting my ex on weekends to ease the pain of the separation. Now I see it was delaying my healing, but a moment was coming when reality would happen faster than I could imagine and bring a whole lot more to deal with than a breakup from a relationship that wasn't working anyway. We had a party the night before and had a few drinks. In the morning I left to go shopping. I borrowed my ex's car and before I went shopping I checked my apartment to feed and play with my cats. It was around noon and off I went to finish my errands. I was coming back from the store heading down a hill and, although we didn't have snow, the roads were wet and slippery. As I turned the corner down the hill, the car started to slide and, as much as I tried to control the wheel, the car started to hydro-plane. There were cars coming up the hill on the other side. It all happened in a matter of seconds and I smashed into the car coming up the hill on the driver's side before I came to a crashing halt.

All I could think about was driving my ex's car and what he would say if I crashed it. The next thing I remember was the ambulance arriving and the police officer trying to talk to me. I was in panic mode and hitting my head on the wheel sent me into shock. I didn't remember much after that until I was in the hospital. I was fine physically other than a major headache and bruised knees, but shattered emotionally.

This was my first accident and all I remember was the police officer asking me all these questions, including whether or not I had been drinking. I was crying and hysterical with my arms trying to cover my face. I don't remember saying no to drinking, just that he kept yelling at me and trying to put something near my mouth. I was told later that I was fighting him and acting very aggressive. I was in shock. I also knew at this time I hit another car and wanted to know if everyone was ok. It wasn't till later that I realized the police officer was trying to give me a breath test and all I wanted to do was call my ex to tell him what happened. He found out from his best friend who drove a tow truck and showed up to tow the car away.

The man in the other car had a few bruises and his 80-year-old mother in the passenger side had three broken ribs. I was devastated and felt life as I knew it was over. Little did I know it was only the beginning and things would get much worse. The details went on for over a year as my guilt and fear became stronger and stronger. The good thing was I finally broke up with my ex and began to live a very quiet existence. I didn't drink and I didn't drive even when I still had my license. I was finally charged with refusing a breathalyzer, driving causing bodily harm, had my license suspended for three years and had to go back to court on the bodily harm charge. I had been drinking the night before. Did that make me drunk? Was I out of control driving? The doctor at the hospital examined me and said I was fine and not impaired; however, I caused a major accident and hurt other people.

As I write these words I can feel my headache coming on and my body aching reliving that moment. Our bodies tell us so much physically about what is going on inside our soul. I am breathing deeply and exhaling the emotions as I put words to paper.

Every experience, no matter how horrific and terrifying, is a lesson and a chance to grow, when we allow our hearts to heal. Writing these words is giving me a chance to look at the situation once again through clearer eyes and I believe that some of the physical issues that have developed since this incident will find a place to heal. I am older and wiser with more experience in my pocket, and so thankful that I have this opportunity to reveal, release, and restore to an even better place.

So let me finish this part of the story. My court date came and my daughter drove alone from Toronto to Kitchener to take me home, because my lawyer assured me the worst that would happen would be a conditional sentence. The universe had something else planned for me.

The judge allowed the prosecuting lawyer to have the wife speak as a witness, for a very long time, about how their life was destroyed from this accident. My heart started to sink as I watched my daughter listening and saw the fear in her eyes. By this time in the trial, my lawyer had discovered most of what the people were saying was not the truth and that they were hoping for a large financial settlement, but the words were spoken out loud in the court room and the effect was already in play.

The words we use and how we speak them have a profound effect on the people hearing them and can heal the heart or cut into it like a knife. I have learned from this event to choose my words wisely, being careful to think before I speak so as not to intentionally hurt another human being. This family was hurt and angry and filled the courtroom with words once spoken, impossible to take back. They were affected by the accident and I am truly remorseful for their pain, but in that moment it was the judge who was affected and now it was his turn to share his feelings.

As he began to speak the courtroom was silent. My daughter sat alone waiting for his decision as my lawyer assured me we were fine. The judge began to say that as much as he understood I was a model citizen with no prior convictions and that conditional sentencing was normally the decision, he had a mother the same age as the victim and today he was going to make an example of me to be sure that others would pay more attention while driving a vehicle.

I barely heard the next words as my daughter sunk in her chair. NINE MONTHS starting that moment, I was sentenced to jail. They shackled me like a convicted murderer and would not let me speak to my daughter. All I could think about was my daughter driving back to Toronto on her own, knowing the next time she saw her mother would be behind bars. I cried and cried begging to speak to her before she left and saying this may very well cause another accident.

It was the longest day of my life. So many emotions going through me I couldn't get a grip on anything. What kind of a person am I and especially what kind of mother, to put my child through something so horrific and not be able to see her or assure her in any way things would be alright. How she would get through this was my biggest concern, and what was going to happen to me seemed insignificant. I prayed that if there was a God he would take care of my child. It was weeks before I could speak to my daughter and I had to believe that there was a reason for all of this turning out this way, and that she was safe and protected from a force larger than both of us. She was.

When we are in the throes of a crisis it is difficult to see to the other side. We get so personally involved with ourselves and it is not until we step out of the box and approach the situation as an objective bystander that we begin to get some clarity. That being said, it is not always as easy to do as it is to say. During the next several months there was a lot of time for me to think about the why's and reflect on how I came to be in this situation. At first in my humanness, I got caught up in my own pity party. I retreated into silence and felt myself pulling away from life.

I can look back at the situation now and know in my heart that I was being protected in a very big way and, as they say, God never gives you more than you can handle. After the initial shock and adjustment to my new living conditions, I had some choices to make. I could stay locked in my pity party and watch the days turn into months of darkness or I could find an alternative. It wasn't easy, but one good thing my parents taught me was how to survive adverse situations of pain, hurt, physical and emotional abuse. This was a time when it really came in handy. Was this why I chose my parents? I remember my mother saying to me once, *"I have never known anyone who could fall down and get back up as much as you."* I was definitely down; all I had to do is get back up. Funny how life plays out, isn't it?! I chose to make the decisions on the day of my accident and now I had more choices to make.

I am an educated woman with a Masters in Psychology, a great work experience in the corporate world, and an entrepreneur. The truth is, I made some not so smart choices that forced me to look deep inside and figure things out and now I had nothing BUT time to do just that.

Was I moving too fast through life and not paying attention to my family, myself, my friends? The answer is YES. Life is precious and moments fly by and are gone, never to be felt the same way again. I cannot look back and say what if, because that time is gone. What I can do is understand that this situation, no matter how challenging, changed my life in a good way and was necessary for me to experience in order to become the person I am today. When I finally got my bearings, I asked for forgiveness and prayed for the angels to stay close and help me find the light again. Before long, I started to teach at the school they had at my new residence. I helped many women learn basic computer skills. I assisted another lady graduate grade 12 by tutoring her in English. Most of all, I wrote my feelings down every day and discovered that my words could help me understand life better, and slowly I began to forgive myself a little more.

When we are deeply immersed in our own circumstances we become so personally involved that it is difficult to see things objectively. We base our decisions on our belief systems imprinted from birth by our parents and peers. If there is anything to learn from my story, it is that life is precious and taking the time to breathe and slow down enough to think things through clearly may help us make decisions that benefit our personal growth. Understanding that, even in the darkest moments when it seems there is no way out, all we have to do is ask for help from our higher power as we perceive it to be. We are never alone in this world. Each one of us is connected in a special way and each experience is simply a lesson to be learned in becoming the person we were created to be.

There were more ebbs and flows for me to experience before I really understood this, but each one gave me more inner strength to love myself a little more each day. It is a work in progress but I can now accept the ebbs as much as the flows, because I am alive and learning that, when we have the proper tools to survive and reflect on our lessons and experiences, we learn to see how they will eventually teach us to thrive.

People come and go and each one has a purpose in being in our lives, even if in the moment it is difficult to see or understand. When we can reach the place of accepting, we can ask ourselves the question, what is the purpose of this person or situation and what can I learn from this? If we don't let the bitterness set in, with each lesson we learn to be more empathetic of ourselves and the world around us. We grow in compassion and knowledge and this gives us the opportunity to help others who may go through similar pain and sadness.

In the moment of despair we cannot see ahead to the time when it is over and things settle down. Months later we look back and are able to see how all the pieces of the puzzle do fit. If we keep an open mind and heart, we will begin to see how beautiful things manifest out of what seems like the worst scenarios.

Earlier I spoke about the relationship with my mother. It continued throughout my life and was a challenge at the best of times, to figure out. While I was in jail, I got a call from my mother that was totally unexpected. She asked for my forgiveness and said to me that she knew she was a bad mother and didn't give me the love I deserved. She asked me to forgive her and my response was," Mother, if I had not forgiven you we wouldn't be talking now." This was a moment that may not have occurred had I not been in this particular situation. It was the beginning of the healing between my mother and me.

My daughter and I experienced an emotional upheaval during this time. I thought she would never see me in the same way again and I was right, but as it turned out it was a good thing. We both made it through this stressful time and many others, and today we are closer than ever.

In sharing this story with you I have been able to heal even deeper, and what once seemed like the most dismal time in my life became an experience that took me to newer heights of understanding myself and the relationships with my family. The question, why did I choose these parents, was answered. They taught me to be strong and never give up the fight. Although life started out with many speed bumps, it was necessary for me to learn not to turn them into a stop sign and keep on going. When we slow down enough to breathe and notice the beauty around us, any situation can be a blessing if we understand that nothing happens by coincidence and everything we encounter, every person who comes into our life, has meaning. We are never alone in this world. Our experiences may vary but when we learn from our lessons the common denominator is we become stronger and more aware of our own ability to cope and survive. Hopefully along the journey we develop the skills to not only survive but to thrive in any situation.

Life can take us by surprise and for me there would be a few more lessons and experiences to figure out, but I know within my heart that I don't have to figure it out alone. I trust my inner voice better and listen for the voices that guide me along this path called life. No matter how many mud pies we make in life, with the help of our higher power, great friends, compassionate family, and a willingness to learn, Miracles do happen. I have been blessed in so many ways that once I could not understand. This portion of my story is a small but important part of the process and sharing with you has brought me closer to living the life I was intended to live with compassion, empathy and the knowledge to understand the deeper meaning of our choices and decisions.

I am not broken, I am imperfectly perfect beyond measure, and each day in small ways life gets better and better!

* * *

*Dubbed a 'boost of happy', Lee ushers her audience to align on a personal and professional level, laughing often and loving self. Lee's eclectic approach of connecting the dots unfolds in her workshops, soul coaching, as an author and inspired communicator. Her words are life-changing, pivotal, and transformational; they have the power to mobilize you. Founder of I Am I Can Self Enrichment Centre and Healthy Choices Wellness Show, Lee believes when you find vibrational alignment within, you personally thrive. You feel good; you look good; you have clarity; you have wit; you have abundance of all things good. Lee resides in Cambridge, Ontario. Her next project will be finishing her autobiography, outlining the six decades of her life experience. For more information visit www.iamican.ca.*

# From Fear to Faith
## by Lisa Browning

When I was a baby, I cried a lot. I was born in 1960, and the concept of scheduled feeding had just been introduced as preferable to feeding on demand. My mother's decision to follow her doctor's advice and incorporate this method into her care of me resulted in my frequently being hungry. And because I cried as a result of that hunger, my mother was often frustrated. More often than not, when my eleven-year-old sister returned home from school each day, my mother would thrust me into her arms, saying "Take her. I can't stand it anymore." So, through no real fault of my mother's, I was deprived of two of the fundamental needs of a newborn – the safety and security of being loved and held, and the safety and security of being fed when hungry. Instead, I was inadvertently treated as a nuisance and a burden.

I never knew my mother's mother, because she died before I was born. But I remember being told the story of my mother frequently coming home, as a child in public school, to find her mother in a darkened living room, with the curtains drawn, staring into nothingness.

My grandmother's depression was passed on to my mother. From the time I, and my brother and sister, were old enough to understand the spoken word, we were told "You are not on this earth to be happy" and "Whatever can go wrong, will go wrong." If we were laughing and playing 'too much', we were told "You're going to cry before you go to sleep."

And so it was. I started my life with an inherent fear of happiness, and a deep-seated belief that I would not get out of life what I needed to survive, let alone to thrive.

Growing up in a family of five, with an eleven-year age difference between me and my sister, and fifteen years between me and my brother, I was often the "forgotten" one. When I was very little, my family would gather for Sunday dinner around our large formal dining room table. Because I was so small, in size and in voice, I was often unheard at that table of adults and teenagers. When dinner was finished, but conversation still continued, I would usually crawl under the dining room table, hoping against all hope that someone would notice that I was missing. No one ever did. And so ... I became far more serious than I needed to be. Play took a back seat to the "more important" jobs of getting things done. I figured, if I excelled, I would become worthy of attention.

My creativity was thwarted in kindergarten. I remember, as clearly as if it were yesterday, the day I got up during naptime, and happily stirred the vibrantly-coloured tempera paints, lined up in cans on the painting easels at the back of my classroom. My punishment for this indiscretion was to bring my blanket to the middle of the room, and serve my naptime while my classmates moved on to their post-nap activity. Their snickers and pointing fueled my embarrassment and sense of shame.

In grade one, I was chastised by my teacher for holding the scissors the wrong way, and sucking on my hair. In grade three, I was recruited to lunchtime detention because I was talking in line, waiting for the entry bell to ring. I didn't show up for that detention, and I went through the remainder of the school year in terror, wondering when Mrs Freeman would track me down and punish me further for failing to serve my time.

By grade four, my deep-seated sense of shame was fully a part of my psyche, and yet I still displayed sporadic attempts at bravery, however short-lived. The day I proudly wore fluorescent blue nail polish, as was the fashion statement of the time, but scratched it off each nail when I was teased by a couple of classmates intent on embarrassing me, was the day I surrendered my own sense of self to the 'more worthy' opinions of my peers.

I continued through public school with the subconscious belief that my only worth lay in my accomplishments. I was an A student, always the first to turn in assignments, and never coming to school without all homework being completed, neatly and with headings underlined with ruler-straight coloured lines ... a double line for the title, a single line for the date.

My mother's depression took on a manic component and, by the time I reached high school, I never knew what would greet me when I arrived home at the end of the day. One bright, sunny afternoon in grade 9, I came home in a particularly cheerful mood.

"Hi Mom", I called out when I walked through the front door.

"You're mad at me," came the response.

"I'm not mad at you," I replied.

"Yes, you are."

"No ... I'm not."

This exchange continued until I could no longer contain my frustration. "I am **not** mad at you!"

I will never forget the look of satisfaction on my mother's face as she said "See, I told you that you were mad at me."

I became uncomfortable when my life was going well. "Whatever can go wrong, will go wrong." In order to stay true to this deep-seated belief, I found ways to self-destruct in the midst of any success.

> **"Who am I to be brilliant, gorgeous, talented, and fabulous?"**
> ~Marianne WIlliamson

I became paranoid, conjuring up worst-case scenarios at every turn of the road. When I became involved in my first serious relationship, I used three different forms of birth control, but still panicked each month, convincing myself that I was pregnant. When that 'reality' failed to come to fruition, I convinced myself that I had contracted AIDS, despite the fact that I never once engaged in risky behaviour.

In first-year university, I met the first in a series of abusive partners. He was athletic, popular, and incredibly good-looking. I never understood why he chose to be with me. The longer we stayed together, the more emotionally distant he became.

We attended different universities, in different cities. Most Fridays, I took the bus to his university town so we could spend the weekend together. He rarely came to me.

One Saturday evening, we went out with a group of friends to have a few drinks and watch a band at the university pub. Out of the blue, he pointed to a good-looking girl at the next table. "I tried to get her into bed," he announced proudly.

"When was that?" I asked, thinking he would tell me it happened the previous year, before he and I were a couple.

"Last weekend," he replied, just as proudly.

I ran to the bathroom and cried. A girl I didn't know asked me what was wrong. When I told her what had happened, she said simply "Dump him. You deserve better than that." I stayed in the relationship.

Things between us went from bad to worse. He made it abundantly clear that he didn't want me around and, the more he showed me how little I meant to him, the more I tried desperately to prove my worth. The epitome of my shame came one Sunday night when I pretended to get on the bus, but hid in the basement of his residence. When everyone in the building had returned to their dorm rooms, I made my way quietly to his room. Just as I was about to turn the doorknob, I heard him tell his roommate "I'm trying to let her down easy."

Anger trumped humiliation. "You bastard!" I screamed at the still-closed door. I spent the night in the same basement room in which I had previously hid, and caught the first bus back to university the next morning. I never heard from him again.

After a series of unhealthy and unfulfilling relationships, I got engaged. My fiancé was an alcoholic, with very little education and no goals or interests that jived with my own. When friends or family commented on these realities, I replied "Well, at least he doesn't hit me."

The marriage didn't last for long. I tolerated his drinking and his resultant neglect of me, until my daughter was born. We had been in counselling for many months, but he continued to live in denial, stating that there was nothing wrong with him, and that I was the one with all the problems. I finally came to the sad conclusion that I had no choice but to end the marriage. We divorced when my daughter was two years old. I spent the next few years alone, licking my wounds and devoting my life to raising my daughter on my own.

I marrried my second husband four years after my first marriage ended. Because I wanted to avoid making the same mistakes twice, my fiancé and I went for pre-marital counselling with two different counsellors, to ensure we were on the right track. My family was pleased, as "he" presented himself as caring, kind, and considerate. The night before our wedding, I saw a side of him I'd never seen before. He was cruel and cold, and I was scared to death. I should have cancelled the wedding, but I didn't want to disappoint those who were looking forward to the celebration. I went through with the ceremony. At the reception, he got very drunk. It was the first time I'd ever seen him that way. I was embarrassed, but tried to make light of it, to ease the discomfort of our guests.

Our honeymoon was a nightmare. It was as if I was spending time with a complete, psychopathic stranger.

Back at home, he often left the house, choosing to spend the night or the weekend with a female "friend". Eventually, the weekends turned into weeks. Ever the dutiful wife, I prepared a week's worth of single-serve casseroles, and left them on the front porch for him to pick up. He never entered the house to say hi, or thank you. He simply took his food for the week, and went back to Connie.

It was only when he became abusive to my six-year-old daughter, taunting her like a nasty child would do, that I asked him to leave for good.

He knew I would have to put my house up for sale, as I would not be able to continue making the payments on my own. When he walked out the front door, he looked me in the eye and said "I hope you end up on the street."

Someone once told me that people who did horrible things (ie Adolf Hitler, Paul Bernardo) should not be given notoriety by having their names immortalized, but rather should remain nameless. It is a good point. And so, the men featured in the following vignettes from my life and relationships are nameless. They know who they are, and that is all that matters.

*Before "he" met me, he had purchased a pair of floor vases, each standing about two feet tall. When we moved in together, they graced either side of our fireplace. One Christmas, as I prepared to change the vases for two Christmas violins, I left them on the kitchen floor, ready to be taken downstairs for the season. My dog knocked one of them over, and it broke.*

*He was absolutely livid. As his screaming reached a fever pitch, I knew it was best for me to leave the house. He followed me out to the garage, with the broken vase raised over his head, threatening to hit me with it. "Go ahead", I said, calling his bluff. He lowered the vase and stormed back into the house.*

*I went for a drive, and tried to calm down. When I returned to the house a couple hours later, all was quiet. He was up in his office, on the computer. On the kitchen table was a large pile of broken pottery. I recognized it as the remains of a sculpture a friend had brought me back from Africa ... a piece that held great sentimental value for me. The pieces were so small that it was obvious he had taken a hammer to it.*

*"What in the hell did you do?" I asked him with incredulity.*

*He looked at me with smug satisfaction as he said "The dog did it."*

* * *

*The first punch was so severe that I fell to the floor. Unaccompanied by words, the sound of the impact echoed through the house. I looked up in terror as "he" approached me. No longer silent, he orchestrated verbal insults with kicks and punches. I put my hands over my head to shield myself, but I could not avoid the incessant blows.*

*The assault lasted several minutes, and I dissolved in a flood of tears. His final words as he left were "You deserved it. You had a glass of wine at dinner."*

*When I knew I was alone, I got off the floor and went to the bathroom to inspect the damage. I had scrapes and bruises over my arms and legs, and an emptiness in my eyes. The most frightening injury, however, was the ringing in my ears. I washed my face and climbed into bed.*

*The next morning I awoke gradually, willing the previous night to be only a dream. The ringing in my ears had stopped and I had a brief moment of relief. When I fully awakened, however, relief turned to dread as I realized I couldn't hear out of my left ear.*

*I went to the hospital and sat in the emergency waiting room. I had never before noticed how many of the posters on the walls addressed the topic of domestic violence. I fought back tears as I realized that I was now one of the statistics. I imagined never being able to hear the glorious choral music that formed part of my weekly church services, or the sound of my daughter's theatrical and vocal performances that I loved so much. I was terrified.*

*"You have a perforated ear drum," the doctor said, without emotion. I wondered at his complacency. Was he unwilling to venture into the dangerous territory of*

physical abuse, or had he become numbed to a situation that he saw far too frequently?

"Am I going to get better?" Unlike my anxiety, my voice was small.

"Yes," the doctor replied. "It will take a few months to fully recover, but you will regain your hearing." This time, I allowed my emotions, and my tears, to flow freely. I thanked the doctor, and I left.

* * *

We had spent the day in Niagara-on-the-Lake. On the drive down, "he" didn't say a word to me. As we walked along the streets, he was always three feet in front of me. When we sat down to lunch at a local restaurant patio, he flirted with the waitress, and totally ignored me.

When we returned to Mississauga, he stopped at a corner store. While I waited in the car, I opened the glove compartment, as I knew there was always gum in there, and my mouth was dry. In the glove compartment, still in the envelope, was a birthday card. I opened it, wondering who it was from and wondering, even more, why it was not brought into the house and put on the mantel with all his other cards. "Hope you have a wonderful day! Love Nancy." I put the card back in its envelope, and closed the glove compartment.

"Who's the card from?" I asked him when he returned to the car.

"What card?" He tried to act nonchalant, but his eyes displayed his discomfort.

I opened the glove compartment. "That card", I pointed.

Minutes of hesitation, and then he said coldly "Nancy".

"When did you see Nancy?" I asked. When we had first started dating, he told me he would never go out with a female friend without me, because he didn't want me to think there was anything going on behind my back. I was touched by the gesture, however unnecessary I thought it was ... at the time.

He could no longer contain his frustration. "I met her on the street last week. I pulled up to the corner where she was, she handed me the card, and I left."

I knew it was a lie.

*When we got home, I went out to the backyard and called my sister, wanting a second opinion. "Do you think it's strange?" I asked, after telling her what had happened.*

*Suddenly, I saw the lights go on in our unfinished basement. "You're done", he sneered into the phone extension, and ripped the phone cord out of the wall.*

*I knew there was going to be trouble, so I quickly weighed my options. I could go to the kitchen, where I had left my purse, but that would mean crossing his path as he returned from the basement. I opted to run to the master bedroom, which had a lock on the door.*

*I managed to get there just before he caught up to me, and I locked the door. He banged on it so hard that he shattered the wood surrounding the lock, but the door remained intact so he could not get in to the room. "If I get to you, I'll do far worse to you than I did to the door," he threatened.*

*A group of neighbours were outside in the driveway, chatting amicably. I opened the window and asked them to call the police.*

*Several minutes later, a SWAT team arrived, and I was taken out of the house through the upstairs window. Safely in a police car, I waited.*

*One of the officers knocked on the front door, and "he" answered, and looked around in feigned amazement. "What in the world happened?" he asked. "I've been in my office all evening."*

\* \* \*

One spring, I attended a wellness weekend at a local resort. After participating in workshops and seminars with a variety of inspirational speakers, I went home armed with a new sense of hope and purpose. I looked forward to repairing the brokenness of my current relationship, and joining with "him" in creating a life of purpose and joy.

After telling him about my weekend, and sharing my optimism and excitement, he looked at me with disdain and said "You are on a spiritual path of wellness ... and I want no part of it."

I was stunned. I could not understand how anyone could denounce a life of wellness, no matter the path it took to get there. And yet, I did not leave. I suffered through many more months of emotional and verbal abuse, without fully understanding the damage that was being done.

This type of abuse is insidious. Little by little, the abuser chips away at the self-esteem of the abused, until only a shell of the former self remains. Because the scars are invisible, the abuse is often ignored or downplayed. "At least he doesn't hit me."

I was often told that I expected too much from other people. Over time, I learned to expect nothing, even though I secretly longed for someone I could trust wholeheartedly, without fear of abandonment or betrayal. I put up with far more than I should have, feeling powerless to change the life I found myself living.

Despite all of this,  I managed to hold on to a fine thread of dignity and determination. "Weebles wobble but they don't fall down." The jingle from a commercial for those pre-school toys danced in my head. I drafted a story entitled "My Life as a Weeble". I knew, in some secluded part of my psyche, that all roads were leading to my highest good.

My health suffered. I was severely dehydrated and malnourished, and I lived a life of hyper-vigilance, not eating, and rarely sleeping.

When we had decided to move in together, we needed to downsize, in terms of the duplicate furniture we owned. Because his furniture was newer than mine, my furniture was either sold or given away.

When the relationship was nearing its inevitable conclusion, I was not allowed to sit on the couch in the family room. "It's my couch, and I don't want you sitting on it," he said. He even went so far as to dismantle the bed in the master bedroom. "It's my bed, and I don't want you sleeping in it."  I slept on the floor, like a dog, while he slept in a comfortable bed in the guest room.

**"We all have our breaking point, when our heart will finally have enough of being lied to and will shut off. It will hurt but it knows when it's time to move on."**
- unknown

I was out for dinner with a friend. During the course of our conversation, she mentioned nonchalantly "So, I see "he" has a girlfriend."

"He", in an act of either stupidity or cruelty, had posted this new relationship on his Facebook profile, while at the same time telling me he was committed to mending our relationship.

I was sitting at the kitchen table when he walked in the front door. "How's Valerie?" I asked, my words laced with cold venom.

He knew then that the end had come. The process of separating was brutal, as his manipulation and cruelty reached its peak. Legal, financial and health issues brought me to my knees, and I ended up in the hospital under "suicide watch".

The weekend before I was admitted, I had made arrangements to visit friends out of town, and was looking forward to having Easter dinner with them. Easter morning, my brother came to visit me in the hospital, and brought me a lily. The nurses immediately confiscated it, as 'Form 1' patients were not allowed to have "foreign" items in their rooms. My silent tears spoke to the nurse on duty, and she brought the lily back, and placed it on the table in my room so I could look at it.

The doctors wanted to admit me to the local "psych" hospital, but I refused. My perfectionistic self  would not allow myself the 'luxury' of time off work, and complete attention to self. I did, however, agree to out-patient status.

**"Fat slut, ugly bitch.**
**You're not worth the breathing space to even consider."**
~the man who shall be nameless


**Abused No More**

Sitting on a front porch that will soon no more be mine,
Thinking of all the dreams we shared until you crossed the line,
Wondering how you could have done the things you did to me,
Praying that I'm granted eyes to see what you must see.

I never thought you could become the monster you became.
You were so kind and loving from the day I heard your name.
How could you throw away a love so precious and so rare?
How could you walk away again, confirming you don't care?

I said I'd never let another bring me down again.
You came so close I almost thought I'd truly gone insane.
But I am strong and will get through the anger and the fear,
And I will be the better one. I'm sorry for you, dear.

You need some help before you take another victim in.
There is no shame in getting help. Denying is the sin.
So for your sake, your children's too, please make that crucial call.
You've lost our dream and, with no help, you'll surely lose it all.

I wish our story could have had a very different end.
You were the one I counted on as confidant and friend.
But when the past is ever-near, the present can't survive.
Now that you're gone, my mind is clear. I truly am alive!

* * *

It took me almost two years to get to a point where I no longer believed that the world was out to get me, that the earth would eventually open up and swallow me whole. With the help of an amazing therapist, and the support of wonderful friends, I reclaimed my power. I became the creator of my life, rather than the victim of people and situations, or forces beyond my control.

In previous years, I had struggled with my faith. Although I loved my church and, more importantly, the people I encountered there, I became more and more disillusioned with the dogma that was being put forth. I didn't believe in the resurrection, I didn't believe that Lazarus was raised from the dead, and I didn't believe that Jesus walked on water.

I left the church, because I knew I could no longer stand proudly and recite the Apostles' Creed. When I discovered a correlation between spirituality and faith, I returned, to the open arms of a community I consider to be family.

**Are you a victim or a creator?**

I don't remember where I first heard the question, but I know it resonated with me. For so long, I considered myself a victim, and my struggles with my faith did nothing to change that belief. Over the years, however, I came to understand that we are all a part of "God". We are all creators, as God is Creator. This feeling comes to me most strongly as I walk my dog through the wetlands surrounding my subdivision.

**I am a creator, not a victim.**

Sometimes, I still have to stop berating myself for not having left sooner, for wasting so much time. What could I have done, had I known then what I know now? The question threatens to haunt me. So, now, I choose to change the question. What will I do in the future, knowing what I know today?

Life today is beautiful. I surround myself with creative people who affirm me, and I take great pleasure in helping others find their own path of empowerment and joy. I spend as much time as I can in nature, because it is there that I am grounded, and receive my strength.

I am no longer that scared little girl, hiding under the dining room table. I am out, speaking my truth to any and all who care enough to listen.

*  *  *

*Lisa is the creator of One Thousand Trees, the website and the magazine, and the sole proprietor of words ... along the path, offering writing, editing, and desktop publishing/pre-press services. She received a Bachelor of Arts in English in 1988, and subsequently worked as an editor for over fifteen years. In recent years, she rediscovered her passion for writing, and has had essays and articles published in a variety of online and print magazines. She is currently working on several books for herself and others, including a book on bullying and verbal/emotional abuse, scheduled to be released in December 2014. No matter what she does, Lisa is inspired to make a difference in this world, and to help others realize their passion and their gifts. She currently lives in Guelph, Ontario. For more information visit www.onethousandtrees.com.*

# The Voice Within
## by Catherine Skiles-Brunner

I am no expert on the human condition, but I could have figured out the secret to being happy. It may have taken nearly fifty years, but I think it was worth it. In addition, I think it's too valuable to keep to keep to myself.

Everyone knows that human development isn't static and that each of us evolves over time. Scientists have proven that we became who we are because of experiences we have and the influence of others we encounter throughout our lifetime. Every experience builds upon another. The world sees the outward results and determines who we are. In the same manner as the world, we too determine who we are in our own mind; we etch upon our psyche a picture of ourselves. We become fairly certain that, if this is how we see ourselves, surely the world must see us this way too. Now, here's the part I want everyone to understand; this perception that is created, this self-identity, it's all controlled by YOU. There is no experience, no object, no job, and certainly no one, who can create the perception of yourself that guides you along in your life. Let me repeat that, there is nothing and no one that has control over your thoughts about who you are and your self-worth. That's a powerful thing to remember. It is often easy to forget.

We all have from time to time a voice that we hear in our heads. A little voice of reason is normal. Everyone hears it from time to time. The danger comes in the power we grant to it, allowing it to cripple us. It begins small and innocent, perhaps cautioning us with words of concern, or acting as our conscience. Unfortunately one day we let a bad experience or thoughtless person give credence to the voice. We have more experiences and they begin to build up. We hear those words or relive those experiences until, left unchecked, that voice becomes a harmful negative weapon we use on ourselves. We build an obstacle that causes us to give up on dreams, doubt ourselves, and eventually lose sight of who we really are at our core. Yes, I know, it's hard to believe. It seems ridiculous that any of us would choose on a daily basis to listen to negative condescending sentiments aimed at tearing us down; ludicrous that we might allow some internal voice to constantly point out our every flaw, our every hurt and every mistake. Sadly, this is true with many of us. We allow that voice to have control over us. In fact, not only do we allow ourselves to listen to that destructive voice, but we CHOOSE to believe it. We CHOOSE to put the opinion of that voice above all other thoughts. We can only hear and live by that voice. All too often we give into it without a fight.

Before we know it, the voice has total domination over us. There is no place to hide from it. It is with us night and day telling us that we aren't good enough; smart enough; pretty enough or worthy enough. It beats down every positive thought we might have about ourself. I know this because I have lived it. I still hear that voice rattling around in my head on occasion. When I hear it start to stammer, I do all in my power to quell its influence.

We are fortunate that we aren't born with that self-deprecating voice. We can eradicate it. I haven't always been influenced by it, but have found that somehow most of my life I have been to some degree held captive by it. I have allowed this negative and hurtful voice far too much power over me. At first it was a quiet whisper, almost nonexistent, but over time it became a roaring noise so deafening that it drowned out everything else in my life.

I think it was around late summer of 1975 when I first started to hear the faint whisper. Summer was a great time of year at that age. The days were long and the sun was warm. I loved baseball. I loved playing it, watching it and reading about it. In the summers I could play all day with the neighborhood boys on the makeshift diamond on the side yard of our Long Island house. On that diamond, there were no social protocols, no cliques and no frilly girly rules to ruin the game. It was just ball playing, laughing and being one of the guys.

As I think about that summer all these years later, I realize that was the last summer I remember being just a kid. It was filled with all my favorite things and people. I wasn't afraid of anything. I was a twelve-year-old tomboy, tall for my age and not yet grown into my long arms and legs. My knees were scraped and my forearms were covered in mosquito bites and perpetually dirty. I wasn't concerned about public opinion or appearances. My straight red hair hung in my eyes. It refused to stay in pigtails. The tip of my nose was sunburned and speckled with freckles. When I looked in the mirror I just saw a happy, carefree kid with the world by the tail. The side yard was my slice of heaven and nothing could ever touch me there.

I admit I had a pretty good thing going for myself; baseball, boys and summer. It was a great combination. The world around me was changing, but I wasn't paying attention. I wasn't caught up in the junior high drama. I didn't notice that other neighbourhood girls were beginning to mature.

While I was playing baseball, they were doing their nails and shopping. But change was coming, and others were noticing.

As the summer sailed along a few of these local girls began to come and sit on the fence to watch us play. They would flirt and giggle. The boys ate it up, playing right along by showing off and peacocking around. The boys stopped taking the game seriously. They wanted to take more breaks, they weren't paying attention and I was getting annoyed. I protested that they were ruining the game. They scoffed and made excuses, and then I realized the boys never acted that way when it was just me around.

In true mean girl junior high fashion, there was teasing that was thrown my way. It was always in such a way that I could laugh it off, and at first I didn't think that I was affected by it. I put up with it. After all, I was tall, skinny and covered in freckles, not the most exotic look. But, I began to internalize every word. I would sit in my room at night and cry. I didn't know why, but I knew that, whatever this feeling was, I did not like it. For the rest of the summer, I would be the butt of the jokes. I wouldn't give into them. I wouldn't run away. I was outwardly unfazed, but I loathed the game, my side yard, and myself. I started to look in the mirror and see an ugly and uninteresting duckling.

I let the experience and the cruelty of those junior high girls give power to the voice. It didn't take long before I gave the voice permission to choose words like stupid, dumb, ugly, and dull to describe myself. I tried to laugh off these situations and I acted like it didn't hurt, but it did. It hurt a lot. I began to act the clown and use self-deprecating humour as a way of beating them to it. Something I still do. I thought perhaps if I say it first, it won't feel like such an insult if they do. It works as a shield, but it still hurts when others label me. Instead of being proud of what made me unique and interesting, I compared myself to all the popular girls. I wanted to dress like them, be like them. I wanted to be noticed too. I wanted to be something that I wasn't but somehow thought I had to be.

As I got older the voice made me feel less confident about myself. I continually made comparisons that weren't realistic, and was disappointed by the results. The reality was that by fifteen years old I stood nearly five foot nine. I had a nice shape. I didn't like to wear makeup. I had to wear glasses because I was very near sighted. I had blue eyes, fair skin and freckles. My auburn hair was straight and I had difficulty trying to find a style that worked. I was smart, outgoing, friendly and enjoyed public speaking; I

147

was a mediocre athlete but loved writing and art. In contrast, the voice told me and I CHOSE to believe that I was too tall and gawky. When I looked in the mirror I saw Howdy Doody. Makeup made me look like a clown. Inside my head, the voice would have me believe that I had to look like a supermodel to be beautiful. We moved to Illinois my freshman year and I had a whole new set of social circles to try and master. It was hard being the new girl and under scrutiny.

In my romantic relationships I didn't have many real successes. Crushes always resulted in avoidance and rejection. They often dated my friends, but not me. In general, I didn't get asked to dances until the last minute, or I didn't go at all. Luckily, I did have a couple relationships worth talking about. They started okay, but ended sourly. One guy asked me to prom and then a week later unasked me. He said he was going with his old girl-friend. The voice told me I wasn't pretty enough. Instead of learning from each relationship breakup, I added it to the list of what was wrong with me. All the while, I walked with my head up, but I was a bit shaky inside. My authentic self was getting lost as I masked the feelings and emotions to survive. One whisper at a time, I let the voice tear me down.

In the midst of high school's trials and tribulations, I met the love of my life, Jim. I thought he was the most handsome person I had ever seen. It was a hot August day, and I was with friends at a gas station. He walked through the door and smiled at me, and I dare say that lightning hit me. I felt my heart pound and my knees go weak the moment our eyes met. We dated a short time, broke up and got back together. To this day I am not really sure why. Unfortunately his family had to move during our junior year 1000 miles away to New York. We kept in touch, but technology wasn't what it is today. We were limited to writing letters and talking on the telephone for twenty minutes every other week through our senior year. He joined the Navy and I enrolled in junior college. We tried to con-tinue our long distance relationship. He asked me to marry him and I ac-cepted, but it was somehow out of our ability to make it work. For the next few months, the voice worked overtime. It was telling me that I was afraid of moving away from my family, of taking chances, of committing to a mar-riage for the rest of my life with someone I felt I barely knew. We fought. Neither of us heard what the other was trying to say. It resulted in a broken engagement that would haunt me for decades. We just couldn't harness the emotion at such a young age. With a broken heart, I gave back the ring, and regretted that choice from the moment I did it. The voice was extra harsh. It made sure I would know how horrible a person I was. It was good at shame, very good.

I dove into trying to make something of my life. I had always dreamt of becoming a successful business executive. I wanted to go to college and earn my degree. I wanted to live in a thriving place with opportunities. I tried to block out the voice for a while and continued with junior college, with hopes of going on for a Bachelor's degree at a four-year university. However, I had to take a year off to earn more money. I dated a few more individuals, experienced a number of ego crushing moments adding to my growing mental pile of inadequacies. All the while, I missed Jim. I thought about him often, regretting my decision every single day. There was a chance a year after our breakup that we almost had an opportunity to re-unite. It didn't work out. I swore him off forever. I spiraled into destructive behaviour and masked my unhappiness any way I could, to dull the pain. I couldn't deny that Jim would always hold a special place in my heart as my first love, and our paths crossed again over the years, but I always kept him at a distance. I tried moving forward just to prove I didn't need him. I was engaged a second time to a sailor who I barely knew, and moved to Florida. I was determined not to make the same mistakes this time. Sadly, I made bigger ones. In the end I came back home, rejected, sad and lost. I was tired of trying to find happiness. I began not only to think it wasn't in the cards for me, I began to believe it.

Shortly after the Florida fiasco I moved back in with my parents and, while working in my old home town, I met my future husband. We had a lot in common. We enjoyed being together. He was a local boy with deep roots. He was older than me by a couple years. I thought he was funny. We decided to marry a year later. I was happy and excited about my prospective new life. We were in love and it was a comfortable relationship. We bought his old family homestead and remodeled it. I reassessed my dreams and settled down in the small farming community to be a wife and mother. We didn't have much, but we were happy. The voice became quiet.

As the years passed our lives grew busier. We had a beautiful baby daughter. We had a house, a nice car, money in the bank, and his career was taking off. I was lucky to be a stay-at-home mom for the most part, but helped out with odd jobs where I could. I was proud of him and how hard he worked. When his job required entertaining people I spared no time or expense to make him look good by being the perfect hostess. I thought of us as a team. It was important to me that he approved of my efforts and of me. I wanted him to be proud of me. I wanted him to need me, lean on me. I made choices to support the family unit, and put my own aspirations aside. All I ever wanted was his unconditional love, just as I gave to him.

In hindsight, I thought I had that. I put everything I had into the relationship and truly believed that he was making the same effort too.

As the years rolled along, I began to feel that I was the only one who made concessions. When schedule conflicts arose I would almost always be the one to give up my opportunity to allow him to keep his commitments. If he didn't want to do something, I made excuses for him. If he didn't want to talk about emotional issues with me, I would tell myself it was difficult for him to share his feelings. If he was short with me, made me cry or said something hurtful, I would attribute it to his job stress or busy schedule. As time went on, I continued to make excuses for him, but began to believe that it was somehow something wrong with me that was to blame. I internalized all those feelings. The voice began to rise again.

As I continue this part of my life's story, I think it important to point out that it's little about how he treated me or the specifics of any situation, but all about how I let his actions and words affect the power I gave to the voice inside me. He is the father of my daughter. I will always be grateful to him for that. He provided for his family and we had on many levels a good life, but it lacked in some key areas. He was who he was in the relationship and I find, today, that I failed to figure out who I was. I waited for someone else to tell me who I was.

Each year, I felt more and more that he showed no interest in anything that was important to me. I came to feel that he saw me as nothing but an obligation. Our relationship lacked excitement and passion. We were barely communicating. I couldn't understand why he didn't see it either. I tried to fight for the relationship. I was confounded why he wasn't.

His attitude toward me was hurtful. I became resentful. I was always sad. I felt unloved. I felt invisible. I heard the voice loud and booming, laughing with delight. Our relationship struggled. To fill the void, I became active in the community. I served on boards and committees. I often over committed. It was a way to validate my worth. I craved something of my own. I found a way to go to college and get my Bachelor's degree at the age of 46. I got a good job 35 miles away that paid more than I had ever made in my whole life. I filled the voids as best I could, but the voice continued to grow louder.

The voice told me I was fat, when he was indifferent to the new dress. The voice told me I was dumb, when he dismissed my opinions or spoke over me in conversations. The voice told me to contain my personality because I embarrassed him in public. The voice told me I was undesirable when he chose TV over me. The voice told me I was uninteresting when he didn't look up from the newspaper when I talked to him. It told me I was invisible when he didn't miss me when I was gone. I tried often to convey this to him. He would apologize but it sounded disingenuous, hollow and empty. He placated me by saying he loved me and would try harder. The voice spoke loudly but I continued to make excuses for him, and somehow blamed myself for all my unhappiness. Increasingly, I began to think about all the dreams I had given up, the goals that I had set and how I had barely achieved any of them. I wanted to be so much more, but instead I felt invisible, and trapped by mediocrity.

I found myself wondering what my life might have been like if I had made different choices. The voice fed my depression and sadness. It fed my anger and resentment. It controlled all my thoughts. It had complete power over all of me. I believed it and lived by its words. I could hear nothing but the voice inside my head pushing me down, holding me back. I no longer recognized myself. I cried driving to work. I cried in the grocery store. I cried laying alone in the dark. I felt empty.

One day, the voice became so loud that I could barely hear anything else but it screaming in my head. It clanged and banged, drowning out my thoughts. It was the day that my husband told me after twenty five years that he didn't want to be married to me anymore.

I caution anyone that they should never ask a question to which they don't really want the answer. During an argument we were having, I said "Sometimes, I don't think you want to be married". He calmly replied, "I don't think I do." It was as if a baseball bat struck my chest. All sound was amplified and I felt the universe crack, and I started to fall into a deep black abyss. My vision narrowed, focusing on his face. I could see him speaking, yet I could not hear him. I felt nauseous and weak. Could he honestly be so callous and unemotional? How could he walk away after twenty-five years of marriage? I was devastated. I asked him "How are we going to fix this?" He replied "I don't think we can." He then calmly and nonchalantly informed me of the laundry list of things I was entitled to in the divorce. Wait! What?! He had thought it all out in advance? He had been thinking about it a long time! He had made his decision long ago and was just going through the motions!

At my urging, he agreed to do counselling, but it was half-hearted. For several weeks we barely spoke. I walked on pins and needles, not sure what was around the corner. I couldn't eat or sleep. I lost thirty pounds and shook constantly. He saw this, but hardly engaged me. I fell deeper in the hole. He withdrew more and I internalized it all. He did not want to fix anything. He revealed things in the counseling sessions that shattered any rose-coloured truths I held about our life together. I had given him my youth, a family, my trust. I had given up every dream I had ever had for myself, for this relationship. In this man, I had placed my entire future, financially, emotionally and physically. Now I was facing life alone. Thrown away like yesterday's newspaper. The voice within fed the fear and shame of my failure to be a good wife. I failed at my marriage. The voice roared with laughter.

I sunk to the lowest point in my life. I felt unloved, unwanted and alone. I was exhausted from the sleepless nights and the emotional and physical toll this was taking on me. All the while the voice grew in volume and regularity. It mocked me with every movement, thought and action. I heard I was a loser, a fat, ugly, unloved waste of time. It conjured up every unkind word from my past to further drive me down.

It all changed, the night he moved out of the house. I asked him come back and explain to me what would happen next. How would this whole thing work? How do we dissolve 25 years? He again recited the laundry list I was entitled to as if reading a menu. I opened my heart to him sharing my fears He told me not to worry, I wouldn't be alone long.

His cavalier disregard toward me brought on a rage that I had never felt before. I felt cheated. I felt used. I felt sick to my stomach. I felt an anger rising from deep within. Yet another dismissal of me caused an unleashing of fury like none I had ever known. I looked at him from across the room with contempt. I screamed at him with rage and chastised him for stealing my life and cheating me out of the future that I was promised. That night when he finally left, it was as if he were a stranger to me.

I sat alone in the quiet house. The voice tried to rear its head only, this time, I kept it at bay. I resolved that I would not be defined by this divorce. I was determined to take control of my life. The question was how? I knew I had to speak up for myself. I had to be clear. I was strong. I was not going to be beaten down and defeated. I shut the noise in my head off. That night I slept for the first time in weeks. I was calmer than I had been years.

I took each day and determined what I needed to do to get through it. Slowly, I could see improvement, but it was a long way off. I spent the next several months dealing with the rumours around town about the divorce. I cleaned out a home that housed 25 years of memories and moved into a small apartment across town. I met with a lawyer, insurance agents, and bankers, and untwined twenty-five years of existence on paper. All the while, I did everything alone. I lived in a fishbowl and everyone could see my every move. I could hide nowhere from the shame I felt. The voice fed into it.

I was bouncing through the Universe without any real direction, and eventually the Universe took control and caused my path to cross with someone that would help set me back on course. From out of the blue Jim reappeared. This time, I welcomed him, slowly at first, but then I couldn't imagine life without him. He was my knight in shining armour. A soothing voice that pulled me in like a tractor beam when I felt my life going out of control. The only thing wrong was that he was 1600 miles away in Arizona. He was going through a divorce and together we helped each other through the difficult times. All we had again was our telephone relationship. It was good, but it was hard to be apart. He was my confidant and an understanding friend. I had the support of many others as well during this time, but I believe that God brings to us who we need in our lives when we need them. He brought back to me someone who loved me unconditionally. Someone who had loved me always. He brought me someone who was not afraid to hold me accountable when I let the voice take control of my life.

We spent hundreds of hours on the phone, getting to know each other all over again. We began in earnest, talking about a future together again. I was always hesitant. I wanted assurances that this time it would work. He could give me none. He told me to live in the moment. I was fearful that he would become tired of me. I always found an excuse why it wouldn't work. Jim was patient. He was kind. He was my rock to lean on. I went to visit him several months after we had become reacquainted. It was as if we had never parted. He made me feel alive and loved. I continued, however, to let the voice hold me back and give me excuses why I shouldn't be happy or with him.

So I lived my life as it was. Talking on the phone, hanging out with girlfriends, spending time with my family. I tried to have as normal a life as possible. But I was lonely and I was unhappy. To fill the hours of alone time, I took up a job waiting tables. I could socialize and make a few extra bucks. Everywhere I went; however, in this small town I bumped into my ex-husband. He was moving on and doing it in my face. It hurt to see. I felt trapped in a revolving door. I couldn't move forward; all I could do was look backward. I felt out of control of my life with feet stuck in cement. I wanted out of that life, but wasn't brave enough to do anything about it, so I wallowed in the unhappiness. I waited for someone else to make it better.

Then in a late night talk I asked Jim to tell me what to do. He confronted me with the statement "You would rather stay comfortable in an unhappy situation, than risk doing something to be happy; You have to decide what is right for you. I cannot." How terrifying that was to hear. How sadly true it was. We hung up and I knew that my whole future hinged on that very comment. I asked myself what could be the worst thing to happen. I realized right then it already was happening. I would be alone, sad and unhappy. I talked with family and friends. The difference was, this time, I didn't ask them what to do. I told them what I was doing. They all wanted me to be happy. They all supported and encouraged me.

A week later, I made the decision to quit my job and move to Arizona. I thought I could find a good job and a place I could start over. In May of 2013 Jim and I drove a truck full of my life across the country. I was a little fearful and a lot excited to see what the future held for us together 30 years later.

Five months later, I am happier than I have ever been. I am reminded daily that I am worthy of happiness. I am beautiful. I am quirky. I am silly. I am fun. I am smart. I am loved.

Is it any wonder that I ended up in Phoenix… rising from the ashes? I think not. A little voice told me this is where I should be … …..

***

*Catherine is a life-long traveler on a path to self-awareness, whose journey so far has taken her on many roads. She is a self-proclaimed late bloomer in her career choices, still seeking that perfect calling, and she intently advocates for programs that empower and lift others to see the potential in their unique and magnificent purpose for being. Her own words came to task when the Universe declared that, after her 25 year marriage suddenly ended in divorce, she embark on a new journey on faith. She quit her job, accepted a new relationship and moved 1,600 miles to the Phoenix Arizona area. Her writing has always been a small glimpse inside her private world but serendipity has declared it now be shared.*

# Never Give Up
## by Heather Embree

*To be beautiful means to be yourself. You don't need to be accepted by others.*
*You need to accept yourself.*
-- Thich Nhat Hanh

Usually most healers are called to these professions because of their own suffering. I certainly have had to go through an initiation process, shall we say, in order to get to what I'm doing today and feeling called to support and give back to others.

My first test of loving myself started when I was conceived. My parents were in a rocky marriage and my mom was often left home alone while my father was out at "business meetings". Her family, through their loving concern, advised her against having a second child, saying that it would bring more struggle to her life. From an adult perspective, I completely understand their reasoning, showing care for my future and the well-being of my mother. But from a soul or energy perspective, this feeling of not being wanted is something that has been with me for my whole life and something I still struggle with to this day.

So, needless to say, I was born in an environment of a lot of dissatisfaction and conflict, with very little support from my mother's family. Also, my father's side of the family had a habit of only being able to love one child – so my older sister got all of their affections, while I was the child who got in the way. Fortunately I was embraced by my mother and sister, so I at least had two nurturing women who were teacher-types and kept me alive and functioning in the world. Their laughter and ability to see the brighter side of things kept my spirit intact.

This wound of not being wanted carried with me for most of my life. It showed up time and again. In the 1970s & 80s, there were still biases and stigmas around things that nowadays we would consider to be acceptable or common place. My family seemed to be at the forefront of every type of stigma possible: my parents divorced, my father was a gambler, my mother was diagnosed with a mental illness and hospitalized, my mother's second marriage was to a Jamaican man, we moved to his "Third World" country, and my mom refused to take us to Church. When we got to Jamaica, my mom was outcast once again because she was a white woman

155

who wore shorts, confirming that she was indeed an evil temptress and white devil of the community. This all contributed to the feeling that there was something wrong with me and my family, and somehow I didn't belong to anyone or anywhere.

Needless to say "The Munsters" was my favourite TV show, along with "The Flying Nun". The juxtapositions are not lost on me.

While in Jamaica, I could feel the energy of hate, suffering, sadness, and injustice. No one explained to me that my white skin was either a threat to the people who lived there or was something that was envied and considered valuable to those of the upper class. Sneering comments of "whitey" and "massa class" (as in, "slavemaster class") were spoken with venom underneath the breaths of people, while at the same time I was getting the privilege of special treatment at school where the teachers dared not beat me, as that was for the kids with darker skin colour. I got to sit in the front seat of the school bus so that my clothes did not get dirty from sitting in the back with the other kids. I hated every minute of living there because I knew that many people did not like me simply because of my skin colour and all of its privileges. I understand. It was unequal and there is no reason why I should be treated any differently than the next person. But five-year-olds don't understand the world this way. No one got to know me for me and I was yet again feeling that I was unwanted and unlovable. And then the pressure of being a girl who didn't ever envision having children was blasphemous and ridiculed in that culture, where women were not encouraged to have bigger dreams for themselves. To cope with these layers of ignorance, I kept my head stuck in comic books and held my breath until I could return three years later to Canada because of a robbery in our home in the middle of the night.

My mother decided to stay in Jamaica for six months thereafter while my sister and I lived at my aunts' and uncles' homes. I cried every night until my mom came back to Canada, in an emotional torment from overcoming many losses including the great possibility of losing my mother and never seeing her again. Even though there were many efforts to integrate me back into Canada, I was still under a reverse culture shock from returning home and feeling out of place. Amongst white people, I was now the weird kid with a Jamaican accent – an island that most people either never heard about or they believed was filled with poverty where people were lazy pot smokers. Fortunately there was a teacher in the school, Mr. A., who was from Jamaica and had a warmth about him with his accent that bridged my two realities, confirming that I wasn't just transplanted from one alien planet to another and all that used to be real was now a figment of my imagination. He was one person who understood what it was like back there.

Because I was a highly intelligent child, I was not considered to be "cool" in Canada with my peers. I can't remember having a true friend until two years later in grade 6 when I got put into a class of "smart kids" who finally understood my strange love of math and language. It was the first time that I felt like I fit in with other kids in my whole life.

On hindsight, these years of social disconnection and experiencing different cultures made me pull back and have to find my inner resources within myself. I learned how to pick up on feelings and others' perspectives and become a peacemaker of sorts. I developed a keen sense of how to discern between a person's words and what they were really saying, not trusting someone just because they were a nun, teacher, police officer or simply an adult. I met adults who behaved like children and children who behaved like adults. I developed a bigger perspective that life has nothing to do with physical appearances and everything to do with a person's heart and way of relating. I met addicts who were generous as all get out and bar fighters who had hearts of courage to stand up for what's right. I met philosophical people who sold peanuts for a living. These people seemed to have far more depth and understanding of what matters than the people I was supposed to respect.

By the time I reached 16 years old, I decided that I had enough with my home life. The adults surrounding me were perpetually fighting and I needed something different. I had grown up past my years and knew I would fare better on my own. This was one of my great acts of courage to stand up for Love and not War. This act of my own personal liberation translated into other self-strengthening acts down the road of life, ensuring I left situations that didn't feel right or were unkind. I didn't want what most people wanted – stability, family, money, material success, etc. I wanted peace, love, creativity and to be happy to be alive.

In my University years, I found solace in activism, standing up for issues of anti-racism, feminism, wrongfully convicted prisoners, freedom of expression and non-violent anarchism. My experiences in life created a part of me that could see the world from a bigger picture and the greater systems of suffering. Activism gave me an outlet to externalize all the ways I was feeling about my life and myself on the inside. I could actually do something about it. I had some sense of empowerment. Through it, I learned how to give to others and get past my own wounds. I learned about the complicated power structures in the world of government and women's history. I developed an attitude or strength of not accepting everything as truth. I questioned, inquired, re-framed my perspective about "another" in order to see beneath the surface of circumstances and see the person more clearly rather than through a label. I felt the deep meaning and importance of advocating on behalf of others, risking one's comfort zone for the benefit and well-being of perfect strangers. I broke down lenses of colonialism and its Christian roots. I realized that good and evil, according to a society, were relative things and developed according to which culture was the dominant force at the time, and that society's view of morality was not based on love and compassion. I developed a deep sense of making a contribution to the community while allowing personal freedoms and human rights. Yet as I continued to progress, I could see that the community I was surrounding myself with was full of suffering. People became disheartened and disillusioned. It felt like struggle after struggle. There was mental illness, addictions, anger and disrespectful, blaming behavior amongst the team of activists. This sense of empowerment brought me a lot of wisdom but not a lot of peace. It disconnected me from the humanness of others, yet again. And I was getting lost in my ideals as a way to belong with others. I didn't have genuine, accepting and interactive relationships with others outside of a "cause". So long as I was "in" with their ideals and actions, then I was acceptable. If I had a different point of view or just wanted to relate with someone for the sake of it, then I was considered to be "part of the problem". I learned that there were many conditions in that realm and I wasn't willing to play by all of the rules.

Because of not having a strong bond with my family and all of its assumptive roles, I was never afraid of interacting with strangers, so I felt at home in the world in many ways. I had a strange trust that many people defined as odd, different, not like most people. I blamed it on the water in Guelph. But I didn't know how true that was until I lived in Toronto and spent time in Mexico, where people would open up to me about their life, in all different languages. I remember when one woman on the subway told me about her broken heart over her lover who still lived in her home of Cuba. She cried on my shoulder and stayed on two extra subway stops because she felt she could open up to me. Ironically, her name was Joy.

This would happen time and again. It came naturally for me to be able to find the comforting words, the solace, the beauty in the person who believed they were ugly and were overlooked for not fitting in to the greater culture. I had a natural sense of oneness with another's life journey --their suffering and human yearnings to be cared for and understood that I saw as a universal truth. However, with this openness in the world I also had to meet that which was terrifying and repelling. I bumped up against rapists, thieves, tyrants who got joy out of hurting others, people only interested in material gain and willing to sacrifice the relationships in their lives, soldiers without a soul, people afraid to extend love and con artists of all sorts. This shook me to the core, where I felt intimidated and powerless in the face of those who seemed to not care at all about others and were malevolent rather than benevolent in their intentions. I doubted myself and wondered who I could trust. I went through a darkness of the soul phase, losing all hope in humanity and questioning everything I stood for. It was a state of deep questioning and disillusionment where I felt I was losing all sense of what I believed was true. Fortunately, as I learned later, I wasn't alone in this spiritual depression; it was actually a healthy thing to question everything on which I was basing my life.

Throughout my life, my mom, sister and I had a "strange" spirituality. We would have vivid dreams, we would go to get Reiki, we had a sense of there being more to this life than the physical reality, we spoke of past lives and we would recognize that we were more than the roles we had to play. We had telepathic experiences and psychic coincidences with each other and we would speak about them in the kitchen with each other then go back to our "regular" lives, trying to fit in to the status quo. We knew the importance of creativity for health and sanity and had a sense of God operating in our lives. I would often consult with my sister if I had a problem to figure out, asking her to do an intuitive reading on me. Once her reading got me out of a serious jam in Mexico when the revolution was breaking out. She gave me her Goddess Oracle cards and I started doing readings in secret for others, where people would end up in tears. We felt a spiritual sisterhood amongst the three of us yet we always kept it somewhat hidden from everyone else for fear of being seen as weird or evil, or fear that we would be "locked up in the looney bin". After all, this had already happened to my mother twice in reality and heaven forbid it happen again to either of us.

I had a calling in my late 20s to embrace this part of myself that I knew was mystical, wonderful, powerful and able to bring peace and harmony back to the earth. I had visions of Celtic goddesses, night dreams of loving beings and I drew on my Native American friends and teachers I had met along my path of life. I knew I had developed enough senses of self-reliance, self-determination and inner strength to shift and change my life in accordance to what was becoming truth for me. It was a lonely path. No book. No support systems. No real guideposts. I wanted to live my life according to the principles of love, care for the Earth, healing others from this illusion of suffering, and bring a sense of joy, magic, wonder and creativity to life. I wanted animals, and herbs, and loving people around me. I brought back childhood memories of playing in fields and feeling superconnected to the earth and the sky and knew that life did not have to be so hard and dreary and dull in the way that others were approaching it. It seemed wrong that people had to age and die. That life was this cruel and heartless. So I did a call out to "God" as I just could not accept and believe it all just ended in biology, cold-heartedness and one injustice after the other and that there really was an empty space in the Universe that just didn't care.

Once I called out to God or whoever was out there, little shifts began to happen.

Through my own awareness, I came to believe in miracles even though I didn't go to Church. But I started to read various spiritual texts in the mystical traditions and in the Christian tradition. I was filling myself up with the hope and knowing that love matters and healing comes when the heart is healed. That there was a place for the broken-hearted. Christ's message and walk spoke so much to me, as I really felt the impulses of wanting the world to know that love is important and the people who are oppressed, vulnerable and doing "small acts of love" are actually considered to be valuable. That the unseen world of love and emotions does matter in our lives and that the bullies and oppressors have a lot to answer for in the name of Truth, God and Love. What I didn't like, as most people don't, is the judgment and shame and lack of understanding that is riddled throughout the Christian tradition. And it did not speak well of the woman's experience of life, death, her wisdom, insecurities and sexuality. So, in a nutshell, it didn't honour what I knew to be true about women and others I have met in life. It took away the sovereign voice and made outspoken people, especially women, appear bad and wrong. It made people feel guilty for being themselves and having natural impulses and desires. It also was a religion that did not own how it dominated, exploited and demeaned other people's approach to spirituality and healing. It disconnected people from honouring the Earth and its creatures. In essence, the history of the religion was heavy and too filled with unconsciousness and keeping people feeling small that it wasn't satisfying my search for non-violence, love, connection, personal power and joy. I just could not be associated with a religion that has hurt many people with a righteous attitude.

I was then guided to read about the mystical traditions of Theosophy, where they speak about Christ as an ascended master and spiritual guide. They personalize God and spiritual powers, showing that every person and being has access to limitless creative, healing and spiritual abilities. That the psychic realm was a valid and spiritual gift, and the invisible realm is alive and well and there to support us. They spoke of angels, spirit guides, mediumship and divination as all respectable means for connecting.

This opened me up to the Spiritualist Church of Galt where I found a spiritual home. They honoured women and people of colour. They connected with deceased loved ones and brought peace and healing to others. They understood inspirational speaking and channeling of angels and guides. Their hymns were full of love and understanding of another world on the Other Side of the Veil. They recognized that writing and art were expressions of the Divine. They saw dreams as something profound and important in the spiritual dimension. All of the secrets that my mom and sister and I held to be true were all coagulated in the Spiritualist Tradition. I had finally found my place after 32 years of searching. I grew in confidence of my abilities, attracted a man into my life who shared and supported my spiritual gifts while wanting me to be successful, and I let go of the fears of what other people would think – especially what the Christians and my family members would think. All of my years of being stigmatized, judged, misunderstood, unseen and cast into a state of spiritual loneliness had now been revealed. Every act of courage of transformation I made, every yearning towards the truth and every fight for justice and standing up for what matters in the heart was all worth it in this place that honoured these struggles. And I was finally supported to let go of self-doubt and stand with satisfaction that what I knew to be true was indeed true.

And not only that, this experience of being an outsider looking in has honed my abilities as an intuitive and spiritual witness, giving me the knowing that it is important to take action for the higher good without worrying about what other people will think. I've been able to break through illusions of fear, self-hatred and faithlessness and instead trust that love is the key. This has helped me to have more compassion while also being able to intuit situations better as I can "read a room" or "a person" based on my life lessons. Not out of judgment but rather wisdom, experience and discernment. I am also more in the mind of serving the Divine, willing to say the loving word or do the loving action without the need for recognition or accolades. Because I know deep within my bones that the invisible realm is watching and working with me, that I have a team of ancestors, loved ones and angels who want to see me succeed in my life mission as a messenger and spiritual/soul healer. And so long as I'm open to listen and follow joy, wisdom, love, wellness and compassion, then I am cared for and quickly guided by my spirit team.

In summary, if there is one message my life path would like to leave on this walk is that every suffering, every feeling of being misunderstood, is an opportunity for growth and strengthening of the heart and honing oneself on the divine path towards one's truth in the world. Accepting your vulnerability and frailty on all levels is the key to your service to others who suffer just the same. There are many bullies out there, overt and covert, and by letting go of false or limiting beliefs about yourself that have been implanted by their opinions allows for your divine light to come forward more. We are, each one of us, struggling to be seen, heard, felt and loved. And there is more support for you than you've been led to believe. All you have to know is that you are loveable no matter what anyone else has told you. And all you have to do is ask.

* * *

*Heather is a metaphysical healer and soul intuitive practitioner in Guelph, Ontario. She has been a regular writer and editor of various genres over the past 15 years, as well as a human and earth rights activist. For more information visit www.blossomingheart.ca.*

# From Surviving to Believing
## by Patricia Eales

It never ceases to amaze me what the mind will do to protect itself. When I walked through the front door of my home after a full day of work on the night of Thursday, March 9, 2006 and saw that all of my living furniture was gone, my first thought was 'I wonder why Steve took the furniture out to be cleaned?' My next thought was 'oh my god, I think we've been robbed!' As I ran around the house I soon realized that the TV and computer and other valuables were still there and it was then that my mind started to recognize that we hadn't been robbed. I had been betrayed.

When I got to my master bedroom and saw that the bedroom suite was gone, the reality started to sink in. The man that I had loved and spent the last seven years with had moved out and taken all of the furniture that we had purchased together. All that he had left was the furniture and other things with which I had come into this relationship.

I left the bedroom, and came down the stairs to see that an envelope was resting on the banister. I opened it to find a card. How typical of the man. He had always given me cards for every occasion and this was no exception. All of the cards in the past had been appropriate to the situation. The cards were never pre-printed with words; he had always added his own. The pictures on the front represented exactly what he wanted to convey to me. Is there an appropriate card for 'I've left you forever and taken the furniture with me'? Apparently there is. The picture on the card was of a young boy sitting on the edge of the moon. To me it signalled goodnight and goodbye, and the words inside confirmed that. *'Sorry things haven't worked out, I won't be back'* Steve

Even though I now knew what had happened, so much of me still didn't want to accept it. How could he have left? We had made love last night, and this morning he kissed me, told me he loved me and to have a good day at work. How could he be so deceitful? What was the reason he left me?

Despite phone call after phone call that I made to him, I was never able to find out the reason why he left. He just told me that he felt it was time to go. He would still take my phone calls, but he would never, ever give me an explanation as to why.

163

It's quite interesting, the journey that had gotten me to this particular place.

The home I grew up in was loving and warm, and my parents loved me, my brother, and each other dearly. The example that my parents gave to me was one of a partnership. There were never overly demonstrative displays of affection between my mother and father; a peck on the cheek, or a warm hug. But I knew that they adored each other, because they could never walk by each other without a touch. A touch on the shoulder, the arm, or a brush of the others hair. I grew up knowing that was what I wanted when I got married.

I married my first husband shortly after my mother passed away at the very young age of 56. I often wonder if the reason I married him was because my mom really liked him, and I thought this would be something she wanted me to do. I'm not complaining, it was a good marriage, and we have two beautiful children from it, but I don't think it was ever like the marriage my parents had, or the marriage I grew up wanting. I felt as though we were more like brother and sister.

When we separated after 11 years of marriage, I knew I wanted more. More passion, more affection. Just more.

And two years later my wishes were answered when I met Steve. He was romantic, he was passionate, and he touched me the way I saw my father touch my mother. I was in love. Truly, madly, deeply.

After dating for about a year, we decided that we wanted to join our lives together. My kids were happy, they really liked this man, and he really enjoyed being around them as well and was very good to them.

I was so blessed. We moved into the house of our dreams, and I lived like a lady born to the manor. Trips, cars, beautiful jewellery.

And passion. Oh, the passion. I felt adored and completely loved. There was nothing this man wouldn't do for me, and I for him.

So, to walk into the situation I did, to say I was stunned would be the understatement of the century. And grief? I had survived my mothers death, and the failure of my first marriage, but I had NEVER felt pain like this before. I don't think I ate for three days, and sleep? I probably didn't sleep for three days either.

Did he leave me for another woman? Was that it? He told me no, there was no reason other than he needed to leave. To this day, I still have no idea why.

The first person I called that night was my brother. I had thought of calling my dad, but there was a part of me that couldn't do that, because I didn't want to tell my dad that another relationship hadn't worked out. So I called my brother. I still wonder why I called him, but I know I wasn't thinking very clearly at that point. To say that my brother and I weren't terribly close would be an understatement, but we had been trying to work on our relationship. He liked Steve and enjoyed coming down to visit us and I really thought we had turned a corner and I could confide in him. I don't know what I expected from my brother, but I didn't expect him to tell me that I had deserved this. Really, I had deserved this? In what way had I deserved this? I was stunned, but sat there and took it, because at that point I was so exhausted that I just couldn't stand up for myself. Obviously, my brother was not going to be the support that I was looking for. I look back and still cringe, but I have forgiven the person I was then.

Day after day went by, and I couldn't put my head around the fact that Steve had left me. There was no closure.

I called friends, and god love them, they said the right things. What an asshole, what a jerk, what a bastard. But no one could tell me why he left.

I called his friends to find out if they knew why he had left, but they didn't even know he had left, let alone why. I called his parents and his family, but they just kept saying they were sorry. I just kept crying and yelling 'why had this happened???'

I would later say to people that someone who loses their partner to death at least knows that it is fully finished. I felt as though I had suffered a death, but he was still out there walking around, and I had no idea why he wasn't with me.

Looking back, I  wonder how I functioned through the period of grieving I went through. I know I did function, if only for the reason that I had two children who needed their mother. I couldn't curl up into a fetal position and wish the world away; I had to get up every day, go to work, and provide for my kids.

Of course, I didn't really function. I was consumed. Consumed with needing to know why. Consumed with trying to plan revenge. Just completely consumed. Daily phone calls to beg him to tell me why he left, ask him to come back, try to get some sort of answers to my questions. All to no avail.

This state of being consumed became all too clear to me when I was called into my supervisors office about five weeks after Steve left me. I wasn't functioning at my job, I wasn't doing what was required of me, I wasn't giving it my all. In short, I was let go. I had been there less than three months, so no notice or warning was necessary.

So, here I was. Abandoned by a man I thought loved me, and now unemployed. Once again, I was a single parent trying to pay rent and put food on the table. I was in a house I couldn't afford on my own, and no job.

This time I told no one. Not my brother, not my father, not my friends, not even my kids. No one knew I wasn't working. Every day I got up, and armed with a stack of resumés and references I went looking for a job. I would take any job, I just wanted someone to give me a job.

I have always been an employable person, always being able to find a job when I needed one. This time though, it wasn't happening. Was it desperation showing on my face? Was my focus not there? Day after day I looked. I got called in for interviews, but I was either over qualified, or not qualified enough. The frustration started to set in, and I'm sure that was starting to show in interviews.

When Steve left, I thought about moving back to my home town to live with my father, but my children had a wonderful school, great friends and were involved in sports where we were living, and I didn't want to uproot them yet again. In fact, they specifically asked if we would be moving because of this, and I promised them that we would stay where we were so that they wouldn't have to leave their school and their friends.

But what to do when I couldn't find a job? Pretty soon, I wouldn't have the money to buy food, let alone pay the rent. I felt I had failed at so much, and the last thing I wanted to do was break my promise to my children. That would have been the hardest failure for me to live with.

Finally, after four weeks of constant and consistent job hunting, I was offered a temporary position as an administrative assistant at a manufacturing plant. It wasn't what I had done before, but it was a job, it paid fairly well and with zeroes staring at me from my bank account, I took it. Finally, I felt as though things were starting to turn a corner.

There wasn't anything else that could happen, was there? Little did I know that there was one final thing coming.

I started my new job on the Tuesday after the long weekend in May, and I really enjoyed it. The people there were friendly and helpful, and in just four days I felt as though I had been there for years. I was so excited that I decided to tell my dad the good news.

My father and I have always had a close relationship, especially after my mother passed away. I had finally told him about Steve leaving, but not about me losing my job. I felt awful keeping that from him, but now that I had the new job, I could tell him what had happened and celebrate the new beginning with him. I knew he would be upset that I hadn't told him, but I also knew he would understand why.

Now, getting in touch with my father by telephone was always an adventure. He would get so many wrong number calls, that he eventually got an answering machine to screen his calls. You never knew what message dad would have on the machine, he had such a dry wit. There could be train horns blowing, or opera music playing over his message. Pretty amusing, really. When we would call, we would always say 'hey dad, it's us. Take your time, we'll wait for you to pick up' and within less than a minute he would pick the phone up, usually with the answering machine screeching in your ear. If he didn't pick up, we knew that he would get back to us when he got home.

So, that Friday night I called and as usual waited for him to pick up. When he didn't, we left a message for him to call us.

My kids and I got busy with all of our activities and on Saturday night I said to my daughter, I wonder if Granddad called back? We checked the messages and there wasn't anything, so we called him again. This time my dad picked up, but I could tell that he wasn't himself. 'What's wrong Dad? I asked. He told me he wasn't feeling very well, and when I pushed him, he told me that he had been having chest pains since the night before. I asked him why he hadn't gone to the hospital, but my father being a very stubborn man, said that it wasn't that bad and that he'd be ok. He said 'I'm

80 years old, and if it's my time to go, then I'm fine with it.' Not the words I wanted to hear, and I knew he wouldn't call an ambulance. I lived an hour away from my father, and didn't want to wait until I got there to make him go to the hospital, so I told my father to get his coat on and be ready, because I was calling the ambulance and would meet him at the hospital.

After calling the ambulance, I drove up to my home town, hoping all the while that my father had gone with the ambulance attendants to the hospital. I had called my brother and told him to meet us at the hospital, but only got his answering machine.

It was probably the fastest I have ever driven, and I'm sure I broke every speed limit on my way. When I arrived at the hospital, I was informed that my father had gotten there just a short while before me, and that they were running tests. I was so thankful that he had gone with the ambulance and that he was in a place where they could now look after him and he would get the care he needed. Soon, I was able to see my dad, and while he was angry that I had called an ambulance, he did finally admit that he was glad I did what I did. I scolded him for being so stubborn. He told me that the apple didn't fall far from the tree, we laughed, and he gave me a big hug.

The attending doctor came by and asked me to step out to speak with him.

His words shocked me. Did I know my father's final wishes? What did he mean? I told him that can't be right, my father is fine, he'll be okay. Weren't they doing everything to help him get better?

It seems that I wasn't the only one keeping secrets. My father had been told about nine months previously that his kidneys were starting to fail, and that he needed dialysis; however, he had refused treatment. The doctor said that it was amazing that my father had lived this long without having the treatment that was required. He wondered if I might be able to convince my father to start the treatment, although he wasn't sure it wasn't already too late.

After a long and passionate discussion, my father finally consented to starting the treatment, but our home town hospital didn't have the dialysis machines. He would need to be transferred to another hospital for treatment and the closest one was an hour away. I was told by the doctors that they weren't sure whether or not he would survive the journey.

I went home that night and brought my children up to see their grandfather the next day. On that beautiful Sunday afternoon, it was as though he wasn't sick at all. We had a wonderful visit and there was lots of hugs and kisses for each of the grandchildren.

Early Monday morning, May 29, 2006, they prepared my father for the trip, putting him under sedation to reduce the stress of the transfer. I was to meet them at the hospital later that afternoon.

When I arrived at the hospital, I was shown in to see my father in the ICU. He was hooked up to every conceivable machine there was, and was still under sedation and unconscious, but the nurse told me to talk to him as he would still be able to hear me. I took his hand, and told him I was there and that I loved him and that the hospital was doing everything they could to help him, but that if it was time for him to go, that he should go, we would understand. At that moment, every machine started to beep, and they ushered me out very quickly to the family room. Twenty minutes later the doctor came in and told me that they had done everything they could, but that he had passed.

When I had left my father at the hospital before his journey to the dialysis unit, I had told him that I loved him and would meet him at the hospital once he got there. My wonderful, beautiful, funny and loving father had waited for me to arrive, and once he heard that I was there with him, his soul departed his body. I knew my mom had come in to be with us at that moment, and had taken my father's hand to go with her. She had waited 21 years for him, and it was time for them to be together again.

I now had to go home and tell my children that their beloved grandfather was gone.

They say that things come in threes and I had just suffered my third loss in three months.

In 1992, Queen Elizabeth II described her year as her *'annus horribilis'*. 2006 had become my *annus horribilis*. At 44 years of age, I had lost a partner, a job and now a parent. It was the trifecta of tragedies.

I remember looking up and yelling at the sky. 'Have I suffered enough? Are you finished? What more can you make me go through? I've learned any lessons that you think I need to learn, I don't want any more!'

I was shattered. I was angry. I was exhausted. However, my father's death had released me. It released me from the victim mentality I had fallen into. It released me from seeking revenge for Steve leaving. It made me realize that I was wasting my tears and time on a man who hadn't had the courage and hadn't thought enough of me to tell me why he didn't want to be with me any longer. It released me to be the person I needed to be, and not what others thought I should be.

My father had lived comfortably, and he had enjoyed his life. He had travelled, had all the things he desired to have, and he had loved and spoiled his grandchildren. When he died, he left a very modest life insurance policy, essentially enough to bury him, and a little extra that my brother and I would share. There was no house to sell, no stocks and bonds, but that was never anything that I was expecting. I would have had my father back in a second over any money that I might have inherited from him.

But apparently my brother had thought there was more coming to us, and was very angry. Here we were again, thrown together against our wishes and forced to deal with the final arrangements for my father. We got through what we had to do, and it was the last time I spoke to my brother for almost five years.

I took stock of my life. No partner, no parents, and no sibling to turn to. I had friends, but they weren't responsible for looking after me.

It was up to me, and me alone.

So, for the next four years, I did what I had to do. I went to work every day to pay the bills, keep a roof over our heads and to put food on the table.

To say I was exhausted was an understatement.

Over those four years, the stress, and the worry started to affect my eating habits.

As a competitive athlete in my youth and early adulthood, food had always been fuel to me. Don't get me wrong, I loved food, but I never ate more than I needed. Other than my pregnancies I had never been more than 5 or 10 pounds overweight.

Now food had become my drug. I ate to ease the worry. I ate to ease the stress. I was eating to avoid dealing with my life. I was 49 years old, single and over 50 pounds overweight. If I kept doing what I was doing, I was going to jeopardize my health.

I started to wonder who would love me the way I was. I felt frumpy, tired, old, and definitely not the slightest bit sexy. I couldn't look at myself naked; why would anyone else want to?

It had come to the point that I was missing out on so much. I got up each morning, looking forward only to when I could go back to bed. I would go to work, come home and either make something out of a package or order in, and then I would fall asleep on the couch in front of the TV. My kids would wake me up to tell me to go upstairs to bed.

There had to be more to life than this. I didn't like my job, and I had no hobbies. God, I was too tired to even think of having a hobby! My doctor was talking about putting me on anti-depressants to help me cope, and I didn't want to go on medication. If I was feeling this way now, what would I feel like at 60, 70 or 80? Who could even say I would live to 80 the way my health was now?

With my daughter in her second year of university, and my son due to leave for university in a year, I was going to be an empty nester soon. When they left, I didn't want to be alone or lonely. I didn't want to just exist, I wanted to live! So, with my 50th birthday looming, I decided that I needed to take charge of my life.

I made a plan. I was going to push myself outside of my comfort zone, and do the things I'd always wanted to do and even some I had never thought of before! The first thing I did was join an outdoor adventure group, which consisted of other single people who were new to the area or in a similar situation as myself.

The first outing that they had planned was a tree top trekking adventure. I thought that sounded like a lot of fun. It was fall, the leaves were changing, and I would be spending time outside with others my age, and hopefully having fun.

When we got there, they gave us helmets and harnesses. The instructors took us over to the training area, where they had us walk on a board about a foot off of the ground. Easy, peasy! I could do this! I balanced my way along and felt quite proud of myself. Then they led us out into the forest and pointed up. Way up. Way, way up. Probably about 20 feet up. Did I mention that I was afraid of heights? No, because I didn't really think it would matter. Boy, was I wrong! But, at risk of looking like a fool, I climbed the ladder. Don't look down, Pat, don't look down. Shaking and sweating, I managed to make my way across the first part. I was so proud of myself! I could do this! On to the next station!

I climbed up the next ladder, but that was about all my shaking legs would let me do. I froze. Completely froze and could go no further. Humbled, I had to go back the way I came and down the ladder. But here is where my story started to change. I wasn't embarrassed, I was empowered! I had stepped WAY out of my comfort zone and done something I had never done before. Sure, maybe I wasn't hopping across like some of the others, but my realization was that I was me, not them, and I had proved something to myself that day.

When I got home that night, I thought about the day. When was the last time I had challenged myself, truly challenged myself? I honestly couldn't remember, and I started to cry. But they weren't the tears of a victim, they were tears of recognition that my life wasn't yet over. That there was more to my story. I may not have conquered my fear of heights, but I had challenged it. Would I do that again? Probably not, but it felt damn good.

This breakthrough soon led to others. I started to get up and move more. I started to eat more vegetables and healthier foods. My energy started to come back, and instead of falling asleep on the couch at night, I was going for walks with my kids and having wonderful conversations about what was going on in their lives.

Even though things were getting better, I was still suffering from emotional eating, and was definitely not happy in the career I was in. I changed jobs thinking it was the company, but I soon came to the realization that it was the job I was doing that didn't fulfill me any longer. But what else could I do? It was the only thing I had been doing for the past 25 years.

It was my son who turned to me and said 'why don't you go back to school?' The idea appealed to me, but what would I take? I knew I didn't want to spend four years getting a degree, so college was the option that would work best for me.

I was asked to think of my passion. What was it that motivated me, got me excited? I soon realized that my health had become my passion. It motivated me and I got excited when I saw the results I was achieving through healthier eating and exercise.

So, four months before I turned 50 I went back to school to train as a Nutritionist. It had been 30 years since I last stepped foot in a classroom, and I was nervous and scared. But when I looked at what I had been through over the last five years, and how I had persevered, I knew I could do it. However, as usual, I couldn't do it the easy way. I was going to school full time, working part time to pay the bills, but halfway through school I had to put my studies on hold for financial reasons. I never doubted that I would finish, but I just didn't know when it would be.

It was around this time that I decided to move back to my home town. I felt it was time to try to make another go with the relationship with my brother. I wasn't entirely sure if I was doing it for myself, my brother or some strange thought that my father wanted me to do this. We did try, and probably tried for a good six months, but sometimes you just can't go back. One good thing though that came of moving back home, was repairing the relationship I had with my brother's ex-wife. We had been such good friends as young girls (our mothers were best friends) but time and circumstances had caused us to drift apart. I now consider her my sister, and while we are not related by blood, we are family to each other.

After putting my studies on hold for four months, I was able to afford to go back and finish school. It was hard and I had to make sacrifices, but I made it through to graduation.

Not long after starting school I was given the book *Eat, Pray, Love.* I read her story with amazement, as some of what she had experienced was so familiar to me -- the emotional eating, the depression and the spiritual quest. But the one part that gave me pause was the point in the story where Elizabeth talked about every city having a word to describe it, and was attempting to find a word that described herself.

Did I have a word that could describe me? What would the word be?

I thought long and hard, and realized that there is no one word to describe yourself, but words that describe yourself at different stages in your life.

Looking back at my *annus horribilis* and the four years that came after, my word would have been 'survive'.

At my graduation ceremony, I crossed the stage to receive my diploma and thought of the hard work, the sacrifice and the tears it took to get me there. I embraced the joy and pride I felt at finally finishing something extremely worthwhile. And as I looked out and saw my two children beaming with pride at their mother who had followed her passion, two words came to me that described my life now.

Believe and Achieve

It's been over seven years, but I have gone from Surviving to Believing and Achieving.

It feels damn good, and I can't wait for the next adventure!

* * *

*Patricia is a Registered Holistic Nutritionist (R.H.N.) and a highly trained and experienced health professional in natural nutrition and healthy lifestyles. She believes that diet, lifestyle and the environment play a key role in our mental, physical and emotional well-being. In her 40's, her high stress, corporate work life, combined with other life stresses, caused her to gain over 50 pounds making her the heaviest she had ever been! Refusing to believe that this was 'normal' and realizing that there are so many other women out there just like her, she went back to school to train as a a holistic nutritionist to be able to help others who are going through the same things as she had. For more information please visit www.guelphnutritionist.com.*

# Maybe Shame is a Colour
by Laura-May Culver

**the light**

All at once, there is Nothing, and, there is Everything.
I reach for the stillness, stir and stretch in the restful, quiet darkness.
Falling in stillness, Light grows and glows warm in darkness from the inside of it All.
It is, as If, it IS,

And the Light whispers:

*Are you Ready?*
*You will forget.*
*I will always BE you, within you, with you.*
*There is no beginning or end.*
*I will always BE. Remember ME.*
*You will know me best when you let go and be still. It is then that I will warm you.*
*I will feel like yourself, your higher self, like a mentor, whispering in the dark.*
*Let Go and Fall into stillness, and I will wash over you with waves of Love and Truth.*
*You are the light.*

{ Flashes of faces. There is a pretty young woman, crying. A handsome man, holding her in his arms. They have visited many doctors with cold shiny metal instruments. The results convey that conception is impossible; the woman's reproductive system has only one fallopian tube, and just a quarter of an ovary. They so want, and need, a child. Both believe deeply in adoption, the man was adopted by beautiful, loving parents. The woman's parents adopted one of her sisters. A lot of paperwork, visits to lawyers, meetings, and anticipation. Finally, in early November, 1968, tucked warm in the bassinet: a baby boy. The woman is so very happy, the man, so proud. }

I ask the Light with my mind:
'Will I be with *them*? How? Is this possible? They have their child! I don't understand.'

And the Light whispers:
*They have their beautiful child.*
*They waited and prayed. He is with them now.*
*But, they are meant to have two.*
*And so, relaxed, receptive and full of happiness, they will conceive YOU.*
*This is your destiny, and all of their's.*
*But, know this:*
*On this journey, your Light (which is who you really are),*
*will dim with human moments of forgetting...*
*If you choose to enter this life, you will experience love, loss, pain, shame, grief,*
*sorrow, guilt, and courage. You will forget your choice and then you will remember.*
*Your experiences, and your choice to be honest about them, will teach and serve*
*you and all those in your life.*
*You will know me when others support and love you. I work through them.*
*I will be with you, and will show myself to you. Sometimes, the forgetting will*
*block your ability to feel me:*

{ In the darkness there is a flash of images from life with this family on Earth }:

### the candy

I am a pudgy ten year old little girl with thick dark hair. It is Friday morning and I walk to the kindergarten boy's house around the corner. He can tell things with his feelings. The adults have asked me to help 'the blind boy' board the bus. I love him and know his truth. He guesses what colour I am wearing based upon the temperature of my clothing. Kids are nice to him.

I get into my assigned spot beside him on the bus and pick at gum that is stuck to the green plastic seat in front of me. It smells like wet rubber. I am having memory thoughts.

I think about Leni, the most popular girl in my grade six class, who tells me on the bus "thanks for the Halloween candy. It is all gone now so I don't have to be nice to you anymore" and turns away to her friend in the seat beside her, laughing. I shrug and look out the muddy window. I demand the tears that are welling up in my throat to stay put. Clenching my teeth to keep from showing my humiliation, I stare at the houses as they pass by and have a flashback to the previous night when I hand all of my goodies over to her after she promised to finally be my friend. I am so happy I skip all the way home from the bus stop.

I am sitting on the bus and I think about when I get home and how I have this self-appointed routine to check all of mom's hiding places for booze so I can get rid of it. The usual place is in the garage; stored beer in the empty dishwasher, and red wine behind the snow shovels. I pull all of it out and hide it. I go upstairs to check on her. I enter her room and see her sleeping or passed out or something. The lump in my throat tightens. I go into her burgundy purse and take some change from her wallet so I can buy myself some candy.

Sometimes she is awake when I get home and wants to go for one of her secret car rides. Mom likes to do this when she has run out of her special candy: Codeine 222s. They are sold in 12-pack little brown vials. Her favourite thing to do is to suck the whole vial back and swig it down with red wine. But dry and straight up is fine too. Just needs to get it inside her. I hate the way her mouth snaps and sticks when the pills make her mouth all dry, like she has cotton stuck on her tongue.

She doesn't really want me to tag along; she needs me to help her get the drugs. She has been getting help at the local centre so she won't use, but she just pretends to stop. She is very smart. We have been doing this 'car ride' thing in this town for a long time now so it is harder to get served at the pharmacies. I wait in the car. Rain hits the windshield so it is harder for me to see if she is getting served. I have to keep low, she insists, so the pharmacy staff can't see me. I know this doesn't work. They all know who I am. But, mom thinks it does and will not listen when told differently. So, I wait for the signal. It is a thumbs down, and my heart sinks. It is my turn. I have to get ready to be dropped at the next corner and walk around to the store. Once inside, I am to ask the same pharmacist for the pills.

We follow the routine. I hate this so much I taste bile. She drops me off and I walk around and into the store. I move to the back and ask for a vial of 222s, please. The pharmacist is called over to the wicket. He leans toward me, places his hands on his hips. I watch his lips part. There is spit attaching them. He frowns deeply at me and slowly says "We know your mother was just in here. You need to leave."

It is like I am frozen there, in front of the cough syrup, unable to move. He does not wait for me to go. He turns his back on me. My throat gets really tight and I feel like I can't breathe. I want my mommy to tell me it is going to be okay. I feel dizzy and sick to my stomach. NO! I scream inside my head. Don't make a scene! He is already pissed off.

Panic grips my throat like a vice grip tightening. I start to shake and vomit rises. When I am sure I am going to be sick, a car passes and shines light in the store, flashing bright on the wicket window in front of me. The light washes over me and I start to calm down. No one has noticed I am still standing there, as if no time has passed at all. I can move freely now, out of the store. It is as if the light is picking me up, ever so gently, and I am coasting or riding on a carpet of care, all the way to the car. I can see this light glowing and perfect, wrapping around everything.

Back in the car, mom looks at me all happy until I tell her I couldn't get the pills. She spits as she yells at me, facing forward. The light fades as I watch the saliva drip off the steering wheel. Maybe shame is little round bits of chalky poison. She starts the car. She wants her candy, and will search every pharmacy until we get her some.

Dad brings a different kind of candy home for mom. She likes her Sweet Marie chocolate bar. Tonight he goes back out to the convenience store to get it for her. Sometimes she dips it in her wine while she reads her latest novel in bed. Today they fight when he gets home from work. I can't hear what they are saying but I know it is not good. I write to God in my journal. I learned to talk to Him at Sunday School. Maybe if I write to God and pray really well, I can make them love each other again.

> Dear God
> Please don't let my parents get a divorce!
> Please! We have a good family and they love each other! I will be a good girl.
> Please make them stop yelling at each other.
> Please. I can't stop crying. The tears are falling and I can't make them stop.
> Please don't let this family break up. Please!

{ Images of the little girl sobbing and rocking herself while lying on her Holly Hobbie quilt fade, and my awareness of calm stillness resumes. I stretch into the warmth, and rest. I know it is my choice to choose to experience this pain and sorrow. Sharp images form }:

**quebec**

It is a late spring evening at dusk. I am sitting on the swingset in the back yard. I am daydreaming, wondering if that boy I like in grade seven likes me back. I have lived in this house and town for a full two years. We have never lived in one town longer than that and I am glad to be settled. I will be in grade seven next year and I have some new friends that like me for who I am. I notice a hangnail on my thumb and bite it. My feet are getting cold so I start swinging. I hear my brother call me into the house. We have to meet mom and dad for a family meeting in our living room. My heart is in my throat. I don't want to go in there. They always call these meetings just before we move again...

Mom and Dad sit beside each other but in different chairs. Mom is smiling in that pasted on kind of way. Dad says "Your mother and I have decided to take a little bit of a break from our marriage. We are going to live apart for a while to see how much we miss each other. You will be moving to Quebec with your mom for six weeks in the summer on a French Exchange Trip, and then you will be moving back up North until we can sort this out." He keeps talking but I can't hear him anymore. I try to get up but I can't move. I think I hate them. And, I know I love them so much it hurts my heart. I bite my lip and taste blood in my mouth. I hang my head. It is not worth arguing. This is not up for debate. I mope and sigh. Mom sighs really loudly and I think I hear her say to me "Don't you want to have an adventure with me, Moopy? Careful, any more moping and you will trip on that bottom lip."

And that was it. I was going to be alone with her. A lot. And, we are moving again.

We leave the house that has a swing set on an early summer morning. I don't look back as we drive around the cul-de-sac that seems to echo little kid laughter and hide-and-go-seek shrills. The drive to Quebec is long. We travel as a family. Mom is extra happy, smiley and enthusiastic. No one is allowed to be sad, she says. It is life, change is good. Buck up! Mom doesn't drink or try to find pills on the drive across province because Dad is there. It is a secret. She is waiting until we arrive. I don't have to go to the pharmacy or liquor store with her as much there because the convenience store sells alcohol. How convenient.

We are expected to speak French the whole time we are there and try to make new friends.

Mom drinks every day of the six weeks. I spend my time pretending that she is fine, just a little tired. If anyone asks me about her weird behaviour, I always say "What do you mean? she is fine."

We avoid any major catastrophe but I can't relax. I worry about her all the time. I yell at her when she lies about heading to the store for wine. I tell her she needs to stop, to grow up, to do her French Homework.

Maybe shame is a plant with sword shaped leaves like the fleur de lis.

{ The images fade and I become aware of floating in warm stillness. Something about this new experience is drawing me. I wonder about this new life. I ask the light to show me more. }:

**the hospital**

9:05 am. The office secretary calls into our grade eight classroom. I hold my breath and stare down at my knees. I pick at a piece of fluff that is on my jeans. I know this is about me, and I don't want it to be.

I have plans. The girl's club likes me today. I want to be popular and have someone to sit with at recess. Maybe now they will stop taking turns walking in pairs behind me, throwing ice balls and laughing, calling me names as I trudge home alone through the snow.

"Ms. Smith, please have Laura come down to the office." The loudspeaker booms and hurts my ears. Blood rushes to my face. Resentment burns in my belly. I close my eyes so I can pretend I am invisible. I hear snickers coming from the back corner. Bumping my leg on my desk, I stumble out of my seat and head down the empty hallway to the office. The secretary looks away, pointing to the Principal's office.

The Principal folds his hands together, taps them twice on top of his big desk, and straightens his back so he towers over me. He breathes very deeply through his nose. I can hear it whistle. He smells like cologne and I know something is terribly wrong.

He cocks his head to the side and slowly the words come out.

"Laura, we have tried to reach your mother today. She is supposed to be here at work. Would you *happen* to know where she is?"

My mother is a French Teacher at this school. They always ask me where she is. Sometimes I have to call the school in the mornings for her. I have to let them know she is sick again and a substitute is needed.

My answer is weak. I lie. "I don't know. I thought she was here. She is not feeling well. I forgot to tell you she is sick. I forgot to call this morning. I'm sorry. She has the flu. She was throwing up this morning I think. I know she has a cold. Or…"

I have to sit in the Principal's office for a long time. Recess comes and goes. No one brings me lunch. I stare out the long window, waiting. Snow is falling and I think about the hole in my boot and the note passed to me in the yard from the girl's club leader, saying I am cool.

The phone rings. It is the police. They have pulled my mother's car over. She was a four hours' drive away from me, intoxicated, headed anywhere and everywhere, looking for pills.

3:30pm. The secretary sighs loudly in my direction. No one is available to pick us up. My brother is in grade nine at the high school. They call a lot of people to see if someone could come. Finally my 'godparents', who I don't even know, arrive in their van. We are going to see my mom at the hospital where the police have admitted her. I am super sweet nice to everyone. I smile and ask how everyone is. Like always, I talk all the way there.

The hospital smells like fungus and puke. We go into my mom's room. There she is, smiling at me. I look at her carefully, scanning every nook. She is tucked tightly under the hospital sheet. I try to figure out if she is still high. I always know because her words come out in a slight bit of a drawl, and her eyes are shifty.

She looks at me and lies. There is something wrong with one of her body parts, she says. They will take her to a different hospital, far away, and keep her there for a very long time.

We are leaving now. I feel happy to get out of there. It is February, mid-school year. I am thirteen. I think I may have friends in this town. I get in the van. We will be living with the strangers until dad can move us away again, back to our old town where he lives. I am getting so good at lying and saying goodbye.

I look out the window. Maybe shame is a colour, like starched white linen. If it had a smell, it would stink of bleach and vomit.

That night, after eating dinner with the strangers and their children, I lie in the bed they have made up for me. In the quiet, the familiar thoughts come through the dark at me and slap me hard on the face: "And where were *you*, exactly, when all this was happening? YOU were having fun with your stupid friends smoking in the grocery store back parking lot, weren't you? Weren't You? What is wrong with you, anyway? Why weren't you with your mom, huh? You are supposed to look after her. Remember? Now look what you have done!"

The thoughts get really loud. My stomach hurts and I want a cigarette. I turn over and bring my knees up into my belly, curling into myself, a small ball. I can feel my breath on my knees under the covers.

After a while I can't stand it anymore and it is getting stuffy. I unclench and let go. Maybe the light will come and keep me company. It never yells at me. I lie there, waiting. After a while, the familiar warmth and glow of light comes over me in waves. I picture in my mind sunlight through the trees, like when you are sitting in the back seat of the car with your parents in the front and the sun glints through the trees, playing peek-a-boo, as you drive along. I breathe really deeply and hear the light say:

*I am here, sweet girl. I will always be and have always been here. Let go and know I am. Look for me within others that want to help you. Sleep, child.*

**Dear Mr. P.,**

**Thank you for being my grade nine teacher.**
**I like that you ask me how I am feeling. It helps me. I like to express my-self. Here is one of my journal entries to you:**

**"Letter from Her"**
**I (we) got a letter from her last night that she had written the second day of school (the 7th) and I really thought about it last night. Maybe she is getting better! She sure writes well. The thing I'm scared about is that she is on medication and when she comes out of the hospital she will still be on these pills.**
**What if she tries \*suicide and succeeds? Lunch, Got to Go!**
**\*she has tried it before**

**And, Mr. P, here is a letter I wrote to her:**

℅ Royal Victoria Hospital
Dear Mom,

I received your letter only a couple of days ago and it took seven days to get here. That is the reason I haven't written earlier. In your letter, you asked me about how I was getting along in grade nine. Well, I am loving it. It is far better than public school. My brother is enjoying Grade Ten also. I'm glad you are feeling better and that you've got an apartment all set for you to move in!! How is your figure? I bet I weigh more than you!! You probably look great by what I've heard. I've joined the school choir. Enclosed is a picture of myself at grade eight graduation night. Don't I look a lot like you?!??? I wanted you to be there but it was just as nice knowing I was being thought about!
I want you to sit down, write me a letter and send it right away!
PS. When are you getting out?
Love, Laura (May) xxxxoooo I LOVE YOU VERY, VERY MUCH!
See you?!!
Love, L.M.C.

**Thanks Mr. P. for being there for me.**

{ The images fade again, making room for another scene emerging from the dark }:

**the last day**

It is early morning and I am on the downstairs couch. I am babysitting two small children. I can't hear the kids so they must not be awake upstairs yet. I pull on my jeans that are jammed into my thighs from trying to get comfortable. I lie back and stare at the brown water stains on the ceiling and see patterns in them like when you lie on the grass on a warm sunny summer day and watch the clouds against the blue sky, making shapes of dragons and angels. I am thinking about how I really like that I didn't have to see my mother for a whole night. It feels like a real break.

I hear mom's car pull in the driveway. My stomach hurts. I stretch my arms out and over my head as I sit up. Running my tongue over my teeth and gums; it tastes like I was sucking on ashes all night. She comes around back and knocks on the door. Hesitating, I open the locks and let her in.

Handing me fresh clothes, she starts in at me right away. "I missed you last night. You haven't been home. It has been two days. I want you home tonight."

All I can hear is 'blah, blah, blah'. I unfocus my eyes and think about how happy I am that I have friends  in this town and that they want to hang out. I want nothing to do with my mom. She is the last person I want to be with.

I am whining at her: 'But, *Mom*! I have the party tonight. You said I can go to the party! I don't want to be home with you, I want to be with my friends!'

She is great at whining too. She retorts: "But, you have not been home. I need you with me. I need you home. You can see your friends another time. I am better when you are with me. Come to the apartment at noon when you are done and we will discuss this further." I roll my eyes and stomp my feet. I say "okay" really sarcastically.

She smiles at me and turns to leave. "I love you, moopy," she says as she moves through the screen door. I scrunch my nose up and grit my teeth. I murmur under my breath that I love her too. I silently scream "aargh!" as I watch her through the window. I feel so much relief as she backs the car out of the the driveway and is gone.

Later, after babysitting, I am with my friend, Julie. We go to the apartment like mom asked. She is not there. I feel badly that I yelled at her and told her I don't want to be home. My throat feels tight as I stick the note to the wooden door: "Call me at Julie's." I start to second-guess myself. I wonder if maybe I should be home with her. She needs me.

We go to Julie's. Her mom says that there have been no calls. After a while, I call my grandparents house to see if mom is there. My aunt picks up. "There has been a bit of an accident", she says. "The ambulance has taken your mom to the hospital. She tried to kill herself again. There is nothing you can do now. It is best you stay there tonight." She says other things but I really can't hear her. She hangs up.

I don't understand. My head is swimming and I am dizzy.

I remember that I have to meet my friend Kee. I am walking downtown to meet her. Nothing is making sense. I walk and walk. I go into the bank to get money for the party. The ladies are talking and I hear: 'Air Ambulance' 'Serious' "Not Good' 'What a shame' 'Could hear the sirens from here'.

I scream at them, "That is my MOTHER you are talking about!!!" They look over and realize it is me. The tellers all know who I am as this is my mom's bank.

Maybe shame is the smell of money and the dark holes of downcast eyes. I run out of the bank and use the payphone to call the hospital. The phone handle is so heavy I can barely lift it. I tell them who I am and that I want to come and see her. They say I can't, she is on her way to Toronto by Air Ambulance. I start to tremble and my feet give way. I lean on the side of the phone booth feeling nauseous. No one comes out of the bank to see if I am okay.

Kee shows up with a big smile. Ready to party? Numbness cloaks me like a shroud. I tell my friends that I am okay, and that my mom will be fine. They tell me that I might as well enjoy myself and we head out of town to the party. In the camper, I drink a bit and pretend to be drunk. I want them all to like me. I can't let this accident keep me from being popular.

That night, at 3am, I have one of those awake dreams. She visits me, softly drifting away, while I lie awake in the stuffy camper. Mom? MOM? I think I can smell her. And then, she is gone. I did not say goodbye.

I am fourteen and I know in the pit of my stomach that this is the last day.

{ I am back with the light in the stillness. In the safety and truth of the light,I know I am ready, but I hesitate. The light shows me more }:

**the stairs**

I sit quietly on my bed for what seems like hours. Barely breathing, I crane my neck, pointing my head toward the door, listening for the bedtime routine sounds my dad and his new wife make just before they turn out their light. I take off my socks, stretch my toes and place them on the thick pink carpet. I stop, listening again. The pendulum clock chimes in the living room.

I look at my journal that sits on the bedside table like it is patiently waiting for my words. I write:

Help me die
The pain is there-I can't stop it
I don't-can't believe this is happening
I'm just fading away.
Life, it feels like, has stopped for me.
Help me.
I hope that place where my mom is
Is a nice place
I am going to be there soon.
Very soon.
Sooner than anyone thinks.
I want to die.
Please let me die.
Help me live.
Help me die.
Let me live where my mom is...
My mom is dead.
Help me die.
Please.

I breathe deeply. My pajamas smell like sweat and baby powder. I move off the bed, opening the door to the hallway. I stop and listen again. Creeping slowly, it takes me a long time to reach the top of the stairs. They feel cold on my bare feet.

I woke this morning, ready to try again. I have something to die for. I am killing me.

Throwing yourself down the stairs doesn't really work. My fourteen-year-old brain wonders if I am doing it wrong. I try anyway. I half fall, half hop. My higher-self mentor, 'me' is strong. She wrestles me, lands me on the second from the top step. I give up, crumpling, unable to move. Anger and frustration burn through my belly and pour tears out my eyes.

I don't want to die, really. I want to understand.

My nose is running. I lick the top of my lip and taste the salt. I gasp and think I taste bile. The edge of the wooden step carves deeply into my side. I wipe my nose with my pajama sleeve and hug myself tight in a ball, bracing myself for the familiar thoughts that are swarming. They always come next, swirling around my head, ready to strike.

Some are mischievous like black flies, creeping into my hair and waiting… "You are so stupid. You stupid, stupid girl. What did you do that for? You can't even do that right? Can you? Stupid girl."

After a long time, the stinging thoughts start to settle down and a different, familiar feeling of warmth and comfort washes over me. I feel tired. I give up, get up and go to bed.

The light comes and whispers to me as I fall asleep:

*I was there on those nights you wrestled with life and the thought of death. For real. I was there when the untrue thoughts came. When you let go, When you gave up struggling, sweet girl, you could feel me once again. I held you—washed the light of my love over you. Once you let go, you could feel me, hear me, know the truth. I whispered your future to you as you slept. Let go and listen. I am always here.*

{ In the silence of the in-between, I was given glimpses of this Life. Back in the stillness, I am in awe of the strength of this young person. I now know that yes, I choose the sorrowful life. And I choose the possibility of the joy it can contain: I am Ready. }

*And the light, in a whisper soft and distant, said:*
*Sweet child, Just let go and Know.*

And the faces dimmed, the colours deepened, and the forgetting began…

* * *

*Laura-May exudes enthusiasm and passion in all areas of her life. She has been known to challenge herself and others to delve deeply into the mysteries of being human; wonder about our life purpose and potential, and, consider the possibility that our personal power lies hidden within the truth of our interrelated Earth community. Founder of Knowself Services ~ Foundations for Life Coaching and author of The Red Telephone Booth Meditations, Laura-May believes in Angels … and so much more. She resides in Fergus, Ontario. For more information please visit www.knowselfservices.com.*

**Maybe Shame is a Colour** *is an excerpt from a larger work in progress. Names in this story have been changed, for privacy reasons.*

# Nobody Can See, Unless You Tell Them
## by Nicole McHenry

I sit and watch my children playing, and wonder what their lives will be like. I wonder how they will handle themselves, and who will be beside them when I am not there to guide them.

Something happens as we grow. We think everyone can see our 'stuff'. And it somehow looks bad to us. We may be coloured by our experiences, yet we think anyone and everyone can actually 'see' our flaws. We think they will judge us for our mistakes, and the things we have 'let happen', as well as the things we were powerless to stop.

Toddlers think nobody can see the truth because they hide it so well. What makes toddlers so incredibly clever ? They truly believe they are. Absolute belief. And then we grow up.

Like many, my experiences have included lovers, liars, abusers and manipulators. I managed myself because of them, despite them, and around them. Abusers and manipulators believe nobody sees their flaws, their bits of dirty laundry. They are too clever. Somehow they work out that we have a different belief. We believe that everybody knows our stuff. And they play on it.

I have had an eventful, amazing life. I am incredibly blessed – and loved. I have nonetheless weathered what was horrendous for me. And survived. I am also very aware that there are many people in this world who would give anything for my charmed life.

Very early on in my life, I realized I had an awareness beyond my years. I knew about things I shouldn't, circumstances, events. I was seeing and chatting with spirit, with no fear.

Knowing is one thing. Understanding is quite another. There were defining moments in my life that came with fanfare, and some with absolute tranquility. However these moments needed context to be understood. This takes maturity. Without that maturity, some of those pearls fell on deaf ears. And that's why patterns repeated.

It took some uncomfortable experiences, and people who behaved badly, to show me that some patterns led to the bad stuff. I found my absolute saviour in the spirit world and my mediumship, yet had to experience the deconstruction to understand the reconstruction that was needed, and why. It is because, when I am ready, the universe will bring what I need. And it will always be that way. My absolute belief. Yet it wasn't always that way.

We are the sum total of all our experiences, standing at the gateway of infinite possibilities, and we can do anything. Anything! I 'eventually' came to realize, that unless I told people all my bad stuff, they didn't see – they didn't know. They couldn't see my choices anymore than you can now. Until I tell you.

My point is that you are not wearing your experiences in a way that will stop you -- unless YOU let them. I was aware that my experiences were banked in my memory banks for future use. In my immaturity, I thought I would conquer that broken self-worth and battered self-esteem if I wore them like a badge of honour, and wheel them out when I needed them. Totally at peace with my reality. The times I wheeled them out was when I needed an excuse or a justification for something. I know that this is true, because I have done the work. I worked on my sense of self-worth, until it was no longer broken. It is still a work in progress.

*It takes time to heal. Time and space.*

The space to reconstruct a whole person from what my experiences and environment had left me with, without any influences around, good, bad, or indifferent. Until I had that, and understood it, it was like trying to build a house of cards in a hurricane with a hailstorm. Disempowering.

*Knowing is one thing – Understanding is another*

I have always been very perceptive. My sixth sense kicked in when I was very young. I knew lots about lots, when nobody wanted to hear anything from a babbling kid. Particularly when it was something I shouldn't know about...and even worse, turned out to be right about !

I saw people who had passed, standing around the living, and knew about their lives and their issues, none of which I had the experience to actually understand. I had many conversations with the dead. Imagine having an uninhibited chat with a fun uncle, a cheeky grandma, or an older sibling. I had no fear. I enjoyed it. My kids are the same.

I used to do palm readings when I was about seven. I recall telling mum and dad to bet on 'Luna Girl' at the picnic races when I was about eight. She of course came first. Chestnut mare. Still remember. I can see her in her stall now. I remember constantly wanting to know what happened to 'the Emerys' who we had met one holidays. A bit obsessed, I just knew there was something about them. I learned later that he had shot his wife and then turned the gun on himself. The kids were all sent into care.

I knew I was different and felt like I was watching my life as an observer, not just a participant. By age fourteen, mum sent me to a psychologist. I needed fixing. She sent me to one of her friends first. There we were, mum sitting on the couch, excited, waiting for 'the magic fix to happen'. Mum wondered why I didn't say anything. Her learned friend certainly knew why. She suggested mum wait in the other room. Shortly thereafter, something I had said in confidence to the 'learned professional' came out of my mother's mouth verbatim. Suffice to say I didn't trust her again.

I went to a psychologist independent of my mother's reach, and he was pretty amazing. I don't recall much of what we did. I know that he listened. He did, however, share a few incredible things. He gave me an understanding that my opinion was important and that, if I was to share that opinion, there would be consequences. Not everyone would like what I was sharing. And he was right. And in fairness, a teenager sharing her opinion was likely to have a few consequences. These days, every time my teens share an opinion, I question whether it is about getting a rise, distract, or cry for help. Just like mine was.

*There are always a few defining moment in our lives.*

They don't all need to be fireworks moments; however, they are a potential turning point. One for me was when the psychologist called my mum to join one of our sessions. She sat there, calm and stone faced -- and lied. She refused to acknowledge, accept, or admit anything I was saying. I was distraught. I was absolutely devastated and bawling my eyes out. He stopped trying to lead any constructive discussion, and told my mum that it is normally the teenager who was sitting there smugly and the parent in a complete state such as I was.

Suffice to say, mum decided he was a crock; however, to her credit, she let me continue to see him. I think in reality I threatened to get dad to fix it. Manipulative toddler – teenage girl. Same same, yet different.

I asked her on the way home, why she had lied and not told him what was really happening. Her response floored me. She told me it was nobody's business but hers and she didn't have to say anything she didn't want to. This moment was a bit of an epiphany for me. In hindsight, my understanding and insight was well beyond my physical years. I became incredibly calm. I realized in that moment, that I couldn't rely on anyone else but myself. Ever. It gave me an understanding that adults tell themselves all sorts of lies to get themselves through with their own experiences intact. Without that, their whole reality comes into question. This is something they have spun over many years, and no upstart teen, whether right or wrong, was going to change that. I was in control of myself, and my reactions. That's all. Such wisdom from a teen.

Another event in my life was when my parents divorced. It got very interesting when they moved on, because we girls were along for the ride whether we liked it or not.

*Enter Manipulator Number 1 – 'the boyfriend'*

My dad married well and refused to go on his honeymoon unless his daughters came along. Wow. Lucky wife two. Lucky we girls on a European vacation. Mum is incredibly intelligent, yet was completely naïve when it came to men. Enter 'the boyfriend'. Charming, dashing, attention-loving, immature brat.

Off on dad's honeymoon we went. No sooner had we driven out the driveway, the sale board went up on our house. Mum's last words to us were that we would be painting our rooms when we came back and life would be wonderful. Of course, by the time we returned, the house was sold, and we were moving into the boyfriend's house.

I had told mum what 'the boyfriend' was like – and how it would all end up. It seems that nobody likes a teenager who knows, any better than a kid who knows. Unfortunately, my mother seemed to have shared such pearls with 'the boyfriend' and I lived with those consequences each day. He had a daughter and son who were certainly no brain surgeons and, although it was not my fault, it appeared to be my problem.

Our day would start with him striding (stomping) through the house in his underwear, with a boom box type radio blaring, followed by the requisite slamming of the bathroom door. We girls got to use the old laundry trough to wash our hair and brush our teeth. The showers were available when he wasn't home. Maybe that's why I love my morning showers so.

My most humiliating memory was as a teenage girl, having to drop my pants and lay over his legs as he sat up in bed and have him smack my bare butt as hard as he could, some 20 to 30 times, for some  indiscretion or other. I knew that having a meltdown was giving him what he wanted. My sister used to just scream in pain. I can hear it now ringing in my ears. I used to just pull up my pants and walk away with my head held high. I did, however, throw my mother a fairly evil glare as I walked past her. It was so degrading. By design, of course. I just didn't understand how such an intelligent and accomplished woman had such a lack of inner strength when it came to a man. What was she thinking? That voice in my head kept me sane. I was reminded by that little voice in my head that, if my butt was that red raw, it no doubt hurt his hand.

*I had learned well, that I couldn't control anyone else, just myself, and my reactions. And that had to be enough for now.*

By the time I was in year 12, I had escaped, and 'the boyfriend' had moved on. I had moved in to my grandparents' unit because I didn't want to live with my 'untrustworthy' mother and sister. I clearly had a few unresolved issues. They travelled to the warmth of the north as soon as it got cold, so I had the unit to myself.

*Enter Manipulator Number 2 - the Black Prince.*

Why, oh why did I not trust my voices? I had such a suspicion about him that I told him I would meet him at 1pm outside the police station. I spoke with him on the phone before we actually met. I wouldn't give him my number or surname.

Looking back now – I was clearly intriguing because of it.

We were a pair who had very different backgrounds and upbringing. You never think it's an issue until you have to manage children together! His mother was a paranoid schizophrenic alcoholic who had really done it tough during the war. She was an incredibly hard worker. His father told me proudly that 'wives were whores, and prostitutes were business women'. He brought his brothers widow out from Poland, divorced mother, married the widow, as was 'quite common after the war' apparently. He then took custody of the two older boys, leaving the black prince with mother, and promptly shoved the older two in a boys' home.

There are transcripts on public record from many abused children who were placed in these homes, which included his brother. His brother was very brave to have bared that wound publicly, after carrying it for some 40 years. Our society lives with the broken children who came from those homes, who commit heinous crimes, suicide, or both. Much healing is needed. Though I struggled being so disrespected by his family, as a medium, I knew what had transpired to make them like that. However what I didn't have the maturity to understand is that I actually sacrificed my self-worth and self-esteem because of it.

*I understood their suffering, yet I didn't have the maturity or experience to understand that I didn't have to accept the result of it.*

The Black Prince was quite charming – in fact incredibly so. Charming, dashing, attention loving, immature brat. *History repeats.* He had seen me coming a mile away. An adoring fan, so naïve, that I didn't actually see the deconstruction happening. He was a bundle of rage that unleashed when mixed with alcohol. However he was so apologetic when he was sober. He didn't actually 'apologize' or 'admit to' anything now that I think back.

Because he was such a strange fish, and didn't get along with anyone, we became more and more isolated. I didn't notice that there was never anyone else around, because immature young love can be all-consuming. I got enough socializing at work, and to be honest, couldn't wait to get away from people and their social agendas. Thinking back even harder, I was seriously buying into the paranoid mindset. I already had issues with trust, so he fed them.

*Abuse works best when you isolate the victim.*

I had a hankering to move to a property. We went to see the property one evening, and paid a deposit. We could only pay $400, because I went to the ATM for some more cash, and it crashed. Ignored Sign No.100. In a reading before I moved, I was told that I would be isolated if I moved there, and it would not be good.

By now I had two beautiful children. The Black Prince was finding having to share the limelight with two little creatures seriously unfair. With two littlies in close succession, I was numb to the spoiled brat he had become, and the house in the country needed some serious work done.

He did less, drank more and, by the time baby number three arrived, he was really struggling. I have never spoken this out loud, however I entertained the idea of not actually having baby number three and just getting out. Even thinking it makes me shudder. I have this voice in my head and this amazing barometer of energy that swings from absolute calm through butterflies, to sheer dread, however I knew I would have precious little missy moo.

I knew I had to work, and started an accounting practice. With an alcoholic husband, a property needing renovating, and three children under five, enter Nanny Megan.

One of my children had a friend with five siblings. Their mum was the best person in the universe. Their dad? No comment. Gorgeous Cath managed to contract an aggressive cancer, and made me promise that I would help her husband with the business accounting given she knew she was about to die. Of course I said yes. Her strength as she was getting things in order. Incredibly humbling.

Nanny Megan was their nanny, and that's how I inherited her. We shared her. I had her school hours, and he had her the rest. The day I had honoured my promise to Cath, I walked away. I did however retain Nanny Megan.

With the work I was doing and the salary from the black prince (that wasn't spent on Jack Daniels), I brought in tradesmen to finish the house. I was beginning to get my head clear after three babies, and returned to spiritual development class.

*Spirit, my absolute savior, yet the downfall of the other. How ironic.*

When I ask a question in my head, I always get an answer. 'Usually' I listen. I asked why it felt so hard to do anything, and I was shown a picture of a sulky teenager, crossed arms, crossed legs, frown, and me trying to walk forward dragging this sulky overgrown teen like a ball and chain. Oh My Goodness…yes. That is exactly what he was like!

He pretended to love my clever ideas; however, as soon as I began to achieve, enter the sulky frowning overgrown teen. Jealous beyond words. He would stay in that mode until it was almost completed, and then he would be okay again. The pattern was always the words of support and encouragement then he would enjoyedly try to destroy everything. It was like sport for him. I was never one to worry too much about security because my belief was that I would always be fine. My office keys used to go missing. I realized later that he would snoop in the office to see what was going on. My office manager just assumed I knew he had been, because she certainly did.

As I sat in development circle I began to get some clarity. I had this two hour window each week, when I communed with spirit and the inside workings in my head. It was a space that had little judgment and no agenda. I began to unravel the intricate web of lies and subjugation that I had thought was normal. Everything that we live, for any period of time, whether good bad or indifferent – becomes our normal. *It was my normal.*

They say that you are a reflection of the five people you wrap around you. That is very true. I recall every time I would do anything around the house, the black prince would make some adjustment, and comment in some way. Every pot I ever put on the stove, he would walk up, move it a few millimeters, check it was better, make that humph sound, roll his eyes, shake his head, walk off. Why had I not noticed this before? I realize that this had been going on for many years. It was incredibly wearing to keep my self-esteem levels up in that environment.

With such an incredible amount of work to do, and three adorable little babies to enjoy, I just got on with it. Every class I went to, I got a renewed sense of self back. One day I realized something. You can only be intimidated -- if you are intimidated.

*And then it happened.*

I woke up one morning when my littlest pixie was about three. I woke up. **Really woke up.** Anyone who has done it will know what I mean. I woke up and wondered where the hell I had been, and what the hell did I think I was doing!

How could I teach my boys that this is how you treat women? I was certainly not teaching my daughter that this sort of behaviour was acceptable. I had to get out. *I was isolated.* Nobody would miss me for days, and with

195

the old mine shafts and national park across the back of the property, I might never be found. Yet I had to take my power back. And my strength would be that he thought he was so clever and had me so well in hand, that I couldn't be planning anything. I would go up to cracks in the brickwork, put my hand in, and pull out another half drunk bottle of vodka. I would leave it on the ground and walk away. The wood heater needed wood fed into it constantly. I would go out and get the wood sometimes. I pulled the bottle out from under the logs, and sat it on the stump and walked away. It was pretty brave to be honest. Confronting an abuser is dicey.

The best was yet to come. Saying the word 'No' was next.

I always wanted to try to help him, as I could see that he was struggling with himself. I tried to get him to see a doctor who might assess him for depression and possibly medicate him. He was the father of my children after all. He had clearly had a few drunken discussions with himself between making the doctors appointment and actually attending. He sailed in and, just like my mother many years ago, he said he didn't know what I was talking about and was fine.

*And I remembered, I couldn't control anyone else, just myself, and my reactions. And that had to be enough for now.*

I left it alone, as I wanted help for him for himself. I had already made my decision. I was out. He came up to me while I was sitting outside and asked me what I thought of the doctor, and how I felt being wrong as usual. I took a moment, and told him that it was now official. All this time I was thinking he was not in control of his behaviour, yet clearly I 'was' wrong – he was just an arsehole. I sat and looked at him. I didn't run, didn't cower, didn't do anything. Inside I just knew I would be fine. Now was not the time to stop trusting my inner voice.

*It takes time to heal. Time and space.*

I had been sleeping with one of the kids in bed with me for many months. Some time ago, in one of his tantrums, he stormed off to the end room and slept in one of the kid's beds. My oldest asked him why he was sleeping there. He answered that he was allergic to something in mum's bed. I took the opportunity to make that permanent.

Part of this was because when I had one of the kids in bed with me I wasn't awoken in the early hours of the morning by him standing over me pressing down on some part of my body through the doona. It was bizarre. He would stand over me and press down gently, just until he woke me. When I woke and asked him what the hell he was doing, there was no life in his eyes, and he would run off.

Looking back now – seriously – how did I think that was normal?

It took me two years to get it right in my head that if he left I would have NO regrets. There were many stages I had to go through, and the last one was getting it right in my head that, if I saw him with someone else, I would not have a reaction. After all, twenty-three years is a long time. I understood that I was not bad or stupid to love someone who was not good for me, or good to me, and until I hit that point of disconnection, I would be in limbo.

Being the local accountant in a country town, I had seen many couples split, and how they behaved afterwards. I saw the stages they went through, and noticed that after around three months of separation, some made the stupid mistake of going back. I knew if I went back, I would never get out. Never. And I also realized it was the ease of connection that these couples missed, rather then the person they left.

I also couldn't stay awake some days. That time was scary looking back. I had a doctor who prescribed me a whole load of medication because I was stressed and struggling. Was it any wonder?! I filled the prescriptions, yet didn't take the medication. I just stuck it in some drawers.

One day I cleaned out my drawers. I realized that the boxes of pills that I had never taken were all but empty. I then got the flashback of the nightly cuppa being made for me. Needless to say I came up with an excuse for no late night beverages. Bladder issues. I also stopped losing hours of my time. I will never know what happened in those times I lost.

*Finding the Patterns brings power.*

I was becoming empowered by the fact that I could actually read what he was doing and it didn't tie me in knots anymore. Such a creature of bad habits.

He would start an argument with me early in the week for no reason. His arguments didn't actually need my input. They were merely a belligerent rant. Later that week he would not be talking at all. He would then get dressed up and go out on the Friday evening. I had worked out that he was ensuring he could go out without me wanting to come with him, with the usual 'my fault' tag thrown in for good measure.

When the black prince realized I was not going to succumb to his charms and his aggression didn't seem to have me cowering any longer, he tried the tack I was after.

'Well maybe I should leave you'.

It took me almost three years to get him to think this was his idea. When the day came, and he finally drove out the driveway, I did the highland jig on the inside, holding my beautiful children close. He seriously expected me to run after him down the driveway. However I was not out of the woods yet. I knew he wouldn't take kindly to me not chasing him, and I battened down the hatches for the next stage. It wasn't long before I was warned that things may become 'uglier', by the psychologist who had seen us separately at a family mediation centre. It is a requirement for separating couples wanting access orders, which was the next step towards divorce for me. It couldn't come quickly enough.

In the days and weeks ahead I was followed, pranked, broken into, came home to open windows, and intimidated by experts. I got so used to it, I would double back and follow the white van that was sitting opposite my driveway every morning. I would sit in a store and wait for the latest person following me to come past again and I would wave and ask if they needed anything.

*I was determined that I was not going to be intimidated anymore, however being safe was equally important.*

For over a year I was *never* home on my own on the property. Never. When the kids went for the weekend or holidays, I slept on my friend's couch. It was bad enough when the kids were home and I would hear him outside. I used to meditate in the evenings, and he used to throw rocks on the roof from the paddock behind me. I was determined to have some sanity and stay in my power. My things were thrown in the dam and he slashed up my sheets. I was so very tired. It messed with my head, and wore me down.

*Remember - I can't control anyone else, just me, and my reactions. And that had to be enough for now.*

I would be driving home from the kids' sporting events and he would be coming the other way after being at the property. He knew I had seen him and he didn't care. Yet he was going to cover himself. He started visiting a friend up the road. One evening my friend rang me in a panic from her bathroom. She had questioned him, and was so scared by the look he gave her that she called me instantly. She was chilled to the bone. I was used to it. I calmly explained he needed an excuse to be in the vicinity, in case he was seen coming from the property. Her husband got very angry when he realized they were being used in that way. She used to check in with me regularly after that.

It was an unpleasant time. I woke to find a dead alpaca in the paddock one morning. One afternoon I came home and the fences had been kicked in. My gorgeous neighbours were driving around the roads trying to catch ten escapee alpacas, bless them. The police weren't interested. I am sure they see this sort of thing all too regularly. His name was on the title, therefore he had as much right to be there as I did. My experience is that after battling to get any sort of intervention order, they are not worth the paper they are written on. You really have to be beaten half to death first.

*I remembered -- I can't control anyone else, just me, and my reactions. And that had to be enough for now.*

The kids were part of a sporting club that raced interstate. I booked a cabin to go away for an event. Everyone at the club knew he was a problem because, after being distant previously, he was all of a sudden trying to ingratiate himself and discredit me, thereby trying to isolate me from anything social. This played his hand a little. I had a call from the club that 'someone' had booked a cabin requesting to be beside us, under the name of Nesbitt. There was no Nesbitt racing. This was, however, the name of a lady who opened her front door and was shot in the face. The park followed up all the contact details and everything was of course, fake. That voice in my head told me I would be fine. And I trusted it. However, I didn't go racing that season.

I sat in development class one evening and I was told directly from a tranced guide – 'you will not lose your children'. I had no idea what that was about. Two weeks later I found out. Just like his father did to his mother, the black prince tried to destroy me by trying to take my children.

I was at work and got a message to call Human Services (DHS) about the 'whereabouts of the children'. It seems the black prince had been coached well. Textbook stuff. He took one son to the doctor and told an incredibly fanciful tale. Next stop, the police station to lodge a complaint. DHS then placed the children in safe keeping of their father. Of course.

I spoke to the children and listened to their frightened voices. I then got on the phone again to DHS and asked what was next. They told me they could come and see me about 4pm the next day and go from there. I convinced them that this was too long, that it would mean another day, and the children were already displaced out of routine. DHS agreed to come at 10am the next morning. I was not going to lose them for another minute! I was told by the tranced guardian that I would not lose my children, however it was still quite possibly the worst night sleep of my entire life. After years in development circle, I have developed the ability to travel to my children in their mind's eye. They know when I am there. It kept us all sane that night. They loved their dad, yet hated the constant troublemaking.

The DHS inspectors arrived and I showed them around. They stood in the corridor and looked at each other, then at me. I asked them whether they had been led to believe that the kids were living in a shambles, and they concurred. It was a thirty something square heritage listed house, fully furnished, warm, clean, and inviting.

They explained they would still investigate further as part of their process, and let me know the outcome. They took all of three minutes outside, and came back to confirm that the children would be returned to me that evening. It felt like an hour. I thought I was going to be ill on the spot. They also contacted the doctor who confirmed to them that the children had clearly been coached. They seemed not surprised. They may have seen these shenanigans before, yet I was living it!

Having DHS on board was the best problem I could have. We were 'all' being watched. I had three months free of abuse, intimidation and bad behaviour. The unfortunate side-effect of the experience is that the children were told I would never find out the fanciful stories they told. It was devastating for them when they realized I had read the report, and knew what they had said.

*Sometimes you need to tell people the bad stuff*

As soon as there was no money to fight over, their father dropped all access and appeared on the doorstep once every year or two. My eldest hit high school, and started to ask questions about his father. In my head I was told that it 'was time', so I took him to the library and we googled. It was harsh to find his father's history on file. However he needed to know the whole truth, not the bits he had worked out for himself. Of all my three children, he always needed to know the whole truth. Psychic children are hard to fib to. He also needed to find out with me by his side, not at school or with mates fooling around on the Internet.

What I told him was what I know to be true. This is your father, it is not you. He made choices. You will make yours. *And nobody can see your father's choices, when they look at you my darling boy.*

We were both in tears. Because he understood himself, he understood me, and why I got out, and the past made more sense. I also 'knew' that he would go and live with his father at some point. He still thinks if he is a good enough boy, he can fix daddy. You don't own your children. You give birth to them and a piece of your heart walks around in them. And you have no control from that moment on. Just love.

*When you are ready, the Universe brings you what you need*

Fast forward to the most amazing man in the universe. We really met by divine design. A complete skeptic and a psychic medium. He asked me once early on whether I had cast a spell on him, because anything that worked so well couldn't come naturally. I thought he was joking. He was seriously asking!

I adore my husband, and importantly, maybe, just maybe, I am not afraid of him knowing everything about me. He looks at me with pure love, and I am not afraid anymore.

I know that nothing happened to me, because deep down I just knew it wouldn't. And that speaks to the reality that intimidation only works if we are intimidated.

This is all part of my experiences, and now you know them too. The bits I wanted to hide weren't so bad at all once I let the sun in. And going forward, nobody knows unless I tell them. And so it will be for you.

Nobody knows unless you tell them.

Blessings XX

*  *  *

*Nicole is an accomplished medium, psychic, healer and teacher, whose passion is taking her to the international stage in an effort to support healing on a mass level. Having studied psychic mediumship with the world renowned Lisa Williams, she recognizes that success in our journey comes through empowerment and insight. She honours her gifts through developing retreats and programs around innovation, leadership and spiritual development -- for the real world. She has spent as much of the last half century working her 'magic' in corporate business development, as she has working in education, and psychic mediumship. She combines that sixth sense into an uncanny knack for assisting people to bring balance to their business and personal life, mentoring them to make the best of opportunities that haven't even presented yet. A wife and mother, she teaches in university graduate schools, and is looking towards her Phd. To connect, learn with, or see Nicole, visit www.nicolemchenry.com*

# My Heart Lives Outside My Body
## by Kelly Bettridge

*"I can love*
*But I need his heart*
*I am strong even on my own*
*But from him I never want to part*
*He's been there since the very start*
*My angel Gabriel"*
*- Gabriel, Lamb*

PART ONE

On the 26th December 2003, I died. If you read the medical reports of my son's birth, none of the words written there will tell you that I died, but I did nonetheless.

They will tell you a story of a dangerous birth where the lives of both the mother and child swung silently between the worlds, then came back again, reunited with life but pieced together very, very differently upon their return.

Up until 33 weeks, I had had a beautiful pregnancy with my second child; a whole lot of weight gain through gestational diabetes but, other than that, I had been enjoying being the epitome of embodying Goddess with very few problems or hiccups.

Then I got the phone call from the registrar at the hospital where my child was due to be born. His voice had an odd tone; determined, serious, staccato.

*"Hi Kelly. I'm calling regarding the results of your recent 32-34 week ultrasound. It seems we have quite a situation ahead of us. You are presenting with Grade 3 Major Placenta Praevia. You will need to be admitted to hospital within the week..."*

The doctor reeled off the facts; the placenta was enlarged and covering all exits and entrances to the uterus, and hence, my child. It was covering the stomach side of my uterus, where they would enter to do a c-section, and the cervix was also completely covered, where the baby exits during a natural birth. The result of this condition was a harrowing classical c-section and the potential for a dangerous hemorrhage, before, during and after the procedure, thus presenting evidently huge risks to myself and my child.

I don't think I said much. I probably said yes at appropriate places and blanked out, listening but not listening, numb to the words, to the fear, to the fact that I wouldn't be having the serene, love-filled, blissful natural delivery that I had had with my first child. Now I was going to have my stomach sliced open, and a baby ripped from my body...if we even made it that far.

As a person, I adapt quickly. I get things done. I deal with issues so that the resolutions are quick, and as painless as possible. In situations like these, my intellectual side takes over and my heart gets bundled in a box, glued together, stapled, tied up with force-field enforced string and buried somewhere far, far away. Eventually, when I'm able, I unpack the box, and my heart cries silently by itself until it can weep no more.

This situation was no different. I got onto task. People were told, sorted out, and given tasks. They all sat in fear and angst, wondering why I wasn't scared for my life and my child's. But my heart was in that box, stowed away until I could allow myself to collapse. I knew that I would need all the strength in the world to stay alive through this, and giving in to the fear and emotions of it all would only weaken my resolve to live. I couldn't even look at my family because I could see the stark frightening reality of a potential death staring me in the face every time I saw their eyes.

One divine Summer morning, I was laying down on the floor with my two year old daughter, Aramaya, feeling the sunlight stream in through my lounge room window, kissing and caressing my face, telling me it was all going to be okay. I reached forwards to get a lego block and I felt a push down on my lower abdomen, and I started to bleed. It was the 22nd December and my child wasn't due to be born for another six weeks.

I called my family, and I was driven to hospital. It was an hour long drive and I felt every bump and pothole in the roads, clenching my legs together, feeling the warmth of my blood drip between my thighs, calling, begging, screaming silent petrified thoughts out to Archangel Gabriel to ask him to stop the bleeding. While externally, I would have projected a picture of peace and resolve, internally there was a war being fought...and I didn't feel like I was winning.

In the delivery suite, midwives and doctors rolled in and out, checking this, measuring that, feeling, poking, prodding, discussing. No one spoke directly to me except to ask me questions. I sat. A lamb to slaughter. A slave to my body. My soul screamed and thrashed about. It wanted out. It wanted to be gone.

I felt like I was a character in my own melancholy tear-jerker movie. As the medical staff moved in and out of the room, paying me little or no attention, I gave up trying to take part in my birth/death and I looked out of the window, seeing the dust particles float and dance suspended in the rays of the sun. I saw the dead moth lying on the outside of the window pane. I saw the clouds streamlined through the deep blueness of the Summer sky. I thought of my beautiful Aramaya. My two year old daughter who I might not ever see again. Tears threatened and I fought them off, pushing my fingernails deep into my palm, drawing blood. I still have that fingernail scar.

Then the silence broke.

*"Kelly. We would like you to stay here until you give birth but I understand you have a two year old daughter, and being so near to Christmas, we are going to let you go home because the bleeding has now stopped. However any sign of more bleeding, even slight, and you will need to be readmitted permanently."*

Relief. Car. Home. Bed.

In the light of the new day, last night's events felt like a bad acid trip. I cuddled and squished Aramaya until she threw me off her, exclaiming indignantly that it was 'too much, Mummy!'. How could I tell her that I thought I was going to die last night and needed to get in as many hugs as I could?

Then it happened again. I bled. The warmth of life flowed out of me and onto the floor, right in front of my daughter. Ninety minutes later I was back in hospital.

Midwives, doctors, specialists, nurses, specialist specialists, student doctors. A whirlwind cacophony of people trying to help.

I dissolved myself into a puddle of nothing and just sat on the bed, waiting to be told something, waiting to feel something. I'm sure I was holding onto someone's hand, but it was probably just my own. The only thing I knew was that I wanted to go home. I didn't care about dying any more; I just wanted to go home.

The next morning, my strength had gone. My well was empty and I was lost. It was Christmas Eve, and I was in a hospital with a baby growing inside me and no safe way for him to be born. After breakfast, a small official-looking lady came and sat next to me on the bed.

*We have had a meeting about you this morning and it is decided that you need to stay here in hospital until your baby is born.*

*I can't stay. I have a young child at home.*

*You need to stay. You live an hour away from this hospital. The dangers are too great.*

*I can't stay. It's Christmas and I need to be at home.*

*If you choose to leave and you bleed, your placenta will turn into a hose and you will bleed out in fifteen minutes, at most. Your baby will certainly die and you will most likely follow. Even if you call an ambulance, they won't get to you in time. Even in hospital, we can't promise that you or your baby will survive this but your chances are very, very good because we will keep a 'bung' in your arm so that we can tranfuse blood into you if you begin to hemorrhage. I'm sorry to scare you, Ms Bettridge, but this is the most serious case of praevia we have seen. You need to stay here. I can't allow you to leave.*

Silence. Tears. Realization. What remained of my strength slid out of me and gathered in a sad, useless little sac of nothing on the floor beneath my feet. I had to stay. My baby could die. I could die. I really could die. It felt too real.

Within ten minutes of the doctor leaving, a golden-haired middle-aged midwife came in and sat with me. I fell into her arms like a small child and sobbed violently. She stroked my hair, calmed me down and reminded me that women are the strongest beings on this planet, that I was born to do this, that my body knows what to do. I still remember what that midwife looks like nearly a decade on.

That night, my mother brought Christmas to me. We celebrate Christmas on Christmas Eve, and so my room was filled accordingly. My family and extended family rocked up with plates of festive food, music, gifts, even a plastic Christmas tree. I could barely look at my daughter. It felt like a final goodbye to me. I was present at my own wake.

Christmas Day came and went. On Christmas night, I watched National Lampoon's Christmas Vacation and drank a glass of sparkling wine that one of the nurses had sneakily brought in to me. As I lay on my hospital bed in a room all alone, something happened inside me. I accepted my fate. I opened my heart and said yes to death and to life.

**26th December 2003 10:07pm.**

My brother and his girlfriend had come to visit me and we were watching a reality television show when the contractions started. We called for the nurse and, within thirty seconds, the emergency call had gone off across the hospital and doctors filled my room. I was hooked up to a bag of blood in case it was necessary and, within ten minutes, I was up in the operating room being prepped for a c-section.

The surgeon rubbed his hands furiously, talking to me as he did so. I liked him immediately. He looked at me straight, unwavering, focused.

*"So, Kelly, you know what we're up against. I'm going to have to go in via a classical c-section which means a horizontal cut externally and through the first layer then a vertical incision internally to avoid the placenta. We won't be talking to you and we will look very serious. I know you want to stay awake but if we think you aren't coping, you will be put under. If you start to lose too much blood, we will put you under. You are young and you may want more children so I will try to save your uterus. If I can't, it will have to go. I will deliver your baby first, then we can work out what to do next."*

I was moved into the operating room and I watched the medical staff set up the instruments, humming and buzzing around me like bees. They were moving fast. I had my epidural in between contractions and lay flat. I felt the first incision, like a slight pressure, not painful but like I was a handbag and a person was rummaging around inside me, trying to find their purse or keys.

An hour later, my son was born. I touched his blanket as he was whisked away. I didn't see his face or hear his cry. He wasn't breathing properly and was taken down to the neo-natal intensive care unit. I sent his father down with him -- to keep him here.

I watched my son leave the room in the arms of another woman and made the mistake of shifting my gaze to look at the floor in front of me. I saw the blood, pools of it running from under the table and blood-red soaked sponges everywhere. I pondered for a moment that the doctors really should wear gumboots because their shoes, although covered in medical shoe bags, were red and probably uncomfortably wet and horribly warm. I slipped in and out of consciousness as the blood flowed from my body. The anesthetist kept asking me if I felt alright, and I would hear a voice say yes. I had reached that point where I wanted to be awake and experience my own death.

I closed my eyes and thought of Aramaya, my daughter, and my family waiting out in my hospital room. When I opened them, I stared at the surgeon who had his arms deep inside me. His brow was furrowed, he had the stereotypical sweat beads across the bridge of his nose and beading up above his eyebrows. Then, I heard some alarms go off and I felt very, very strange. As my eyes started to close, I saw two extremely tall beings super impose themselves over the two surgeons and place their arms inside my body. It was Gabriel and one other. I felt peace, and lost consciousness.

Three hours later, I woke up. My baby was doing well and on assisted breathing with oxygen. I was alive. I had lost close to three litres of blood, and my organs had started to shut down. I didn't care about any of that because my eyes were now open and I was alive...I wasn't going to die.

The surgeon came in to see me and shook his head.

*You're one strong little lady, Kelly. You lost a lot of blood and your blood pressure fluctuated like we've never seen, despite the drugs, but you never lost consciousness until right at the end. It was all successful considering the situation and your uterus stayed intact. Well done, girl.*

Two weeks later, Perrin-Gabriel and I left hospital. The months to follow proved to be intense on every level. I developed post natal depression, post traumatic post natal stress disorder, which I have to this very day. My son's birth changed me. It lifted me up, chopped me into teeny tiny little pieces and threw me into the gutter to die, then it picked up again, filled me with strength I never knew I had, and breathed a new life into me.

I left my children's father when Perrin-Gabriel was one and Aramaya was three. I wasn't the person who I had been before Perrin-Gabriel was born. I had become me. He was born so I could give birth to myself.

**Part Two**

*"Making the decision to have a child is momentous. It is to decide forever to have your heart go walking around outside your body."*        *-Elizabeth Stone*

Every year on the evening of the 21st February, I start feeling odd.

I snap at everything and everyone that I love because I know they hold my life, and my sanity, in their hands. During that evening, I am blindingly aware that my heart and emotional stability maintains equilibrium only in their ability to keep safe, be well and stay alive…and so, I can't help myself getting angry with them. I don't know why. I never understand why, no matter how hard I deconstruct the feelings. Maybe I blame them for making me love them so much.

Six years ago, my heart decided to once again take up residence outside of my body. Six years ago, on the evening of that first 21st February, I was 34 weeks pregnant with my third child.

After a harrowing second pregnancy three years earlier, which nearly took my life and my son's, and resulted in post natal depression, post natal post traumatic stress disorder, I had (bizarrely) gone back for another dip in the beautiful fertile waters of my own version of feminine heaven.

It was about 8pm and my other two children had gone to bed. I was sitting up watching television, feeling peaceful and enjoying some zone out time.

Then, WHAM! A huge elbow kicked through my stomach. Well…it felt like it had. I felt a searing pain run across my bellybutton and looked down at my belly. The baby was kicking with such crazy force that it was like she was having her own private protest rally about being cooped up inside for so long. I could see my belly being stretched backwards and forwards and little elbows and feet trying to kick their way out of my uterus. This is not an exaggeration. Neither was the pain.

You know when you read about those pregnant women who say they just knew something was wrong. Well, I just knew. I knew my baby was in distress but there was no way I was going to verbalize it, because saying something would mean I would be manifesting it, making it real. So I did nothing. At the time I made a joke about the fact that my baby was a feisty individual, just like her Mum, and was making it known how much she hated being in a place that she couldn't get out of. Eventually the baby settled down but I remember laying there for hours absolutely petrified that tomorrow I was going to give birth. Another premature baby, another near death experience…or maybe not so near death this time…

All my life, up until this point, I had felt certain that I would not live past the age of 30. I had thought that my traumatic birth experience with my second child at age 28 was the one that was going to get me but, given that I was within a week of turning 30, I really started to believe that this pregnancy, this labour, this baby was going to be motherless very soon. It just seemed too coincidental.

The next day, the 22nd February, carried on in typical stay-at-home Mama Kat style; school drop off, a bit of grocery shopping, paid some bills. I knew I was in labour though. I could feel the tightening. Years ago, a friend of mine had told me how a friend of hers had staved off early labour by squeezing her legs shut. What a nonce. I actually tried it. I squeezed and squeezed my legs shut. I prayed. I begged. And then I called my obstetrician.

*"Hi Liz. I think I'm in labour."*
*"WHAT? What are you doing? Get to the hospital. I'll cancel the rest of my appointments and I'll be there as soon as I can."*
*"No, it's okay. I'm just going to pick my kids up from school, wait until D gets home from work, then we'll head off once my Mum finishes work."*
*"Are YOU serious? Don't be ridiculous. You know your uterus could rupture. Get to hospital now."*
*"Really? Oh. Okay."*

Then … Phonecalls. Kids picked up from school. Mum racing home from work. Trip to hospital.

And .. waiting on the gurney being prepped to go up for another c-section to deliver another premature baby.

210

This time there was no large hemorrhage. My previous scars had held together and I came through it really well.

My baby, Romany, was born breathing (barely) at 6 pounds 2, having just reached 33 weeks and 6 days. I don't remember meeting her. I remember the nurse saying "hold out your hand before they take her away". I think I touched the blanket she was wrapped in. I heard a lot of people fussing around her, and watched the doctor's face to see if I could decipher what was going on. My heart had well and truly jumped out of my chest and was hovering somewhere over the isolette crib in which my little girl was cocooned.

Someone, a doctor or a midwife, told me that they had to take Romany away, and I told my (now ex) husband to go with her. Someone had to keep her in the world, making her want to stay with us, giving her a reason to breathe. It wasn't until two years later that my ex-husband told me that, on the way down to the NICU ward, in the lift, our baby had stop breathing twice. The first time, the midwife couldn't get the oxygen working. Just writing that sentence makes me want to run and jump off the highest building. Loving your children from the moment they are born, and then entrusting their safety to another ... it is the single most difficult thing I have ever done.

About twenty minutes after Romany was born, she was brought into my room, still in an isolette, although this one looked more like a science fiction suspended animation tank, accompanied by two ambulance officers.

*"We thought you might want to say goodbye to your baby before we take her off to the Other Hospital."*
*"What?"*
*"She isn't breathing properly so she needs to go to a better equipped NICU ward."*
*"Okay."*

I think I waved goodbye. What do you do?

Then I shut off. I'm pretty sure that, if my heart, my emotional heart, had a colour, it turned black and drew the curtains in on itself. A different hospital. I hadn't even seen her properly, let alone touched her.

Four days passed with me in one hospital and her in another. I expressed milk via pump six times a day and fresh milk was delivered to Romany

six times a day. That was the one thing that I could do that the health professionals couldn't and, by gods new and old, I was going to do it well.

I would get reports from those who visited her.

*"She's incubated. She's the biggest baby there. She's stable."*

Mixed emotions reigned supreme within my fractured spirit. Why had
they seen my child and I hadn't? Resentment, anger, jealousy, rage, self-
pity. She was my child, not theirs. How dare they know more about her
than I do.

It felt like they were talking about a random child. Not mine. Sometimes
I had no feelings. A black heart. Curtains drawn.

I guess my family knew I had shut down because all of a sudden one morning a doctor came into the room:
*"You have depression? We have been told that you do, and we've found you a bed
in the same hospital as your daughter."*

I didn't have depression, well not yet. But it was pretty obvious that I had
abandoned my own heart and needed to be reunited with my child...who
I had not seen yet.

And so, I moved hospitals.
And I met Romany.
And I felt nothing.
I wanted to feel concern. I wanted to care. I wanted to cry.  I wanted to
cry.

She was in Level 8 NICU. Three babies around her had died that day. They
were all really sick and so tiny. She was massive, but she just couldn't
breathe. She had a weird beanie on her head, lots of tubes everywhere and
had been incubated for days.

I found out that someone had given her formula that morning, and I can
tell you that if I had had a loaded machine gun there and then, I would've
gunned that midwife down. MY MILK was the only thing I could give MY
BABY. It still hurts.

For three weeks, little Romany worked her way from a Level 8 to a Level 2 NICU baby. Then she came home. My crazy little feisty bundle of curly-headed mischief.

This is the sixth year of the anniversary of her birth. The 22nd February never gets any easier. Each year I relive it...the lack of control that we have over our hearts. How fleeting life is. The fact that all we can do is love... and hope, pray, beg that it is enough to keep the ones that we love safe.

I don't think my heart has ever jumped back inside my body. It still hovers around my children wherever they go.

* * *

*Kelly Bettridge; Manager of Her Own Crazy, Frequent Loser of Common Sense, On Call Freedom Fighter, Cheer Squad to the Underdog, Often Oxymoronic, A Continent Hopper, A Wistful Child of the World. Kelly is a British-born Australian Mama Kat to three kidlets, living and loving it up in the Upper Yarra Valley of Victoria, Australia. She has been a freelance journalist and fiction writer for the past 15 years, is a yoga and school teacher, a healer and psychic medium and has owned a successful esoteric business and therapy centre. From a young age, she has been able to feel the veil between the worlds and knows that she lives with one foot constantly in another dimension.*

*She blogs at www.kellybettridge.com and at Angelica Minx (www.angelicaminx.com), writes regular columns for several magazines and chooses to live her life with enough love and fabulous insanity to fill several books.*

# Unmasked
by Marcey Gray


**Escape Artist (1995)**
She cried on the bedsides of those unprepared,
with thoughts in tatters that could not be repaired.
For years made to mask the madness in mind,
She decided at last to leave this world behind.

So alone in a room, she decided to hide,
and buried her troubles in what she knew wasn't art;
A wall painted black to run from the shadows,
of the people who would never come looking.


Rather than my own life, my arduous history now seems more like a heart-wrenching Reader's Digest article, once read while waiting in a doctor's office. Years spent in despair; knees to chest under heavy blankets moist in tears, and feet left aching from pacing midnight floors, are now but memories out of focus -- challenging to recall.

My journey with mental illness began at age eleven as my life began to change at a pace that spun me into a whirlwind of confusion. I had always enjoyed interacting with other children in the schoolyard; pursuing each other in unsuccessful efforts to tag another with a kiss, clambering on the monkey bars, and twittering as friends lost their footing in games of hop-scotch. Then unexpectedly, I lost interest in, and could no longer relate to, my peers and their meaningless amusements. Much the same happened with my creativity.

Able to occupy myself for hours colouring, painting, and writing stories, soon the colours faded and the words were lost in limbo. In my head, I recited a repetitive song: "One of these things is not like the others; one of these things just doesn't belong..." and in most every situation, I found myself not like the others, not belonging. The awareness of being different - of not belonging but wanting to with every fibre of my being -- and the distress of being judged for my "unnatural" behaviour terrified me and soon my battling thoughts had my stomach in knots.

214

For the most part, my inner turmoil remained obscured to those around me, or identified as the actions and behaviour of an introverted child. My exterior symptoms, however, were increasingly obvious. Harder to suppress were the sweating episodes of insufferable abdominal pain and nights spent restlessly, in spite of Ibuprofen in double doses and a boiling hot water bottle pressed tightly to my purpling belly. A ping-pong match of visiting this doctor and that ensued, and before my issues could be determined, my parents and I moved away from Guelph. An isolated house on the Bruce Peninsula, far from all I had become familiar with in my short, young life became my new home. I tried to find some optimism, given our new home was down the road from where I had spent my childhood vacations. I told myself it could be a fresh start with new dreams. However, I did not fit in there either.

On my first day at my new country school, I entered the classroom and clumsily zigzagged through a maze of desks to my assigned seat as eyes burned into the back of my head. Classmates excluded me whenever I tried to ease my way into their in-groups, closely knit since kindergarten. I acted normally as I thought was expected and attempted to intermingle with other obvious outcasts; they would not have me. Words, or at least the right words, never came out. As a means to combat the banishment, deep frustration and shame that arose from not knowing what deficit drove others to shun me I withdrew into a shell and started missing school.

On days when I was present for roll call, truancy officers frequently called me in to the principal's office. They interrogated me about my recurrent absences from class, either because I had escaped to the library with my textbook or because I had not found the courage to step foot on the school bus the morning before. Sitting uncomfortably, only inches from the officer, I imagined a blunt, glaring flashlight pointed in my eyes as he repeatedly asked me the same questions expecting me to answer differently each time. I told him I was sick, but still in the midst of seeing copious doctors, I couldn't explain *how* I was sick – no one knew. Again, the right words just wouldn't come to me. He shared a story about his own son, who had an unexplained illness that was precipitated by a food allergy. "He was fine after he stopped eating beef," he spouted, and suggested I try the same. A beef allergy; I wish it had been that simple.

The gut-twisting fear of being an outsider had been difficult; now quiet giggles and whispers engulfed the classroom each time I returned from the principal's office. The trepidation developed into continual, crippling anxiety attacks – tense muscles, heart palpitations, and racing thoughts.

My parents decided, undoubtedly from their own frustration, to withdraw me from school and arrange for home schooling.

Aside from minor allergies and two treatable physical ailments, allergists, endocrinologists, gastroenterologists, psychometrists, and many other "ists" had not been able to find a solution to my other issues. At twelve years old, I had my first appointment with a psychiatrist. She was a middle-aged woman with still-auburn curls permed tightly against her scalp wearing the stereotypical white, cotton jacket that glared at me from behind her desk. After explaining my concerns to her, she advised my mother, who was sitting beside me holding my hand, that I needed to get out of the house more often– perhaps take a bus to the mall or the library. She looked down into her lap and scribbled notes on a clipboard as I attempted to explain the remoteness of my home. Only recently having taken up practice in Owen Sound from Toronto, she clearly could not comprehend the nature of my circumstances. We didn't have a single stoplight, a convenience store or even a gas station; we certainly did not have public transportation to chauffeur me to her suggested destinations.

While several doctors had suggested that my symptoms were imaginary due to boredom, a need for attention, or abuse at home, I had hoped this doctor would have an alternative approach -- *listen* and "fix" me. Fix the racing thoughts of failure and inadequacy that no twelve-year-old should feel. Fix my mind that spent nights dreaming of never waking up again. Fix my brain's looping record, convincing me that I should be fearful of everything around me. Instead, she asked me to draw. So, I drew.

I drew a picture of an anthropomorphized cat in a basketball jersey and jeans. She looked at the pencil drawing and asked, "Why are the cat's paws in its pockets? Is he hiding something there?" Without so much as the passing of a second, I told her, "No, I just can't draw paws". Taken aback, not having received an answer that would lead her to an intense revelation of depravity or abuse, she looked disappointed. "Well then," she said, returning eye contact to my mom, "There is nothing wrong with her. She is mildly depressed -- most likely from the move. She'll be fine. Here's a prescription." Another prescription from another doctor who could not help me. As with the others who came before, she sent me on to a succession of additional specialists who would eventually do the same.

**Journal Excerpt: June 22, 1993**
Time will tell what happens to me, or what I do to myself. My life has never been or will ever be what I had hoped. I will never truly be happy, truly

carefree or truly "ok". I will wear this mask while I cry out from behind it. I will keep pretending to be happy around those who expect me to be, while I slowly fall to pieces from the inside out.

By age sixteen, in isolation and loneliness, 1260 unbearable 12-hour days passed by in the woods while my parents worked. I kept my brain active by listening to monotonous voices on CBC radio, reading textbooks issued to me through an independent learning centre and consuming books signed out of the local library. Without Internet or cable, I engaged in writing letters to pen pals in faraway lands, often fabricating stories about a life I *wish* I had been leading, in order to keep them attentive and writing back to me. Barring travels across the province, sightseeing through doctors' office windows, I seldom left the house. I was desperate for human connection and angry with my parents for moving me to the place that I viewed as a prison. I felt trapped; murderers got less "time" than I did. "What did I do to deserve this?"

**Neurosis (1998)**
Rapt in a fiery hell
Tied up
in barbed wire
Surrounded
by mental bars
Chains on my hands
Shackles on my feet
in the dungeon
of my mind

In time, a friend of mine who had stayed in contact with me after the move invited me to return to Guelph for a weekend. I was ecstatic with the idea of seeing her and visiting my extended family, but understandably my parents hesitated given my condition. Eventually, after dealing with weeks of hearing my relentless pleas, they swayed and I returned to Guelph. Throughout the next year, I visited for a few days each month, staying with my friend's family, or my aunts who generously offered me a place to sleep. While still continuously filled with anxiety and fear, pain and insecurity, I was relieved to hear the loud city noises, enjoy human interaction, and have absolutely no idea what our family of investigative raccoons was doing back at home in my absence.

During my visits, I concealed the truth from everyone. Veiled by a perfected, concocted smile, I hid everything that no one would ever be able to understand. At that time, I didn't *want* them to understand. I didn't want to afflict them with the same worries that bounced around constantly in my frontal lobe. I didn't want them to feel the same shame and embarrassment that had built up inside of me for years. I didn't want them to reject me too.

While I was secretly jealous of their ordinary lives of high school, dating, and dances, they were resentful of me because they interpreted my visits as "skipping off". How could they have known otherwise, that time spent away from home was for the sake of my own sanity? The few friends I had left, and the acquaintances I met, often approached me with questions and comments difficult to answer. "How come you're lucky enough not to have to go to school?" They didn't know how deeply it hurt when I heard those words. I wanted nothing more than to burn my home-school books -- to have friends, to go to my prom, to have the typical teenaged life I coveted. Visiting Guelph was an escape from the isolation, poking and prodding from doctors, and the only time I had any sense of what it truly felt like to be this idea of "normal" I had invented in my head.

At age seventeen, my aunt, who was oblivious to my mental plights, knew that the soul-crushing isolation alone was detrimental to my well-being, and invited me to move back to Guelph to live with her. Her condition: find a job and pay rent. A job? I was barely able to function, let alone work a full-time job in order to support myself. Yet, I knew I had to if I ever wanted to experience some semblance of real life.

Throughout the next decade, I worked full-time menial jobs, took college courses through correspondence, and managed to have a social life. I tried the best that I could to cope with emotions that were overpowering, vicious self-deprecating thoughts, and physical pain. I had become so numb to feeling anything but, that episodes of frustration-induced dish-throwing, catching my breath between tears, and carving hateful words into my forearm with any sharp object I could find had become *my* normal. Much like an elastic stretched to its limit, I couldn't hold on anymore. One afternoon alone at home, I slid to the living room floor and every piece of me shattered.

For eight years, I had avoided seeing any doctors. Just the thought of returning to forgotten familiarities was terrifying. Again, I would face the invasive analyzing from years past, but pills were scattered on the counter and if I didn't make that call, the morning would never come.

### Hostis (2006)

From where, please tell me, did these feelings arise
This inexplicable sadness that cripples my eyes
And tires my mind into unbearable languor?

How did this anger breed from nothing that was
Into a furious evil sprite that grips me in its claws
Beating me until only I am blacker?
If anyone were haunted then surely it's me -
For what else in this earth could strain such misery
In a self who was once so pure?

Someone, please advise what I am to do,
When days of anguish seem to amass -
Death being a choice easier to endure?

My hands shook violently as I picked up the receiver and dialed the number of a local mental health centre. The droning voice on the other end asked questions to determine if I was ill enough to receive their treatment. As I waited on hold, my heart battled against my rib cage in an attempt to escape my body; the attempt eventually thwarted by the returned voice -- "Your appointment is scheduled for March 26." Three months I would have to wait. Three months wondering if I would make it there.

I conquered the hazardous temptations of a running faucet, a stocked medicine cabinet and a full kitchen drawer, and finally found myself sitting in a waiting room surrounded by stale air and muzak foxtrots. "Marcey Gray", soon ricocheted off walls layered in cracks of institutional white. I panned around the room hoping someone else would stand in my place. Realizing there were no other Marcey Gray's there to face my grim expectations on my behalf, my knuckles regained their colour as I released their grip from the chair's arm and followed behind my caller. This scenario played out again across the city as the ping-pong game began anew.

**My Life (2006)**
Fed Up
The embodiment of gloom
My life
Living in a corpse
Hostile from loss
Hour to hour
Beliefs so common
Relentlessly amend
Tears
Deluge my eyes
Searing my cheeks
Burning their ache
Into welts of shame

As a child, my mother supported me during doctor's visits. She held my hand, received contact from often-distant eyes, spoke for me, and listened to medical jargon I could not understand. This time, I was alone. I was an adult, and the doctors were more willing to offer their frank opinions. From files stacked in foot-high folders upon their desks, they narrated the story of my life written in chicken scratch and faded, printed sheets of yellow. They read about my deficiencies and my flaws, fingered through dog-eared Diagnostic and Statistical Manuals of Mental Disorders and finally told me:

"You're a hopeless case!"
"It's time that you understand that this is not going to get any better!"
"You can't function like a 'normal' person. How do you expect to lead a 'normal' life?"
"You need to come to terms with reality; you're going to be sick for the rest of your life."
"You're a hopeless case!"

One at a time, mental "ists" proceeded to stick a series of invisible jam-jar labels on my forehead and determined a future for me that I was not willing to accept. I had not come to terms with "reality", because their conclusion of what my reality *should* be was not my own. Yes, I was sick. Yes, I needed help. Yes, most people thought that I would spend the rest of my life as a burden to all those who ever laid eyes upon me, or from behind closed doors had said in low whispering voices, "I feel so sorry for her".

**Awash (2006)**
The deep end sings to me
Clear indigo abyss
An endless span of possibilities
Whitecaps of faith
I know if they should tumble away
Always, they will turn back
No worries I will have
Floating in this void
Where my life lay
In a gulf of my own
Where nothing is solid
To soar free a forever guarantee
A sea of wishes
Of dreams
And chance
If only I could swim.

Without a job, in the deepest pit of despair I had experienced to date, and against the advice of my parents who were two of the few who could see beyond the mask, I married my best friend of twelve years.

At the wedding reception, before fifty of my closest relatives and friends, I stood silently shaking -- hiding inside of the heaviest, most beautiful dress I had ever touched. I was terrified, but words finally began slipping through my lips as I tried to keep my quivering voice balanced and loud enough to be heard across the expanse of the large room. As my speech neared the end, tears began to well in my eyes, but did not leave, as I stated, "I've had a hard life, but I made it." The faces of those in attendance began to contort in bewilderment and even though they made no vocalization, bouncing around beyond their eyes looking to other guests in the room, echoed a wave of "Huhs?" and "Whats?"

It had been the first attempt of many at starting a dialogue with those still unaware of my *real* life – unaware of the years I had lived as a very suc-cessful, silent actor. Jokes and sarcasm had hidden my pain. Smiles and well-rehearsed lines had hidden my most disheartening thoughts. Makeup had hidden the tracks burnt down my cheeks from tears I had cried alone. No one had ever realized that each time I stood before them, I was taking a stage. I held myself together for as long as I needed to in order to give a believable performance. When the curtain closed behind me, I fell apart.

221

### But, Do You Know Me at All? (2007)

Wide, bright eyes and a contrived smile cloak my face,
which conceal the wounds and trials I cannot erase.
For though I may struggle, and oh, how I chase,
a genuine happiness can't be found on this face
Though I may walk with esteem and counterfeit grace,
I cannot compete in this most critical race:
who can be most joyful outside, while inside a bare space?
A genuine happiness can't be found on this face.
I've tried to find contentment in every which place,
only to grow weary with the steps I retrace;
searching for anything real to replace
the genuine sorrow that hides behind this face.

I had hoped those scandalous words would encourage a conversation in the days following my wedding. "What did you mean by that?" I had hoped someone would ask, even out of simple curiosity. Yet, no one did and the act continued. Still, no one knew the truth of my clandestine life.

Fifteen years had passed away since that day on the playground when I realized that my life had changed. In that time I had allowed and accepted into my head the presumptuous opinions of teachers, principals, doctors, social workers, and various other professionals who read my life on a page and determined that I was hopeless. One night, while lying awake in bed with random thoughts swirling around in my head, I realized that I had become what they had predicted. I had been relying on others to reassemble my broken pieces, yet not once had I attempted to fix myself. Having heard so much negativity about my circumstances, I had not even thought that fixing myself was a possibility. I had read passages in self-help books that stated recovery was possible, but the despairing words from the professionals I had entrusted with my care made recovery seem fictitious. Then, my A-HA moment happened, and I understood that I could take back my control and take responsibility for my life.

I knew it wouldn't be an easy feat; getting out of bed before noon was still a struggle and self-deprecating, obsessive thoughts of worthlessness consumed my every waking hour. However, if I was ever going to recover I had to be the one to put that first foot on the cold floor, stand up straight and take on the day.

With a new-found determination that I couldn't remember experiencing before, I began devouring books about recovery and weeding through doctors to find one suitable for *me*, who wouldn't dictate to-do lists based on his or her opinion, but rather offer support in my new journey. It took time, but I found her. While blunt and brutally honest, she helped me devise a plan for my next steps forward. Baby steps. I talked and she listened, and not once did the word "hopeless" escape from her mouth.

I began visiting a weekly cognitive behavioural therapy group, which helped wonders in teaching me how to think differently about my life and my fears. The ongoing therapy and support of the group enabled me to leave my apartment more frequently, but I found that I was still quite anxious and unhappy; I still felt like something was missing. Then, one day during a CBT class a musically-inclined young lady in my group started talking about an organization called Spark of Brilliance that had helped her rediscover the creativity that had stagnated with the onset of her bipolar disorder. I contacted the founder of the program and she agreed to meet with me.

Our meeting was the first I had had in years with anyone outside of my small circle of family and friends, and those I saw during treatment. As I sat at a quiet café table seated opposite this beautifully dressed woman, with eyes as soft and kind as her voice, she surprised me by her first question. She didn't ask me what was wrong with me, my diagnoses, or about my limitations; she asked me what I wanted, what my goals were and how she could help me. I could feel from the caring in her tone that she was sincere and passionate.

It took days for me to build up the courage to go to my first workshop; uncertainty, like a pile of boulders, pushed down on my chest and the doorknob on my apartment door burned with an invisible fire.

**Journal Excerpt: June 16, 2005**
…I walked into the workshop expecting to hear cries of "woe, is me" like most of the other support groups I have been to. Instead, I heard laughter and people talking about their favourite music, their pets and their families. What? Could there really be a place for people with mental illness that didn't revolve around the illness, but rather offered a place for people to be… people? I think I found it here. When I took off my jacket, I felt like I left my diagnoses on the rack with it. For two hours I created art. For two hours I felt free. For two hours I felt like I belonged. For two hours, I could just… *be*.

Little by little, with the help of paint and a brush, I opened the gates to my emotions, my heart and soul - expressing the depth and intensity of the pain I had experienced through strokes of increasingly vibrant colours. It was freeing and refreshing. While we didn't often share the stories behind the artwork we created, and didn't have a professional analyzing our choice of subject or colour, we had all experienced separately yet together, the creation of our own lives, on canvas.

Words of shared encouragement and a consistent focus on ability rather than disability helped crack open my hardened shell, and I found my voice. Laughter began dancing from my lips and positive thoughts trumped the negativity that had previously wrought my thoughts. I was experiencing a joy I thought had been lost forever. As the months and workshops raced by, I found my self-confidence increasing; my sense of belonging had returned and I was eager to take on new experiences. Ideas started germinating, excitement for what was to come began brewing and I felt an inner peace exploding inside.

In such a very short time, I had rediscovered so much of my potential previously overshadowed by a constant focus on my presumed shortcomings. Unfortunate circumstances may have stolen a great deal of time and pieces of who I may have been had I not been ill, but I was ready to break down the walls and fight against my odds.

Wanting to give something back to the program, I dedicated the next year to Spark of Brilliance endeavours. Using self-taught skills, I developed the program's first website and newsletter, facilitated creative workshops and encouraged participants, who I knew had talents and potential hiding beneath fragile surfaces. By giving back to the program, my confidence continued to increase, allowing me to venture farther out into the broader community. Gaining additional skills and tools through volunteer opportunities with non-profit organizations further empowered me, and allowed me to gain meaningful employment.

Rediscovering art and being involved in programing that focuses on one's strengths and abilities rather than on perceived deficiencies were essential parts of my healing, recovery and personal growth. I believe that, with encouragement received from others and my participation in the arts, I found the ability to communicate thoughts, feelings, and experiences that were otherwise difficult to express. As the colours I used became more vibrant and brush strokes became freer and stronger, the pieces I created became tangible depictions of my progress and healing. Art helped me open up, to see myself as a free and creative person again, and improved my overall quality of life.

While at one point the word recovery was incomprehensible to me, the word that now remains incomprehensible is the word "never", for there is always possibility for healing, growth and evolution, no matter how "hopeless" the case. Less than a decade ago, I was still being told I was a hopeless case – that I would *never* hold a job, that I would *never* lead a normal or productive life, that I would *never* be a contributing member of the community, that I would *never* recover – I have proved everyone wrong.

Through sharing my story with others in the recent past, many have called me a success. I have a hard time seeing myself as successful, as I have yet to paint a masterpiece, write a best-seller, or get lucky in the stock market. However, I have done many things others expected I would never do.

Told that, due to isolation experienced at such a young age and social anxiety issues, I would never have the ability to communicate effectively as an adult, I have since performed improvisational theatre and stand-up comedy, presented to audiences in the hundreds about mental health and the arts, and have publically shared my story with thousands more.

With my history of being unable to function "normally", professionals predicted that I would never be a contributing member of society. I have since volunteered with causes related to seniors, people living with AIDS, rescued animals, and of course others living with the challenges of mental health issues. I have independently published books, been a keynote speaker at the Guelph Mayor's initiative and other mental health related forums. I have won the Access Recognition Award for breaking down mental health barriers for others in my community. I have a small freelance design and creative consulting business and I am honoured to be gainfully employed with the program that played a huge role in changing my life-- Spark of Brilliance.

I'm generally quite modest when it comes to sharing my accomplishments with others, but my small successes (in the grander scheme of things) are important to share because, much like so many others facing the same challenges, I was explicitly told I would never do any of them.

My journey through mental illness has been one that I would not dare wish upon my worst enemy, yet I am thankful for the experience. It has made me a stronger, more compassionate and understanding person and I appreciate even more the little things in life that many people take for granted. I am thankful that I have lived through it in order to help educate those who do not understand mental illness, and to empower those that live with it every day. Although I have faced immeasurable challenges and barriers, and many times felt like giving up, I don't regret it.

Recovery is an ongoing process, and while I will in fact be sick for the rest of my life, I don't see my situation in the same negative light reinforced throughout my life. I still live with the symptoms, but I have learned to cope with them and no longer *define* myself by my diagnoses. I may have severe depressive disorder, obsessive-compulsive tendencies, social anxiety disorder and agoraphobia, but that is just it – I *have* those things. They may be a part of me, but they are not *who I am*.

With all the masks packed away, the shame and embarrassment faded, I am now happy with the person I have become. When I think back on all the years filled with hundreds of opinions like "you will never" and "you can cannot", it was the two or three "yes you cans" that made all the difference. When it comes to my potential, I have eliminated the word "never" from my vocabulary, and the only time I ever accept hearing the word "never" from an often-argumentative brain, is when I remind myself of a quote by Winston Churchill – "Never, never, never, never give up."

While it was my decision alone to take responsibility in and of my life, I could not have come as far as I have without the support, guidance and compassion of others who love me...unconditionally. Sincerely I thank those who brought light into my life when the shadows consumed me. I dedicate my story to my enduring parents, Heather and Richard Gray; my loving husband, Marlon Joefield; my tenacious aunt, Judy Carroll; my mentor, friend and believer in possibility, Judith Rosenberg; and to all the friends I have met along the way who have stood by my side.

### The Story of my Arms (2010)
In scars upon my arms
were etched years of false belief,
Of words indelibly imprinted in my mind.

When the bottom was reached,
My heart beseeched,
There was so much more I was worthy of.

For all of the things I was or was not,
The things I would or never could be,
I finally understood that life was worth living,
Simply because I was loved.

I've had a hard life, but I made it. Now, let's talk.

* * *

*Marcey is an artist and crafter, and Program Coordinator for Spark of Brilliance. Spark of Brilliance is a community-based mental health program of the Self Help Alliance, operated by CMHA Waterloo Wellington Dufferin, that promotes healing, recovery and discovery through the expressive arts for those with a lived experience of mental health issues and/or addiction. She resides in Guelph, Ontario.*

# Identity
by Danielle Hughes

We all wear different masks. Masks that help protect us from the world, that present the face we want everyone to see. I have hidden for years behind different faces to protect myself, hide my experiences and to satisfy the expectations of others.

I have not always hidden myself from the world. Maybe it was my naivety, but I believed that I could be accepted just as I was. That who I was would be enough. I grew up with a confidence in who I was, as an only child within a large extended family. I was supported and encouraged to engage my imagination and to trust in all my senses. No one laughed when I said I had to put water or honey out for the faeries who lived in the garden, no one laughed when I said I knew there was a spirit of a little girl living in our house. I was raised with complete love and faith in my family and myself, until that all came crashing down on me.

Growing into adolescence is always difficult; for met it was doubly difficult. I had to adjust first to being a big sister, which I loved despite the changes and the increased responsibility. I was a big sister, and that was pretty cool. But around that same time, I watched my parents change. With added responsibilities of a growing family and owning a home, they became disconnected. They began to argue, fighting constantly, something I had never really seen before. As the fighting became worse, I learned to take on my first mask to the world. I had to pretend as if everything was normal, as if everything was good at home. I didn`t know how to talk about it; I had never seen anything like it before. I felt like, if I just said to myself and to the world enough times that everything was okay, then it would be.

It was during a fight that I was given a truth about myself, a piece of information that no one should have to find out through anger. I was told that, although my dad raised me, he was not my biological father. The solid ground beneath my feet crumbled. Everything I had thought about myself seemed to come into question. In the aftermath of the fight, I learned that my parents had met when I was three months old. My mom became pregnant when she was seventeen. She became not only a teen mom but also a single mother because the man who provided half of my genes refused to have anything to do with us. It was after I was born that my parents started dating and I gained my dad. There was still a small part of me that felt un-

228

wanted. There was someone out there who created life, my life, who did not want me. It ate away at me from two sides, on the one hand I felt abandoned and unwanted and on the other I felt guilt that I even cared. I was afraid that I lost my dad; that he had told me in the way he did because he regretted staying with us. My mind was filled with a constant stream of Who am I really? Does it really matter? Is it my fault that my parents are going through difficult times? Does my dad hate me? Is it my fault that he is unhappy? My mom tried to help, saying things like "I think dad fell in love with you first, then me". These little things meant to comfort only twisted me up a little more. Inside, I felt burdened. I felt like we were there because of me, and I was the one who should fix things. I felt responsible in a way that only a child can for the discontent of my family and, as things spiralled more and more out of control, my guilt grew stronger and stronger.

My world was consumed with fear. Would there be another fight tonight? What will get broken this time? Will one of us be hurt in the crossfire? I wished I could talk to someone about it, but I did not want to betray my family or hurt them. I had to keep it inside; I had to find a way to make it right. If I could just be enough, accomplish enough, do things right, things could go back to the way they were. I began to take on different titles, masks, to try and not only fill my own void but to help bring my family back together. I became focused on being a dutiful daughter, a protector and big sister, an excellent student, a creative writer, a bookworm.

The titles, the masks, only deepened my disconnect. I developed intense social anxiety and had difficulty creating and maintaining friendships, I felt alone and depressed. I was in a deep dark hole, and felt completely alone. I became numb with it, unable to feel. I was an automaton running on autopilot. The only light in my life was my siblings. They gave me a sense of purpose, a sense of knowing I was loved and needed.

As I grew into my teen years, I began rebelling. My rebellions were small ones, hidden well; I still functioned on the levels I was needed to. On weekends, I began drinking. I spent my time trying to find feeling at parties. I thought I had everything under control, as I didn't let my weekend activities affect my weekday life, my school, my responsibilities. I don't remember a lot from that time; many weekends were blurs filled with bits and pieces of events. I didn't see how lucky I was; I had a group of friends I spent time with who were loyal and who looked out for each other. This drunken haze continued for a couple years, until I began waking up and seeing how I was wasting my time. I had a moment of clarity part way through the year I was 16, I went to fewer parties and began to spend more time with my books and my poetry. I discovered beautiful books about women's Mysteries and began to study Wicca and paganism. I found strength and purpose inside myself and through the beliefs. I was introduced to the concept of manifesting your own desires.

It was a quiet time. I began to search within for my own answers and sought to find myself. I studied, I spent time outdoors, I began to feel a small amount of confidence. And then the bottom fell out of the basket again. The issues at home continued to escalate; I tried to share how I felt and thought we should do family counselling. I was shot down, told I had no right to feel the way I did. I had no reason to feel anxious or upset or torn apart. The rift I had been slowly healing tore open again and I stumbled on my path again. I discovered drugs, specifically, ecstasy. In those colourful little pills, I found escape. I had no care in the world, no hurt, guilt, anger. Everything was beautiful, bright and alive....even if it was just for one night. For six months, I spiralled down further and further....depending more and more on those weekend escapes. I lived for Friday, for those sweet moments of surrender. I never allowed it to interfere with my week day responsibilities....I went to school, did my homework, babysat, all on autopilot. Waiting, just waiting, for the next rush of happiness, of removing myself from this world and being completely in my own.

One day I woke up. I can't pinpoint the exact moment or thing that opened my eyes, I just know that I did. I was scared, afraid of what I was becoming, of being dependent on another substance to achieve some semblance of happiness. I just knew it had to stop. What kind of example was I setting? How could I be a big sister, be responsible for two precious lives and be headed down a road to addiction? So I stopped. I returned to my original form of escapism....books. I started reading again, everything and anything I could get my hands on. From romance novels to philosophical texts, I drank in the written word like it was water. I attempted to be more social again, spending time with others and truly talking...or, in my case, listening. I still had trouble connecting and sharing myself, but I could listen and I could offer different angles on a situation. I was able to be a voice of reason for others even with my own world in shambles. I was able to help my friends overcome their obstacles. It felt like I was finally doing something worthwhile...I could actually make a difference somewhere. I had found a purpose, something that made me feel good about myself. I found my way back to me.

I returned to my theological and philosophical readings. I loved religion and philosophy, I loved bringing them together. I returned to my studies of women's mysteries, I loved the ancient, earth-based traditions. I studied Shamanism; I felt a connection to it and to the honouring of Nature and the seasons. And as I focused on the things I loved, I found my life changing. At home, things were still messy, but in my personal life I started dating for the first time. I was 17, a late bloomer I suppose, and someone had looked at me and thought, I want to know more about her. It was an amazing feeling, my first love. I saw the world around me differently; it wasn't all ugliness and shadows. There really was beauty in the world....not just in books. I stopped feeling so anxious in social settings; I relaxed and had fun. Experiencing love changed my perspective. Love breeds love, and it opened my eyes to see all the good in my home, my family, my roots. I was not bombarded with the bad; I was filled with the good memories.

I remembered things like when we first bought the trailer. My dad bought it as a surprise for my mom, and took me out before the park was open to see it. It was a place we could go to get away in the summer, with playgrounds, trees, a river and swimming pool. We went together and kept our little secret until dad brought mom out to see it. It was our little secret, our surprise. I was always made part of everything, from baking with mom to fixing the car with my dad...I would be outside for hours watching him tinker and passing tools. We would go for drives, just to get away, for hours. Or I was with my grandparents out for breakfast on Sunday mornings then to the country for a drive around. Or visiting in Brampton with family. I didn't need anything; I had my family and I knew that was all that mattered. When I found out that I was going to be a big sister, I was scared of how things would change but excited to have a new person to love. I loved being a big sister. I would do anything to protect my siblings, to give them the same love and faith that I was given. I wish they could have been there before things fell to pieces. I was finally starting to find my way again, when everything went to hell.

We were all so close, which made it difficult for me to see and understand why things had fallen apart so much. We stopped seeing family in Brampton, my parents were arguing more and more each day. It took everything in me just to try and give my sister and brother a small portion of what I had when I was growing up. It was while I was in the early stages of first love that my family life hit rock bottom again.

I can't explain the fear and anxiety of watching two people you love tear each other apart. The helplessness of knowing that what is going on isn't right and that it needs to stop, fighting with what you know is right and family loyalty. I felt like Judas, that night. I had the kids in the basement trying to hide them from the fighting. I did everything I could to keep them away from it, playing movies, music and games. Until everything went out of control, and I heard the house being torn apart. Every minute something else was broken. The house was a crescendo of crashing, banging and shattering. I slowly made my way upstairs; I tried to reason, cried and begged for it to stop. The kids were scared, I was scared, and this needed to stop. I stood huddled and scared in the corner of the kitchen again, watching my world torn even further apart. Hateful words thrown like hand grenades, pushing and shoving each other out of the way. I stood frozen, unable to do my job, unable to protect my siblings. The fight continued to escalate, I was terrified. I had never seen it so bad, I was afraid they would really hurt each other. No one would walk away and let it be. For hours, the house was a raging storm of yelling and hitting and throwing. There were no breakables left to break, furniture was broken. I couldn't take it anymore, the phones were smashed completely unusable. Something had to stop, I went down to check on my brother and sister and found Miranda gone. She was nowhere in the house I searched high and low, but no one would stop to help me...it kept getting worse and worse. I panicked... I hit the panic button on the home security system. I didn't know what else to do. That night, my dad was arrested and taken from the house for domestic violence. That night, I lost my faith in love.

I closed my heart off again; I couldn't risk feeling that fear. I couldn't risk having my relationship fall apart like that. I walked away from my first love shortly afterwards. I just couldn't have that in my life.

I was afraid to read, to believe, to begin a road to being me again. Every time I thought I had found a light in my life something bad happened around me. I couldn't risk hurting anyone else, so I shut down and shut off everything. I went through my days on autopilot again, believing that I wasn't meant to have anything more. I didn't know why or what I had done to deserve a life without love, I just knew what happened every time I began to rebuild myself. I retreated inside, doing what was expected of me but not truly showing my whole self to anyone.

I finished high school and started college. I began the Social Service worker program in hopes that I could make a difference in someone else's life.

After all that I had gone through I felt I could help others going through their own disasters, and I also hoped to gain new insights on how to rebuild myself, my life. The first year went by quietly; I did well and I felt hope again that I could have people in my life. I slowly opened my heart again. I picked up my books and started studying, searching again for higher meaning in life. I was still drawn to metaphysical and New Age traditions; I also started learning energy healing and got my Reiki I certificate. I didn't feel comfortable doing treatments, but Reiki was the first step in a long journey back to who I was. At the beginning of my second year of college, I got sick. I wasn't able to attend school and I missed more than the limit of days allotted to us. I had to put my schooling on hold. I had a lot of time to think and consider, and I realized that I didn't want to finish Social Services, but I also had no idea what I wanted. I got back on the mend and got a job.

As I was feeling better, working, my parents decided to move to Petrolia. I was almost 19; I had my life. My work and everything I knew was in Cambridge. I just couldn't go. I stayed behind, and my family moved two and a half hours away. I felt alone, and in a strange way abandoned. I was angry at them for leaving me. I didn't know what I wanted and I didn't know how to be on my own. I made a huge mistake and fell for someone who lied to me about who they were. I stayed because I didn't know what else to do. I fell into an emotionally abusive relationship. I was working full-time, supporting both of us, doing all the work around the house and being told I wasn't doing enough. I stayed. I had felt like I lost my foundation, and didn't believe in my right to be loved, to be treated well. I gave up three years of my life, until I just couldn't take it anymore. I found within a reserve of strength and courage I didn't know I still had. During that time I had people brought into my life who were like-minded, who searched the metaphysical world like I did. I found several teachers, who helped me bring myself back into focus. I found the courage to leave, moved to Petrolia to get myself together.

The time I spent in Petrolia was healing. I found forgiveness. I discovered that to heal is to forgive. To let go of the past and to move forward with the lessons....not with reliving the memories over and over like an old movie reel. I knew the pain of making mistakes, of being human. I was reminded that parents are people too... people who are trying their best. My parents were trying to heal themselves and each other by creating a fresh start. I understood that, and worked hard to release the feeling of abandonment. I worked, I researched and I decided on a new life path for myself. In my heart, I knew that I wanted to help others and to learn more metaphysical healing techniques. In my mind, I knew that I needed to find security and build a safety net for my financial wellbeing. I decided to go back to school. I chose a health field and plotted my course to become a Respiratory Therapist, knowing that down the road I really wanted to have my own healing place and to build on my Reiki to help others spiritually. I opened my heart again through holistic healing; I began meditating every day. Meditation, affirmations and self Reiki treatments brought me back to my heart centre. I felt myself healing and growing stronger. I found my strength not through controlling the events that happened around me but by accepting them as they were. Taking each moment as a learning experience, I found myself.

I moved back to Cambridge, returned to school and worked reception at a health and wellness centre. I had the two things in my life I felt were most important. I was studying for security and gaining experience and learning new holistic techniques for what I love. I found balance in my life. I gained new love which had its ups and downs but ultimately gave me that final pillar of strength I needed to truly move forward in my life.

I know who I am today. I may be a daughter, a sister, a friend, a love, a philosopher, a witch, a healer, a bookworm, a survivor and a writer but I am so much more. I am at the core a child filled with the wonder of life. I am myself. I accept who I am today and the winding road that has brought me here; I am a work in progress, an ever-changing masterpiece of the Universe. I am a light in the world to help guide others to themselves. I am a teacher and a healer. I accept my titles not as masks to hide behind but as accomplishments of all that I have been through, and the strength of the human spirit. I accept myself as a multifaceted individual who does not need one definition. I am Danielle Elizabeth Sennhauser-Hughes and my life, my story, myself are still healing, growing and evolving.

* * *

*Danielle offers the world a shining light of joy as she helps other find their heart centre. She is a Holistic Health Practitioner specializing in Energy Medicine at Let it Heal Cambridge. Through deep inner study and learning from holistic and spiritual teachers, Danielle has developed her unique heart-centred approach to bring healing into the lives of others. Continuing her work with spiritual development, Danielle writes a monthly column in the Cambridge Citizen and is a contributing writer on Lightworkers World and One Thousand Trees Magazine.*

# I am More Than Enough:
## The Journey to Revealing my Inner Truth
by Candace Stryker

### Who am I *Really*?

This is a question I thought I knew the answer to for so long. Recently, however, the answer feels unclear. Life has a way of challenging us. Of making us question all the things we thought we knew; knew about ourselves, about life. Of humbling us and opening us up to new possibilities, if we are open to them. Well, life has brought me to this place again.

I started out as this shy little girl who always thought there was something wrong with her. I took what I could get out of life, and from the people that came to me. *Well, I should be grateful to have at least somebody, no?*, I told myself. I didn't feel worthy of more. I devalued my skills and, well, myself. It was likely the internalized mantra I grew up with ... *Never enough*. Whatever I did never felt like it was good enough in the eyes of those I most cared about. I tried harder and harder but their satisfaction never seemed to come. As I grew from a little girl to a woman I continued to strive for other's approval. Sometimes this approval would come and sometimes it wouldn't. When it didn't, my little girl feeling would come to the surface again. *Not enough...AGAIN, I'm not enough!!*

I came from a troubled home and I did everything to resist the direction my family wanted me to take. I insisted I could do everything my own way; I couldn't give them the satisfaction of having any power over me. I did things my way, but inside I was still dying for this sense of approval. *"Yes, you are good enough"* was what I secretly wanted from all my actions. And each time I didn't get it I felt let down. Then I tried again. I guess it was my self-righteous desire to be righted. To do things the way I always felt they should be done. To prove to others that *if they only saw the world as I did, everything would be so much better.*

I transferred this feeling to all my work. I never felt good enough for my work, for my friends, or even for my husband. I searched my mind for another reason they were with me. *It couldn't be because they liked me/valued me; they too must have these same expectations of me for 'more' that I have on myself,* I believed.

235

I felt like an imposter most of my life. *If people knew me and what I'm really capable of, they wouldn't have so much faith in me.* Everywhere I went, I wore this mask. I was presenting an image to the world to try to hide all that Ifelt was wrong with me. *"If anyone ever saw these dark parts of me they would surely reject me,* I imagined. I saw myself as inherently bad and trying to cover it up. *Oh those good things I did…well, they were just to make up for these bad parts of me, that's all they are,* I figured. *They aren't the real me…the real me is bad and no one would like it.*

For so long I believed my thoughts that told me I was a bad person. I felt like I was living an image I had created of who I wanted to be but really wasn't. It felt as if I had a dual personality, and I never felt real or authentic. I became lost in the negative self-talk and I never felt like I knew who the real me was. Eventually I couldn't take living this dual life any longer and I started to expose my shameful parts. It was here that I was finally able to start the process of letting them go. I slowly began to open up to people about the workings of my mind; who I thought I was, the past that I felt limited me, all the wrongs I have committed, and all the pain that I carried with me. It was a slow process at first but it felt so great. It was liberating! I began to feel free and closer to my 'real' self. I could see through the stories of my mind. I could begin to see them as simply part of the human condition. The specific details of my story were mine, but the feelings, the sense of shame, of unworthiness, of guilt, and vulnerability, were not just mine; they were everyone's.

**The Story**

For so long I identified myself as the 'victim' of my story. I was the girl that was never good enough, that no one liked, that no one understood, that felt alone and isolated in her beliefs about the world. I felt I was misunderstood. That surely other people can be happy because they've had a happy life, but me…well, it wasn't possible. *If only they had my life,* I thought, *then they would understand why it's so hard to be happy.*

Growing up I internalized my pain and punished myself for not being the person I thought I should be. I didn't feel safe to express all the shameful parts of myself with others, so I kept them buried deep on the inside. To deal with this pain I needed an outlet, however, and eventually I succumbed to an eating disorder. It was really a means of trying to control my environment. Of maintaining some sort of order to my world that felt chaotic and always out to get me, a world that I felt was determined to

236

make me suffer. The world felt cold and lonely. I felt I had to prove myself to a world that continued to reject me. *If I'm smart and beautiful, I can't be rejected.* And this belief helped me feel safe as I moved through life.

I shied away from others as I didn't feel worthy of their love and didn't feel safe being 'me' around them…the real 'me'. *If others get too close they might see my dark shadow,* I told myself. I was afraid that the part of me I tried so hard to hide might be exposed. So, for the most part, I hid from people. The friendships I did have felt distant and superficial. I settled for less connection in order to protect myself from being truly seen.

I harboured inside me this shame; this sense that not only did I do something wrong, but that 'I' as a person was wrong. The shame prevented me from seeking and obtaining what I really wanted deep inside…to be seen. To be accepted as I was. The voices in my head informed me that it wasn't safe to be vulnerable, to expose myself; it believed that my shame was mine alone and made me inherently 'less than' others. Hiding from others felt like the safest place to be.

I told and retold this sad story in my mind over and over. I stayed stuck in the pain, in the suffering. The story itself became my identity.

Eventually the pain became too much to bear, and I developed an eating disorder. My desire to control my environment (the food, the people, the conditions of my life) became so stressful that I couldn't take it anymore. I remember one day getting off the bus and it felt like so much effort just to walk home. I felt like what I imagined I might feel at 80 but I was only 20. That was it … I knew in that moment I had to get help. I joined an eating disorder self-help group. I told my boyfriend, I told my family, I exposed my secret. The most powerful part was being able to connect with others who were experiencing similar challenges. Being able to share my story and see others around the room nod and say, "me too", and being able to hear their story and being able to nod and reply, "wow…me too!!". It was then that the shame lost its grip on me. I knew I wasn't alone. From there, healing became possible

Just as I felt I had healed one pain, however, another pain emerged. I let go of the eating disorder, the social anxiety disorder, and I felt the desire to bring life into this world. I was ready, I believed, so we tried…and tried…and tried…and nothing happened. My friends would share their celebrations of new life and I just couldn't be excited for them. I wanted to and I pretended I was but I felt threatened. The feelings of 'less than' emerged again. Now I wasn't punishing myself, but I believed God was. *He must know about all my selfish ways, all the 'badness' inside me, and has deemed me unworthy to bear children.* The pain surfaced again. The suffering came back.

There was nothing I could do. Some things in life just are. I realize now that I thought having a child was another way of proving myself to the world. I felt a child would validate me, prove me worthy of existing. It would allow me to create another human being the way I felt a human should be...just like me. I was unconscious to all my self-righteous ways.

I carried this pain and sense of inherent unworthiness into my marriage as well. It felt unsafe to face the world alone so I clung fearfully to my spouse. *At least he is with me...protecting me from this scary world.* His presence validated my existence. *I have a husband so I must be loveable. At least I can appear this way to the world if he is beside me.*

But even this can't work for long. I can see now how my need to control my body and my social interactions was bound to manifest in other ways as well. I attempted to pass along my sense of 'rightness' to my husband, feeling like I needed someone to agree with me about how things 'should' be, to prove my worth ... to finally feel 'good enough'. So I tried to mold and shape him too into the person I felt he should be. I guess at some level I knew I was doing this and I harboured a subtle inner shame about this too. This was just another way I was 'bad', and another reason to hide myself from others. *They might see my motives and think less of me,* I imagined. *How can you not even love and accept your own husband when that is what he gives to you?* I would sulk at my inability to offer this to him.

Eventually my disbelief in his love for me drove me to seek it in another. I wanted to be needed, valued ... and I never felt I obtained this from my husband. He was always the one I needed. *To be worthy I must be needed,* I mistakenly believed. *And someone out there must want what I have to offer.* With time, this belief manifested itself as another man; a man I felt finally needed me. Although we never started an intimate relationship, the feeling was there, the desire was strong. I believed I was 'in love'. But the fear of leaving the 'safety' and 'security' of what I had felt unbearable. I couldn't. A part of me yearned for the independence of leaving the comfort of the known for the risk of the unknown...but...I just didn't have it in me.

Then my worst fear came true. My husband asked for a separation. *He* wanted to part ways. The pain this caused was enormous. I never felt like I could do it on my own…survive. I literally felt like I 'needed' my husband to protect me, to provide for me. It was how my whole life had been to that point, depending on others to keep me safe in the world, believing others knew more about the world than I did. When he asked me to leave, the fear, the pain, and the insecurities in myself all came to the surface. It was as if this pain I carried in other parts of my life spilled over into all parts of my life.

This pain was fear…fear rooted in my old mantra of 'not good enough'. It was as though this belief I carried with me actually made me act in ways that confirmed it was true. I was like a detective, continuously on the look-out for all the ways I failed, all the ways I didn't measure up to this ideal to which I held myself. I could not love and accept my husband, I could not love and accept my situation, I could not love and accept anyone fully, because I could not love and accept myself. I was still not 'good enough' in my own eyes.

**How did the journey to healing began?**

Many changes in life seem to happen slowly and incrementally. These were big challenges I encountered, but their transformation of me was a slow progression of realizations, and surrendering to what I could not control.

What I see now is that it is most often not one dramatic thing that changes us, but rather the constant shaping of us by life itself. It is the little things that happen every day that shape us into the people we are. For me, there was always this background desire to escape my pain that I believe drew me into healing, into the spiritual realm. I was never really religious, or raised in a religious home, but a part of me felt there must be something more to this life, that this pain cannot be for nothing. There must be a purpose to it all.

I felt this inner urge drawing me to explore the spiritual dimension but I didn't know where to start. I tried self-help books ... but I wanted a community; a community where I felt safe to express and expose myself. I was searching for a place where I could finally feel like I belonged.

I experimented with meditation, I went to counseling, and I allowed myself to gradually expose my shadow self to different people. Over time, I transformed. It wasn't one thing but a combination of everything that led to this transformation. A slow process of letting go and letting life be my guru, my teacher ... allowing it to mold and shape me. Being open to possibilities and opportunities as they presented themselves.

## The Realizations

As I opened myself to life itself...everything around me became full of meaning and purpose. Every person, every situation, and every action had meaning. They were opportunities to see my patterns, to learn and grow. No longer was the world against me, the world was now my teacher. *I am here on this earth for a reason*, I now believed, *and it is up to me to take the opportunities and obstacles presented to me, and use them to help me see myself more clearly*. The people, the situations presenting themselves to me each and every day were there to help me practise being the person I really was; the person I always wanted others to see me as but didn't feel I lived up to. The loving, kind, and generous person, the patient, beautiful, and trusting person. The voice of my 'bad' self wasn't really me; it was the conditioning of my mind, the past replaying in my mind of 'not enough'. With this realization I could finally let the ideal image of myself go. I could finally rest in 'me'...as 'me', without needing to be any other.

## Realization #1 – I Can Change My Perspective

As I once again fall 'victim' to the story in my mind, I can see now how easy it is. To remain stuck rehashing the stories of the past, the struggles to achieve the dreams of the future, and the challenges that continue to present themselves as we move through life. I can see it now. It is a story. It is a series of thoughts I'm choosing to believe that are not necessarily true. This is how I healed myself the first time around, with the eating disorder. I stopped believing my thoughts. I challenged them. *Is it really true that I can't trust myself around food? That I'm too big? That ALL food is bad?*

Not only did I begin to see that my thoughts are not necessarily true, but that they are based on a set of assumptions about the world. I was living my life through the eyes of fear. Scared of what other people thought of me, of making a 'mistake', of missing out on something. So instead of relaxing into life and going with where life wanted to take me, I resisted. I felt most comfortable where I was, with the story I knew, with the pain I carried. I had no idea it was all just a story. It was really in hearing other people's stories that it clicked for me. My story is just that; a story based on what I've been taught to believe about the world. I wasn't the only one who has experienced pain, shame, guilt; we all have. As I finally felt brave enough to share my story, other people opened up and told me their stories too. I started to see I wasn't the only one who has struggled through life… all of us have to some degree. My story wasn't mine alone, it was ALL of our stories.

Through the sharing of stories I also began to see that other people have had pain but they have chosen to see it differently. Some have chosen to rise above their pain and some have chosen to suffer; it all depends on how they decided to perceive their situation. *If others were able to rise above their pain, why can't I?*, I wondered. How could I transform this pain, this suffering, to help others, to free others from their pain, to help us see our universal human experience and not suffer alone, as others have done for me? Looking for how this pain has shaped me for the better…slowly began to my dominate thoughts.

### Realization #2 – I have nothing to fear!

Once I realized I wasn't alone, I began to walk through the world with a new mantra … *I'm fearless!* I repeated this short statement to myself as a reminder of all the times I felt fear in life; the times I would feel myself holding back from what I really wanted, and from being me, in the fullness of who I am. I began to challenge those fearful thoughts. *Are they really true? What is it I am really scared of? What is the worst thing that could happen even if I 'failed'?*

These two words, *I'm fearless,* …have helped me come face to face with all the little fears I encounter as I walk through life. All those times I stop myself from speaking up when I have something to say, from dancing the way my body wants to move, from saying no when that is what I really want to say, when I see my actions coming from a place of fear, from a place of limiting assumptions about the world and who I am supposed to be in the eyes of others. It is from here I feel empowered to act differently, to act in line with who I *really* am and what I _really_ want; to act from a place of love…self-love.

### Realization #3 – Becoming Aware

Not all the time would I act on what I really wanted but it was *the process* of increasing my awareness of my thoughts that began changing me. I became aware of my actions/inactions and questioned what they were all about. I began to notice what was really stopping me; all those limiting thoughts that were holding me back. At first it was mostly small things where it didn't really matter and I could live with the results of possible failure or exposure, but then it grew. Suddenly I began living from my heart. From a place that felt true, that felt authentic, that felt loving. No longer did the fear have the same control over me.

I began acting not out of a place of heroic bravery...*I'm NOT going to let these thoughts stop me!* but rather from a place of gentle continual awareness of the falseness of my thinking...*Hmm...will anyone even remember this if I make a mistake? Will I even see them again? Do I want to rule my life with how I 'assume' they want me to act?*.

The more I became aware of my thoughts, the more I challenged them; the more I acted authentically, and the more I loved me...all parts of me. I could see that, even though I wasn't perfect at everything, I really was doing my personal best. And, oddly, the more I acted authentically, the more others actually liked me! I finally could see through the myth that *being me* wasn't *enough*.

## Realization #4 – I Can Be Now Who I Desire To Be

Through this transformation, I also realized that there is power in simple everyday decisions and experiences. In each moment we are really given the choice to be the kind of person we want to be. Once we know the qualities of that person, every experience, every decision, every conversation, and every interaction is a chance to let that person be expressed. No longer do we have to live in the state of waiting for the world to support us before we act. No longer do we think, *if only the world would support me, I could be that person*. We can begin to see the world as supportive. Each moment is a gift to us, providing us with the opportunity to let that glorious person inside us shine! Every moment transforms from a challenge to be overcome, to an opportunity to grow and act from a place of love.

I find it helpful to reflect on my life as if unfolding backwards. What would I have really wanted my life to have been about?To have added to this world? What would I want to be thinking about myself as a 90 year old? Seeing my life in this way helps me overcome the fear, the doubt, the worry. I know that I did what I came here to do...lived as the person I wanted to be. I know, by doing this, I will have no regrets, for it keeps me mindful of the bigger picture of my life. It empowers me to do *now* what I most value in life, to *be* in each moment the person I desire to become.

Life really is a series of moments, and I have come to believe that it is *how* I choose to act in those everyday moments that will matter most to me when I'm old and gray. Was I fully *there* for people? Did I do my best? Was I loving? Kind? Patient with myself and others? Was I a giver to life? So often I believe we wait for those big moments to prove that is who we are, but I can see now that it is these small moments that matter most. It is the accumulation of all the small ripples that makes up a person's character. Ironically, the more I can honour that person I want to be, the more I *am* her now.

### Realization #5 –My Challenges are My Biggest Gifts

As I look back over my life thus far, it is apparent that all those challenging moments, those times I resisted and felt life was hard and unfair, have gifted me with something. With courage, with strength, with patience, with compassion, and with confidence that I can handle whatever comes next. They have made me into the loving person that I have found myself to be, the loving person that I always was, but that remained hidden behind the past conditioning of 'not enough'. When I can see things in this way, I have to like all that I've been through, for it has molded and shaped me into the person I am today. It is not that I actively seek out challenges, but more that I feel able to welcome them when they happen. My resistance to life has diminished. Seeing that, even in the hardest of life's circumstances, they too offer gifts eases the suffering I once felt. For all the pain I've felt in the past, all the suffering I went through, I can now see it had a purpose.

### Realization #6 – I Can Be Loved Without My Mask

The most beautiful part of it all is that, the more I've let go of my mask, the prior conditioning of my mind (through the stories I've told myself about myself), the more it inspires others to do the same. It is as though the freedom and love it brings me to live freely as myself shines a light for others to follow. I've now come to see authenticity as a gift we can give to others. The more real and authentic we are, the more it gives other people permission to feel safe enough to let their real and authentic selves shine too.

When I finally exposed those deep dark shadows I carried within me, the more I actually felt loved. I felt like this huge burden had finally been lifted off of me. I felt light and energized. I felt free to be me. For I now know it to be true that I am loveable to others. I know that it is possible to not only be loved *despite* my flaws, but even more so *because* of them; because I owned them.

**Realization #7 – I Can Trust in Life. Nothing is a Mistake.**

There is this amazing power that happens when we decide to trust that whatever happens is exactly what is supposed to be happening. That all the lessons we need to learn will be given to us. To believe that we really cannot make a mistake. This is one of the most freeing discoveries I have made. Prior to this belief, I felt paralyzed by even the smallest of decisions (what to eat, what yoga mat to buy, what to be working on right now). I felt like there was a 'right' answer and I had to figure it out. Slowly I began to simply trust...trust life to provide for me exactly what I need in each moment. That there was nothing that I was 'missing' or 'not getting', that there was nothing 'wrong' with me, and that everything was exactly as it should be. *"Could it be that mistakes are not really possible?"*, I continued to contemplate.

I slowly became more and more like the cows grazing in the field, emanating this sense of peace and contentment with life. This sense of oneness with where and what they are doing. It freed my mind from the worry and anxiety of getting it wrong, of missing out on something, of the fear that was in the background, shaping so many of my decisions without me even realizing it.

Everything I did was there to teach me, to guide me. I could see that other life forms are being looked after, so why, I began to wonder, would I be any different? The cows, the birds, the trees...they do not worry but yet they survive, they live, they are. Ahh...it is safe, I came to believe. I could let go, I could trust, I could see how supportive life truly is. It is the judgments I had about my life and what should or should not be happening that made me feel uncertain, that made me feel like mistakes are possible. But other life forms don't make mistakes; they just are...and *how different am I really?*

**Realization #8 – We Are All Created Equal**

I've also realized there is no worse or better of anything. I am no worse or any better than any other person in the world. Our stories may be different, but our desire for happiness and to avoid pain and suffering is ultimately the same.

Everything exists in comparison to another; without the other there would be no way to judge it. All of the ideas of what is good or bad, pretty or ugly, are simply a matter of conditioned perceptions of the mind. An agreed upon truth shared by society. When I observe the cows grazing peacefully in the fields, their tails wagging, I see no shame in them of their bodily functions. They do not hide from one another; they do not feel bad for their natural impulses. They do not try to be anything other than they are. They run if they want to run, they eat what they want to eat, and they sleep when they want to sleep. How simple but how profound! They do not strive to be anything other than they are; something that I feel most of us truly desire for ourselves, to be and do what we truly want to do, to be free of trying to control life.

In these moments I can see that it is the human mind that judges these experiences that brings us shame, that makes us feel 'less than', and that makes us feel fearful of each other's judging minds. Because of this we cannot relax into who we are and it is this that prevents us from truly enjoying the experience of life.

**Realization #9 – When I Truly Love Myself...I Whole-Heartedly Love Others.**

I used to feel that another's success somehow diminished mine. I would hope to be the first one to achieve, to get it right, to have the most likes, to be the best at whatever I did (in the eyes of whoever was judging), but then somehow things began to shift. I'm not sure what exactly happened but something inside me began to love a little more. Maybe to love myself more? Later things never felt like they were in short supply; I wasn't in competition with others, I was there to cooperate and share in others' successes, as they were there to celebrate and share in mine. I would see others on their way up; they would come tell me all the exciting things happening in their life and no matter where I was in my own life, I would fill up on their happiness. No longer did their story make me feel 'less than', rather I continued to feel an equal. It was like I got it...I *really* got it. There is a plan for all of us. We each came to this earth to do something, to contribute something in our own small (or big) way. What one person does is part of their own life's purpose and has nothing to do with my story or purpose. Actually, sometimes I now use their successes as inspiration to affirm that *yes, if they can do it, so can I!* To keep me dreaming and believing in the story I'm creating.

**Realization #10 – My truth is uniquely mine. No one has to understand it but me.**

Sometimes our own truth (the story we're creating) doesn't make sense to others, it never fully can…just like their truth can never fully make sense to us. We are each on our own journey. It is humbling to see the world from so many different perspectives. When we can honour our own truths, we can be there to help others follow their own truths (without impinging judgment). Our journey is the only one we can ever *really* know and understand. And this realization can free us from the desire to 'correct' or 'mold' other people into our view of reality. When we become free to be ourselves, we can let others become free to be themselves as well…to follow their own path.

**Realization #11 - I am everything.**

Over time, I have slowly begun to see what brought me all the joy, love, and peace I was feeling. The reason I was so happy was that I began to see myself as imperfect, to see myself as containing all these opposing dimensions in me. I was everything…the 'good' and the 'bad' all rolled into one being. I was sometimes clean and sometimes messy, I was sometimes a conformist and sometimes totally unique, sometimes a doer and achiever and sometimes content with simply being. When I could see myself in this way I began to accept myself more fully, as the fullness of the being I am. I wasn't perfect but neither was anyone else. I wasn't exactly what I wanted to be but I was doing my best.

**Putting it All Together: I am enough!**

The world looks and feels so much different from when I was that shy little girl always looking for approval, wanting to be noticed, to be acknowledged, to be good enough. Now I just seem to know, in some deep part of my being, that there is enough for all, that I'm good enough as I am, that my life makes a difference (even if it is just sharing a smile on the street), and most of all that it is safe to trust life. God/The Divine/The Universe/Holy Spirit (whatever you want to call it) is there with me even when it feels far away. It is there unfolding its plan through me. If I can open and allow it, I am a channel for this energy to flow. When I can be in this place…everything seems miraculous.

What I love most about this part of life is that all the comparisons, the judging, and the placing of people on a scale of either above or below me seems to have disappeared. I just am. I am me and there is no one like me. Others are just themselves in their own unique way. It suddenly seems almost impossible to compare, because to compare would mean to diminish someone's greatness (others or our own).

Without this feeling of 'less than' or 'more than', a whole new way of being in the world opens up. A way in which we can genuinely encourage and love one another, and want the best for each other. It is freeing not to feel like your worth is relative to the success or failure of others. Your worth becomes all about you; what you decide to make of it. It is a matter of knowing that simply by existing you matter.

Suddenly you can see beauty in another and it doesn't become a threat to you; you can see it and appreciate it. Suddenly someone says something brilliant and you can honour that person's creative genius without secretly harbouring resentment for not being 'the one' to come up with the idea. Suddenly you see the world as supportive, kind, and full of creativity and beauty.

How can one person be 'better' than another? Maybe in terms of outward possessions, beauty, or achievements; but these too are all relative to the perceiver, determined not by us as individual people but by society…judgments of good and bad, right and wrong. Without the mind, without the inner critic…the judge in our heads…everything suddenly becomes what it truly is, a unique expression of The Divine. And this is a beautiful place to reside.

With this outlook the world comes alive. Every person and every experience you encounter becomes more interesting and enables you to see the uniqueness they offer the whole…the gifts they share.

It is interesting how the human condition wants to judge, how we voluntarily place ourselves on the measuring block of beauty, of fame, of success, of 'stuff'. Something is inherently wrong with this picture. When we see the world through these eyes, it feels like we won't 'get' our share. We aren't enough, we have to prove our very existence. Life feels stressful and forceful….we have to 'make' things happen to keep us happy.

When we come to a place of loving ourselves we can begin to see the world through eyes of abundance and love. There is enough for everyone. There is enough love, enough gifts within everyone to have a place in the whole. There is no one that lies outside the whole; we can begin to value our gifts as they are without needing to have them externally validated to prove our worth, to prove our very existence.

For so long I resided in this place. Feeling like I was nothing unless my job, my friends, my relationships, my beliefs made me more than others. I had to be 'more than' someone/anyone in order to feel worthy. But what about those people at the bottom? If my worthiness depends on someone else being inherently 'unworthy', what does this really say about me? Why would they be here, on this earth, if they aren't worthy of anything? That couldn't be possible.

When we no longer compare our worth to others, we find a place of inner peace. The striving, the yearning for more dissipates. We become more genuine and authentic in our actions, and love flows naturally from us as we now see our worth being connected to the worth of all others; everything we do as working in cooperation with the whole.

I guess the real learning is that, the more I've been able to trust and accept myself in the fullness of who I am, the more I've been able to live from an authentic place. And the more true I am to me; the more love, peace, and joy I feel, and the more I can genuinely share it with others; the less judgment I've come to harbour toward myself or others, and the more I've come to see that I am enough. I'm not perfect…but I don't have to be.

The more my mantra has shifted from *I'm not enough…to…I AM more than enough.*

\* \* \*

*Candace's passion is to bring joy into the lives of those she touches, to help people overcome fear and self-doubt and begin to live the lives of their dreams. She writes weekly messages that inspire us to think differently about our lives, to trust life, and to live life authentically and passionately … to live the lives we have been called forth to live. She lives in Baden, Ontario.*

# From Surviving to Thriving
## by Trischa Newfield

*"Oh, God, please help me believe the truth about myself,*
*no matter how beautiful it is."*
The Truth - Macrina Wiederkehr

Do you remember the child's nursery rhyme verse, *"sugar and spice and everything nice, that's what little girls are made of"*? Well, this is my story of wanting to be made of everything nice so I could be loved and valued for being sweet! Mmm…sweet like sugar!

That *sweet road* led me to becoming abused physically, sexually, emotionally, and religiously. As I recant my personal war, you will see a glimpse of where I began, what I experienced, and my perception of the events that took place in my life. Women, children and men around the world experience the horrors of abuse. What allows some to pick up the pieces and rise in triumph?

Determination, courage and wisdom shaped my life. I never set out to be a statistic, or to allow abuse to dictate my earthly experience. I consciously and systematically decided that the sum of my experience would not be my equation. I changed my script and became the landowner of my existence. This journey connected me to others that are seeking freedom from entrapment in order to pursue a life called "inspired." I am grateful for these supporters who have become my cheerleaders. In the darkest hours of my life, I was never alone. They stood by me, provided safety, compassion and love, and they have cheered me on to thrive.

When the cells of the body, mind and spirit were so overwhelmed with negative experience, often it was difficult to trust others or even one's self. I spent years feeling numb. Real joy, excitement, curiosity, and self-recognition vanished.

Today is different. I am excited about living. I cherish and accept who I am and how I feel. I acknowledge my gifts. Resolving the issues of abuse and why I attracted those elements into my life was an intensely painful process but it has led to many rewards. I could easily name many of the abuses: there were police reports, hospital visits, scars, bruises, pain, tears, broken furniture and broken hearts to identify that. Where the battle wounds were of a mental and emotional war; there were no names for that but my spirit was lost and my soul was numb. That journey of discovery would be the most penetrating.

I had great difficulty stopping the cycle of abuses. I would ask myself over and over again - *How did this happen? Why did it happen **again**? Don't other people experience harm in their life; why did my experiences infuse me with paralysis? Where, when and how had my true image of self receded within? Didn't anyone notice? Didn't anyone care?*

The signs should have been obvious, but somehow I could not predict the next attack or how to stop it from happening. It was like I was dead inside, despite being very much alive. My sense of self became my husband, my family, my friendships, my children, my home, my job...but my soul was gone. Eventually as I surrendered to it all, I experienced a crack in the armour of protection that I had carefully crafted and guarded. I began to experience transformation, which I call healing. Life opened up endless positive possibilities for me. My past life began to fade and my new life, ordained as it was to be, emerged.

With baby steps and one day at a time I began to walk in peace, compassion, wisdom and essence. I learned that my obsession with being sweet led me to an inauthentic life of people-pleasing that ultimately led to my life of abuse. I came to understand that I lived in a war zone, not overseas, but in my home, in my workplace, in my school, and in my church. I started to identify that:

•This kind of in-house war breeds humans suffering on the most intimate of levels and it leads to post-traumatic stress.
•Survival is a primal force.
•Changing my thoughts in the present can change my future.
•Women need to unify, and our duty is to be supportive and loving to each other, to raise our offspring in divine intelligence, wisely guiding and protecting all children from violence.

By the time I was two months old, I knew the world and everyone I depended on in it were not safe. I cried every night, and the only way to console me was for father or mother to bring me into their bed. This disturbed father's sleep because he worked the early morning shift. Complaining to a friend at work, both father and friend formulated a plan to stop this nighttime behaviour. The story is told that in the dark and stillness of the night my father lay in wait. As soon as my fussing and crying began, my father stood over me and shouted for me to stop and spanked me. I never cried at that time of the night again!

Between seven and eight months of age I knew that if I performed I could get applause and make people laugh. I was a store demonstrator of the *"Jolly Jumper."* Mother, still prideful, recants the story.

One day, father happened to be in the store and saw a crowd of shoppers gathered. They were laughing, giggling and pointing. To his chagrin he saw his baby in the middle of the department floor strapped into a strange contraption bouncing and jumping. He promptly took me out of the *"Jolly Jumper"* and carried me to the car shouting, "My child is *no monkey* in a zoo!"

By the time I was one year old I felt the effects of the liquid elixir of my family. For my first birthday party my grandfather made me a wooden red leather padded rocking chair. Encircled by my parents, grandparents, uncles and aunts, the photos show me sitting in the rocking chair, in a pretty ruffled dress with a beer bottle pressed to my lips. Those pictures still serve as a reminder to what may have contributed to my future great escape. Alcohol, shame, guilt, and violence became the world I lived in.

When I was five years old and my brother was four, my perception of the inner circle of my family changed when a relative came to live in our home. Two incidences of sexual abuse by that person occurred: one involved an act on myself and one an act on my brother. I held my brother's hand and we waited outside on the front steps until our parents came home. I told my father what happened, and Dad – a Korean War veteran with a violent temper— proceeded to go into *combat mode*. If I close my eyes and think back to that day, I can hear the sound of fists pounding flesh. I can see a swollen almost unrecognizable face. I can see blood, and I can hear Mother's screams and cries. Although I didn't see that relative for many years, the damage was done, lessons were learned, and a pattern soon developed.

My parents tell of their own chaotic life; which perhaps is why they joined a radical religious group, which promised them peace, love and an end to wickedness. Father— not a religious man— was enticed to join in order to save his marriage. Mother seized it to save herself. This led to another kind of abuse for me. Family and friends that did not join were not to be fellowshipped with. And with one phone call or letter the people I knew and loved were gone in an instant.

At the age of six on a hot summer day, our new church friends were visiting when their much older son came into my room, shut the door and molested me. I could hear parents' laughter and voices. I remember hoping and not hoping at the same time that the door would open and that my father would rescue me. That did not happen. Once the friends left I told dad what happened. I expected him to react like he had before but this time he only said he didn't know how to tell his new church friend. He looked like he was going to cry and told me not to be alone with that person. In my young mind I think I realized that I was never going to be protected by Dad again.

From that time on until I was 24 years old my parents would never know about the many people who hurt me sexually and physically. If asked, everyone would tell you that I was a sweet girl. I was developing into a real chameleon.

At the age of 17, my family forced me into a religiously-arranged marriage. In small-town USA, on my second night of marriage to a high school athlete and wrestler, this 210 pound solid mass of muscle methodically placed a pillow over my face, and began punching and choking me in a fit of rage. As a relative lightweight,weighing less than 120 pounds, I was unable to defend myself. I stopped struggling and laid motionless until he stopped.

This was not an isolated incident. Each time he committed these acts of rage towards me, which included not only physical abuse but forced sexual attacks; he would fall at my feet and weep like a baby asking my forgiveness. I kept the secret for fear of another attack. Three years later I gave birth to a healthy baby girl even though he pushed me down a flight of fourteen stairs, kicked and choked me and once left me in a field to die.

When that man interfered with our daughter, I gained the strength to leave and to tell the secret. My daughter and I lived with Mom and Dad. I joined a Battered Women's group and learned a great deal more about domestic violence, psychological terror and sexual abuse. Soon I found an apartment and began a new life with my daughter. Although the divorce was long and ugly, the day came when the Supreme Court of Canada's Justice granted the divorce, awarded me sole custody of my daughter, and mandated a 500-metre no-contact restraining order and judgment. My daughter was finally safe. I was numb.

The sexual abuse she experienced from eleven days old until she was three years old was severe, and my journey with her was complex, intense and confusing. I continued to be in and out of therapy, but never stayed long enough for anyone to completely transform the metamorphosis of my soul. Before a therapist would get close to uncovering the *real me*, I'd leave. I believed that if you got to know me you wouldn't like me and that when you didn't find me sweet you would abandon me. I was convinced no one would ever stay with me. To survive I had to bury myself. People saw only what I wanted them to see. Truth and honesty were pieces of my clothing that I could put on and take off as need be.

Shortly after the divorce, unable to cope with my life, I made an unsuccessful attempt of suicide. Not long after that I met a man who rescued me from my life. I clung to him like a life raft. I was excommunicated from my church. I could have nothing to do with my religious community, including having no contact whatsoever with my parents, my brother, my aunt or cousins. My friends were not allowed to talk to me or even make eye contact with me. I was dead to everyone's sight, including God's. I was made to believe that this was done in the name of God, love, and righteousness. For me this was confirmation that I could be abandoned— that I was nothing.

We were married and I felt a new kind of excitement and happiness. Life was exciting and refreshing. He adopted my daughter. We were both safe now. Then three months after our wedding he violently crushed me like a pretzel in a fit of rage. The violence escalated. Unlike the first husband, this man was a daily drinker and drug user. He never once apologized for hurting me. It was always my fault. Soon life became increasingly unpredictable and isolating; both my daughter and I walked a tight rope. I could not reach out to my parents, although they did stay connected to my daughter. The drugs and alcohol were different beasts that I had never known. I did the only thing I was equipped to do – SURVIVE – one awful day after another.

Two years later I was pregnant, busy in our flourishing home renovation and building business, looking good on outside appearances but sinking in quick sand. The business money was missing and unaccounted for and I soon realized that my husband's addiction to drugs and alcohol were eating up any profit. The incidences of domestic violence escalated. When the baby was eight months old I ran away to a friend's home on the island, taking my two daughters with me. I started to feel safe, but he found me and sweet-talked me into coming back to the mainland.

Life was civil for a while but the cycle of violence returned with a vengeance. I began to live in and out of suitcases; my daughters were my only concern. Each time that I would do better, he would find me and I would go back with him. It was like a revolving door with no change in outcome. Over the next few years I had two more babies. What kind of a life was it for them to see and hear? I didn't know what to do but survive and hope it would stop so we could get back the sweet life.

The last year I was with him I was admitted to the hospital nineteen times. I was beaten so badly that when shown police photographs I couldn't recognize myself. Of course, he was no longer living with us but on one of his many attempts to break in a neighbour called the police. Four RCMP officers attended the scene. As providence or divine intervention would have it, a friend's husband was one of the attending officers. He took me aside and said he shouldn't really tell me this but because he knew me he would. He said my children could not grow up seeing this kind of savagery; they deserved better and the system had been flagged to apprehend my children if I allowed the abuser back into my life. He told me to pick a spot on the map and get out.

That was March of 1991. On July 2, 1991 selling 95% of what I owned, with $1300 in my pocket, I was on a Greyhound bus with a one-way ticket from British Columbia to Ontario, in search of a new beginning. I held in my hand the court-approved documents, which permitted me to leave that province with our four children. Arriving in Hamilton, Ontario on a cold wet stormy Friday evening, my four daughters (ages 3, 5, 7, and 14) started a new life. I never saw that man again.

When the dust settled and I could finally breath again, I began seeing a therapist. My feelings of worthlessness began to break apart and I was shedding that skin to become a productive happy member of society. I felt joyous, happy and free.

At age 37, being only a high school graduate, I enrolled at Mohawk College. I achieved the Dean's Honours list. I received a large cash award from the Soroptimist Society, which offers grants for the advancement of human rights and the status of women throughout Canadian Colleges and Universities. I changed my major and received a scholarship for women in technology. I worked part-time at the college. I provided a stable environment for my children to grow up in and felt that our lives were on the road to recovery. I decided that my own use of alcohol was a crutch and gave it up. This enabled me to soberly learn more about my life's path and about myself.

Years later I married for a third time. Although red flags appeared closer to the wedding date, I still went ahead with it thinking it was pre-wedding jitters. Some years later I realized this marriage was not a true and honest partnership. I made a mistake. I raised my concern to him, secretly hoping he'd change and we'd be happy, but it became apparent that I was the only one in the partnership trying to make it work. I decided to divorce. That too was long and painful. However, I stayed true to myself and to the commitment that I'd made to myself years prior, *"I will not come this far to die like this."* I forgave him and I forgave me. Today my life is beautiful. I am free. I am true to myself and I am happy. I recognize my humanness, I give myself permission to change my mind, I look at my obligation to my **own** life, I commit to living my life authentically, no secrets, no deception. I recognized my mistakes faster than I did before, and I was healthy enough to gain my power to end that marriage with dignity and grace. I felt no weakness to return to a situation that was unhealthy.

During this transformation from 1996 on, I worked on myself. I started to gather tools for the toolkit of my life. Miracles sprang up all over the place. I was introduced to Young Living Therapeutic Oils. Within a short time of using these oils I started to feel physically and mentally better. Some of my negative emotions were clearing up. I thoroughly researched the founder, his philosophy, his mission, and his personal integrity. I agreed with his commitment in taking care of our planet while harvesting and distilling oil from roots, bark, leaves, branches, buds and flowers. I learned that the living oils are a rich blessing from our Creator to aid our health: mentally, spiritually, emotionally and physically, and that this man was in partnership with the Creator to help the living, whether it be humans or animals, to have a more healthy life. Not only was my physical health improving but also my mental health was becoming clearer, my emotions were starting to match my truth and I was becoming more authentic. It was contagious; I shared the oils with my children and parents.

I learned the concept of forgiveness. This opened me up to a new kind of freedom. Forgiveness brought about a kind of serenity that I had not known before. Compassion for the way the abusers in my past were raised and empathy towards their own wounded spirit helped me to forgive them but in NO way did this excuse them from their actions of wrongdoing. Forgiveness is not about the acceptance of evil. Some acts are so premeditated and reprehensible that there is no acceptance. I made sure to protect myself from these abusers even though from a distance I forgave them the horrors they carried out. My understanding of forgiveness never meant that I condoned, accepted or excused their behaviour. In order to live a spiritual life and continue to grow, I had to be aware of their pain and forgive them, to be aware of my pain and forgive me.

These acts raised my higher self to become light from the burden of hatred, enmity, strife, conflict, rage and destruction. Today, forgiving is a habit in my life; I will not allow my cells to store negative emotions or keep sensations of pain, anger, shame or guilt. Moving forward from those negativ ties created space in mind, body and soul and I fill up with love, patience, pleasure and delight. Therefore, I am conquering my once aimless survival with creating my life of thriving.

It was then and only then that it occurred to me that survival is an instinct, something built into the core of our physical bodies and organs. We hear experiences of people who have been told by doctors that they will never walk again, that they will live only a few more days, that they will never survive a particular disease or tragedy. Yet, certain individuals defy all odds, they walk again, perhaps going on to winning a medal for accomplishing a task they were told they could never accomplish. Some recover so completely from the message of doom that they outlive or surpass life expectancy. What explains this transformation? I came to believe that at our deepest core level we all have the ability to use our mind to control our matter. I concluded that all beings are given this blueprint for success. I decided to tap into my mind and deal with the pain once and for all. I was determined to become positive in spite of the blackness and emptiness I felt.

I began a quest of enlightened masters to teach me their techniques. I devoured ancient scripts like I was starving. The more I searched, the more inspirational people were coming into my life. One turn led to another and to another until my inner motivator was fueling me with *life*.

I started to read the words and thoughts of Louise L. Hay, and through her exercises I became a more positive being. I sat in workshops with Louise and Marianne Williamson, Christiane Northrup, Wayne Dyer and more. I attended workshops with Shinzen Young and listened to countless CDs from Eckhart Tolle, Thich Nhat Hanh, Pema Chodron, The Dalai Lama and others. In their example I've been given gifts that have changed my life in a miraculous way. I feel today that I am a new person. Yes, I am still the being that the Divine intended me to be when I came to this planet, but I am living whole. Abusers are not a part of my life. If they present themselves, I recognize them more quickly, I stand up for myself and they leave. I am learning how to be open and receptive to change and to count on daily miracles. I am grateful.

My testimony of transcending negativity and turning hopeless despair into positivity remains something to which I am committed. It is a daily practice. I give myself permission to feel and to honour every feeling that a human can. When I honour the negativity that arises in me I do not carry it as baggage. I thank the negative for showing up, but then tell it to leave. That simple practice has healed me from the empty, dark, overwhelming pain that I had once lived with on a daily basis. I recognize my past feelings, memories and experiences but I am aware that, "This is *now* and that was *then*. The past can no longer hurt me without my permission. I am a beloved child of the universe. I am loved. I am safe."

My story, my life, and my presence are an opening for others. Being on solid ground and having the ability to safely look at the past is a very healing endeavour; despite the fact that it does uncover old feelings of fear, loss, pain and helplessness. At times I cannot go deep in examination without assistance from a trained professional. I am patient with myself. I remember that the brain only wants life to continue. In order for me to marry my present wish to live, and my sense of the world, with a sense of security, peace and happiness, I must be aware enough of what pain and terror are. In identifying this, I can acknowledge peace and freedom when I experience it. Simply put, when I know hot I will know cold, and when I know cold then I will know hot.

I practised standing in front of the mirror looking into my own eyes repeating positive affirmations of self-support and self-love. I have a network of core friends from all walks of life. Some are in metaphysical groups, formalized religion, the business world; some are academics and scholars. Some are younger than me, some are my age, some older, and some are illuminant grey-haired wise ones.

My parents and I have made peace with the past. They've relaxed their judgments, and today I am happy to share that those 80-year-olds are my very best friends, and I am theirs. In my youth I carried resentment, fear and negative thoughts about my parents. Today, I am so blessed that they have been here long enough to really see me, and I them. It has taken my whole life to be able to see things more clearly. It has been a journey that I am proud of. I went through the fire and came out of it refined and blessed. Today my dad and I know that both he and I are survivors of war, and we both know that we are war heroes. He survived the bloodied battles of war in Korea, and I survived the bloodied battles of war in my home, my tribe and my country. I remained in "shellshock" for years, and I knew his "shellshock." He gets that. He is gentle, kind and very open with me. He too is being helped with his post-traumatic stress syndrome by using the living oils.

My mom, once very unapproachable and rigid, is a wonderful loving caring mother, grandmother and great-grandmother. She demonstrates her love for me in numerous ways. There has been tremendous healing in our life and it is beautiful.

Even now, there are times when unexplainably the darkness of the night settles on me— when the winds of doubt sweep over me, when the pebbles of life sting me, when torrent rains of tears wash over me or the fire rages inside! When these emotions race within me, I slow down, I beseech heaven and higher self, I remove negative attachment, I reach for empowering oils, and I change my thoughts by focusing on other words. At times I simply say, *"Trischa! Just get up, get out and show up."* I may have to use this type of self-talk just to get to work, to travel, or to be with friends or family. I realize it is not the person, place or thing that has caused my unrest. I honour my word by keeping commitments and agreements.

The blessings that have presented themselves in my life by doing just that: getting up, getting out, and showing up, are monumental. I've met new friends, heard amazing life-changing stories, and I've come to know more peace than ever before. The miracle for me is that the Divine Source in the universe (my manifestation of such) cares for all creation: the animals, the birds, the insects, the vegetation, marine life, the oceans and the air we breathe. I remember that the divine source of all things created cares for every living thing including me. I connect with my inner child by looking into my own eyes every day. I say things like, *"I love you, Trischa. You and I are in this thing called LIFE together. I will never abandon you, and you will never abandon me. You and I are safe."*

Our personal history can be erased from living that torment when we embrace our nature of divine origin. The greater the level of violence, the greater the inner pain, the greater the need to remember that the incident is over and let it go.

Domestic violence and abuse are not only women's issues – they are also issues of men. 85% of all women who are abused (which is in the billions) are abused by *men!* Speaking directly to woman I say, *"We birth the human race; we birth females and males – We need to be skilled and proactive in their up-bringing. Our males need to be taught to respect, love, and honour women of all ages.* This is a vast responsibility, but our Creator knew which gender could handle it! Be proud and responsible enough to accept the task with due diligence.

As I recall my journey from childhood to present, I see that my inner courage strengthened me to go through trials that now help many. My courage rubs off, and in some way I feel that my example helps others to heal, grow, and move. For if I, so broken, bruised and battered, was able to rise from those ashes, then others too can gain the courage they need to thrive in their lives.

I remain committed to helping this planet's largest population -- women and children. By words and example I teach women to protect and care for themselves and their children. One protects what one invests in so I help women to invest in themselves. Because I walked as you have, I've felt hatred towards myself as you do and because I have moved beyond that, this equips me with the tools and the vocabulary to help you.

Please remember you can live a life that is more than SURVIVING, a life in which you are actually THRIVING. Take back your power, never say, "WHY ME?" There's NO power in why. Commit to building friendships and partnership with other women. Put heaping helpings of love into your family. Spread this love into your streets, into your cities, into your provinces, into your countries, and into your world.

With honour and grace I hope my words will act as your helper, that you will forge a new life path leading to your empowerment. I am grateful for the opportunity to share my story with you, and I support your courageous journey in creating your new life.  You too can live an inspired life in which you are thriving!

* * *

*Trischa was born and raised in British Columbia, has lived in Quebec and Ontario. She currently resides in Hamilton, Ontario. She writes, speaks, motivates, and encourages audiences of all ages to connect to each other and heal their "war wounds" of life in order to create a life worth living. Living, in her belief, is not just about breathing, eating, sleeping, and time spent in waking, but is really meant to enjoy, create, participate in, and help others.*

# Memories, Milestones, and Moving On
## by April Burrows

There is a part of me that wants to avoid completely the details of my life that have led to being invited to be a part of this book. Not because I'm still deeply wounded, or because it's a secret or I carry shame; actually, it is just the opposite. I have told the details of my story numerous times, to friends, counsellors, the police, a crown attorney, a counselling class, not to mention the public retellings which have included police training sessions on working with survivors, a women's conference, and an AGM for the Women in Crisis organization. There was even a long article in the newspaper, sharing my experiences with the police.

Basically, a very helpful part of my healing journey has been to speak my story out loud. At first, when I thought about writing my story I wondered if it would be like ripping a scab off an old wound, but it has not been like that, at least not to date. There are consequences, however; to my family, my kids (who were young when I went through my court ordeal), and for my family of origin (who probably still find it hard that our dirty laundry got aired and they had no choice in the matter). Honestly, it's just not something I spend a whole lot of time thinking about anymore. But I know there are likely things that I do or think that are related to those early childhood experiences that affect me and I'm just not cognisant of them.

Simply put, I don't want these details to be the focus of this story I am about to tell. The details are not who I am, but they do deserve a place here because they are part of my experience and therefore are part of what has made me the person I am today – both the good and, well, the shadowy side of me.

Here's the background:

When I was a young girl an uncle of mine was inappropriate with me. It never even dawned on me to tell anyone. I cannot relay the full impact; however, I do know that it set me on a course of self-denial and created in me a blind spot to self-care and self-preservation. Due to an inability to understand boundaries, I found myself in a couple situations where I would be taken advantage of and I was oblivious to the potential worst-case scenarios. Yet, on many accounts, I look back at the times where things could have been much worse ... at least that's how it might appear on the outside. Oddly enough, I had several girlfriends who confided in me that similar things were happening to them, but I never shared my own experiences. I was a listening ear and a confidante. I think I appeared always to be in control, fairly confident, for the most part likeable. I always had a job and did well, and got rewarded in my workplaces with good hours, raises etc. I was a good worker. But there was an internal drama that continued to unfold. Many times I thought of suicide, and some of my behaviours and friendships were quite risky.

It wasn't until my 30s, around the time my kids were about two and four years old, that it really all sunk in, and launched me into a deep depression. That was also the time I approached the police. I was keenly aware that this was a family issue and that I was not the only one who experienced this. I wanted to make sure that we exposed this in our family so that no one else would be hurt. Unfortunately, the other females who the police approached to corroborate my story and to build a case all said that, while they had indeed sustained similar abuse, they were not willing or able to join their voice with mine to lay charges. There are six of us in total. So I did it on my own. It was more than a two-year process and, if it hadn't been for my court support person at Women in Crisis, nothing would have come of the offences. At her insistence, after a year and a half, the police finally talked to my uncle. He confessed and shared the five other names of those he had violated. He got two years' probation. Recently, I found out that quite a few of my family members never did learn what had happened, so in some ways what I had hoped would result from my coming forward (exposure and healing within our family) didn't even get addressed.

However, I believe that if we follow our guidance (which for me is God, along with my inner Self), we tap into the intuition and knowing we need in order to trust the process and not get hung up on the outcome.

What this journey forced me to do was to slow down my life and take stock of what was happening. What did I need to take care of and deal with now? What did I want my future to be?

So -- I got the story of hurt out of the way and now I want to share my story of healing. At least thus far.

My healing journey has been assisted by a number of counsellors, therapists and mentors over the years. Some of them have influenced me in deeply lasting ways, and I am profoundly grateful.

At one point I was seeing a Jungian therapist. One thing that has really stuck with me was a comment she made about our auras. She said we are born with an intact beautiful bubble or aura but, when violation happens (sexual or otherwise) to someone at an early age, that aura is shattered and we spend the rest of our lives putting the pieces of the aura back together again.

I don't know a thing about auras and such, but what I do know is that each of us is brought into the world as a perfectly whole human being, and when the adversities of the human existence happen it feels like our sense of self is shattered. That image really resonated with what I had been experiencing and feeling about my life. It validated my struggle, it validated my challenge with feeling like, even after I shared my story, I wasn't able to "just pick up the pieces" and move on. It's really not that simple. The beautiful outcome that this description had for me was a lifting of a veil of darkness. It gave me an understanding that I wasn't "damaged goods", but instead that I was on a journey to collect back the pieces of myself that had spilled away those many years ago. It gave me hope because I understood, and I knew I would overcome it.

*"The wound is the place where the Light enters you."* Rumi

Near the end of my sessions, one of my counsellors who is also a great teacher, shared with me about a framework he had heard at a workshop. It was about the three stages in the journey of survivors. Those stages (or milestones, as I see them) are "Victim", "Survivor", and "Authentic Self". My counsellor asked if this made sense in relation to my personal experience. Indeed it did. It was so very affirming of what I had experienced over the past few years that it gave me hope that I was heading towards something I believe we all need to head towards -- becoming my authentic self. It was so cool to think there was so much more in me that God had created me to be, and that it was something I could achieve. I guess I am a true seeker in that sense as I'm definitely still on the authentic self-discovery journey, although I can stake my claim to a few things.

Here's how these three milestones were experienced on my journey:

## Victim

***"I told my story."*** Once I finally acknowledged what I had actually experienced, my need to stuff down my emotions, my anger and my shame began to go away ... slowly. Unfortunately, part of my story was that my sharing was entrusted to someone who used me to meet her own need to be needed. She was a minister who felt she had the skills to walk with me as a mentor and counsellor. This part of my journey still brings knots to my stomach but I have a feeling, now that I'm sharing it, the hooks can be released.

If I were to offer advice here it would be to:

• Trust your gut. No one but your family has a responsibility to you to be your family. Anyone else who claims they will always be there for you may or may not. For me, I often felt really alone, and that I didn't belong. If someone suggested that I did belong, I lapped it up and became overwhelmed with my need for that closeness. This frequently led to more hurt. In the end, you need to find the source within yourself. For me, that source is God. It's when I could claim those things for myself that new and healthy relationships began to emerge.

• Find a person to talk to that understands the kind of experiences you have had and knows how to help you do your own work. No one can do your work for you. My counsellor at Women in Crisis was such an angel for me. For more than two years, she helped me by providing tools, encouraging creativity, and by being deeply present to me. I will be forever grateful for her presence as I dealt with my family, the courts and that wonky minister, and then got on with my life.

*"I am the beloved."* I was raised in a Christian tradition. My childhood relationship with God was one of God as judge and punisher. What I had been told as a child was that I was a sinner who needed to be forgiven, and that I had to ask Jesus into my heart in order to avoid eternity in hell. I saw movies like "Mark of the Beast" that scared people into conforming to Christianity so they didn't experience the end of the world and the hell it would bring. I saw exorcisms and I was exposed to adults who essentially talked about this good and wonderful God but who did not so nice things to people. The day I realized that God was not and did not want to be my judge or punisher, but was my companion, friend, lover even, and most of all saw me as The Beloved, was the day that my sense of freedom to explore my true potential and the divine within me truly began to blossom. This journey to spiritual healing was just as significant as that of emotional healing from the sexual interference.

• I think we are spiritual beings created to be in relationship with God, Self and Others, and through that we will find wholeness. For as long as I can remember, even prior to my religious understanding, I always felt within nature and within myself that there was something drawing me towards love and knowing. When in relationship with all parts we will find delight and challenge too, but that's how we stay humble and can create new and wonderful transformational opportunities.

• My Spiritual Director was the person who listened me into life. Her wise yet gentle counsel about my relationship with God guided me through my experience of depression, anger, and frustration, and gave me a safe place to explore the loving God that was calling me to be – *key word BE* -- myself in my fullness.

## Survivor

*"It doesn't have to be this way."* My work with my counsellor and my Spiritual Director allowed me to see that I survived my experiences, and I don't have to let them have control over my life any longer. This realization gave me such deep hope, yet at the same time unleashed some anger towards my uncle, my family, the church and all those related to the events in my life that caused me such pain. During this time the court drama ended, my uncle was charged and I began to tramp across the large chasm from survivor to authentic self. It's not a short journey, at least not for me, but it's a very adventurous and challenging place. This is a place of exploration and grit and courage and surrender. For each of us this journey is different, but for me it is where I was finally allowed to feel, to fall apart, and to pick myself up again. Even as we cross over the bridge from survivor to the authentic self and plant our feet on the other side, we may find that a part of us has been left on the bridge.

## Authentic Self

*"This is the person who I am created to be."* Being the person others decide you are, the world pressures you to be, or people want you to be, forces you to stay small so they feel comfortable or superior to you. Being my authentic self is heaven; being my other self is pure hell. Dr. Phil calls that other self the Fictional Self, which makes sense to me. I don't think we ever fully arrive or stay in the place of our authentic self but rather I think this is a place of intention. An intention to believe in yourself, believe in the Oneness of all people, and the goodness of and in people. An intention to

believe in the strength of the spirit working within and between and beyond all of ourselves in search of a deeper, more real truth about us all.

*"Our deepest fear is not that we are inadequate. Our deepest fear is that we are powerful beyond measure. It is our light, not our darkness that most frightens us. We ask ourselves, 'Who am I to be brilliant, gorgeous, talented, fabulous?' Actually, who are you not to be? You are a child of God. Your playing small does not serve the world. There is nothing enlightened about shrinking so that other people won't feel insecure around you. We are all meant to shine, as children do. We were born to make manifest the glory of God that is within us. It's not just in some of us; it's in everyone. And as we let our own light shine, we unconsciously give other people permission to do the same. As we are liberated from our own fear, our presence automatically liberates others."*
~ Marianne Williamson, Return to Love: Reflections on the Principles of "A Course in Miracles"

I share this quote because it rocked my world. I knew without a shadow of a doubt that God was calling me to discover my true essence, my true Self and the gift of who I am to the world in a very enthusiastic way. I was standing, however, in a point of tension; a tension between being my true self, which could be an ultimate "hurray", joyful experience, and worrying about how people would treat my true self – the fear of rejection but most critically the fear that people would affirm my inner critic's loud booming voice that says "Who do you think you are? You are not good enough and you are unredeemable". But ahhhh, what Marianne is saying is that I can focus on those who might be uncomfortable or even threatened by my clarity, wisdom, vision, creativity and discernment, or I can focus on the possibility that others may be inspired by how I live my life and in turn let their own light shine.

Many years ago, right after I completed the prayer journey of "The Ignatian Exercises", I worked on articulating my personal mission statement. What I discovered is that I am here to "provide opportunities for people to experience God". This has manifested in many forms -- from workshops with women combining creativity and spirituality, to my one-on-one work as a spiritual director, to my volunteer work and, most recently, through my new business where I am endeavouring to demonstrate that business can be contemplative, conscious and sustainable. Most importantly, I seek to live out that mission by being as open and present to the people around me as I can be. Silence really is golden sometimes.

**Stepping into the light is a letting go process ...** and that first step into the light is a doozy. What it meant for me was letting go of what I thought I wanted, what I thought I was, who I hoped I would be. I clung to who would be there with me and surrendered to God in trust that all God wants for me is that I might know in the core of my being that I am loved-- that I am the Beloved!

One of my favorite poems addresses the process of change, and allowed me to say to myself "I did the best I could with what I knew". Now I know more so I choose something different. I choose the struggle to find, explore and discover my true essence. I don't walk unconsciously but choose to see things as they are with all their bumps and ruts.

*"I walk down the street.*
*There is a deep hole in the sidewalk.*
*I fall in.*
*I am lost... I am helpless.*
*It isn't my fault.*
*It takes forever to find a way out.*

*I walk down the same street.*
*There is a deep hole in the sidewalk.*
*I pretend I don't see it.*
*I fall in again.*
*I can't believe I am in the same place.*
*But, it isn't my fault.*
*It still takes me a long time to get out.*

*I walk down the same street.*
*There is a deep hole in the sidewalk.*
*I see it is there.*
*I still fall in. It's a habit.*
*My eyes are open.*
*I know where I am.*
*It is my fault. I get out immediately.*

*I walk down the same street.*
*There is a deep hole in the sidewalk.*
*I walk around it.*

*I walk down another street."*

~ Portia Nelson, There's a Hole in My Sidewalk: The Romance of Self-Discovery

266

As a practitioner of Ignatian Spirituality and a Christian (although I think of myself more akin to Christian Mysticism – who knows why I feel the need to justify that…) I found myself imagining being in the Jordan River with John the Baptist and being called into the water to be baptized. The sky is brilliant blue and the air is warm and sweet and a whispery, gentle voice says "this is my beloved daughter in whom I am well pleased." No matter if I fall in a new hole or an old familiar hole I am loved -- nothing can separate me from the Love for I am of Love and for Love and from Love.

As we ALL are.

## Stepping into the light casts a shadow.

One major "ah ha" that I discovered in my journey to cross the bridge from survivor to my authentic self is that, when we step into the light, we automatically cast a shadow. There is a big part of my personality that thinks I must be perfect in order to become who I was meant to be. The idea that a shadowy side of myself might stick around, show up or even act up was not a comfortable thought for me. Let's be real -- not *"was"*…*"is"*. It *is* not comfortable for me at all. However, what I have come to realize is that living in the shadow, in the grey area, is a place of grace. You no longer have to choose right or wrong, or take a stand or make a judgement. All we're called to do here is to be present and join in those things that are life-giving. The things that lead us to freedom, hope, joy and love.

## Dancing with the Divine

I have no idea how my early experiences show up within me on a day-to-day basis. I don't know if people can tell, if there is an uncomfortable edge to me or if I float more gracefully through my life. I'm guessing it's a combination of those things and many other things. What I do know is my job on this planet is to continue dancing with real life, with all its ups and downs, joys and sorrows, hardships and successes. Life is a dance of discernment between the things that draw me towards God and the things that turn me away. Between those things that draw in life and hope and those things that stroke my ego or perpetuate self-denial. I dance with the divine within as I explore and embrace the ways of peace, wisdom and awareness. I dance with the divine as I honour and care for myself. I dance with the divine as I care for the planet and do my part to serve and inspire others.

**We can't do it alone**

Whether we are survivors of sexual, physical or religious abuse, adult children of alcoholics, or have experienced some kind of relational dysfunction, we need each other. During my darkest days people described me as courageous for going to the police and sharing my experiences. Honestly, the most courageous thing I have done and continue to do is take the risk of including others in my life, ask for help when I need it, work at friendships of mutual sharing and support, and be real about who and how I am at any given moment. Some of these relationships go well and others don't. That's part of life. Sometimes I make bad choices and sometimes I make brilliant ones. Sometimes people outgrow me and sometimes I outgrow them. But without certain key people who supported me, taught me and cared for me, I might be in a different place. And without the challenging people I would also be different. Each provides me with an opportunity to learn and grow. So I do and must acknowledge that my journey and all of our journeys are shared, for better or for worse, in some way or another, and it makes it a lot easier if we take the risk to figure out how to share them well.

**Leaving a Legacy**

One hope that I have is to be a catalyst for change and for healing. I feel it's time to "Bring it on"! To shine! Not for the sake of glory but, as Marianne Williamson said, "to inspire others to do the same". And "who am I not to be?" I choose to face whatever adversity I did and will have but, despite it all, I want to walk with courage and gentleness in this world. I have always been keenly aware of the struggles of women around me on this planet. I ache for those struggling with mental illness, those who are marginalized, those who are horrifically mistreated, and so in writing my story I commit to being accountable to the gift that I have -- this strength and power to do something with my life that makes a ripple or a wave or a tidal wave of change that brings hope, healing and relief to women wherever I find myself each and every day.

**Praise Be to You for Life**

*Praise be to you, O God for life*
*    and for my intense desire to live;*
*praise be to you for the mystery of love*
*    and for my intense desire to be a lover;*
*praise be to you for this day*
*    and another chance to live and love.*

*Thank you, God,*
> *for friends who stake their claim on my heart,*
> *for enemies who disturb my soul and bump my ego,*
> *for tuba players,*
>> *and story tellers,*
>>> *and trapeze troupes.*

*Thank you, God*
> *for singers of songs,*
> *for teachers of songs,*
>> *who help me sing along the way,*
> *...and for listeners.*

*Thank you, God,*
> *for those who attempt beauty*
>> *rather than curse ugliness,*
> *for those who take stands*
>> *rather than take polls,*
> *for those who risk being right*
>> *rather than pandering to be liked,*
> *for those who do something*
>> *rather than talking about everything.*

*God, grant me grace, then,*
*and a portion of your spirit*
*that I may so live*
> *as to give others cause*
>> *to be thankful for me.*
*Thankful because I have not forgotten*
> *how to hope,*
>> *how to laugh,*
>>> *how to say, "I'm sorry",*
>> *how to forgive,*
>>> *how to bind up wounds,*
>>>> *how to dream,*
>> *how to cry,*
>>> *how to pray,*
>> *how to love when it is hard,*
>>> *and how to dare when it's dangerous.*

*Undamn me, God,*
*that praise may flow more easily from me*
            *than wants*
*thanks for readily*
            *than complaints.*
*Praise be to you, God, for my life;*
*praise to you for another chance to live.*

Adapted from Guerrillas of Grace – Prayers for the Battle by Ted Loder (I changed the word Lord to God)

* * *

*There were many angels on the journey, but I want to take this opportunity to thank those that often don't get thanked; those who professionally supported me during my darkest days: Cris Vrooman, counsellor at Women in Crisis; Lorraine Dykman, Spiritual Director; Geoff Sansom, counsellor; and Linda Lauder, court support from Women in Crisis.*

* * *

*April is the owner of FLOW Office Wisdom, a trained facilitator, Ennea-gram Coach, and Spiritual Director, and the Canadian Ambassador for the Enlightened Business Foundation. She is passionate about organizational and spiritual clarity and loves to journey with groups and individuals in the deep work of discovery and the action that comes from such dis-coveries. For more information visit www.flowofficewisdom.com.*

# Supported Charities

*The following charities were selected by the writers in this anthology, and will receive 25% of the proceeds from all book sales for which they are designated as preferred recipient of the purchaser.*

## Anselma House/Women's Crisis Services
www.wcswr.org

Women's Crisis Services of Waterloo Region offers a variety of programs to help women and children move beyond violence. We operate a residential program at our two shelters; Anselma House in Kitchener and Haven House in Cambridge plus regional outreach services, for abused women and children.

## Because I am a Girl
www.becauseiamagirl.ca

Because I am a Girl is a global initiative to end gender inequality, promote girls' rights and lift millions of girls – and everyone around them – out of poverty.

The Because I am a Girl initiative was founded by Plan International, one of the largest international charities in the world. Founded in 1937, Plan has supported girls and boys in the developing world for more than 75 years through collaboration with children, their families, and their communities.

## Chicks for Charity
www.chicksforcharity.com.au

Chicks for Charity has simple beliefs. Give back. Enjoy life. Laugh a lot. Be thankful. Cherish your family and friends. Share the wisdom. Girls nights. That's what Chicks for Charity is all about. Chicks for Charity raise community awareness through uniting women from all walks of life. Chicks for Charity encourage all women to harness the power of "giving back". Organized fundraising events inspire women to donate time, talent and money to better communities. Through our collected efforts we represent

271

an example to younger generations; we will encourage their involvement and nurture their confidence to ensure that the power of "giving back" is sustained.

## Dress for Success
**www.dressforsuccess.org**

Dress for Success is a global not-for-profit organization offering services designed to help disadvantaged women find jobs and remain employed.

The mission of Dress for Success is to "promote the economic independence of disadvantaged women by providing professional attire, a network of support and the career development tools to help women thrive in work and in life."

## Family Transition Place
**www.familytransitionplace.ca**

Since 1984, Family Transition Place (FTP) has been providing critical services to women and their children who have experienced abuse and unhealthy relationships. Inside FTP's doors, women find a warm and welcoming place where their safety and well-being is the most important thing in the world. Whether they need a safe place to live, or the services of a professional, skilled counsellor to assist them on their journey, FTP is there to help.

## Food and Friends
**http://www.childrensfoundation.org/food-and-friends**

Food and Friends supports local children through student nutrition programs. Their mission is to initiate, facilitate and support quality, sustainable student nutrition programs.

They provide breakfast, lunch and snack programs for students in a supportive, nonjudgmental environment where they feel cared for and safe.

# Food4Kids
www.food4kids.ca

Food4Kids provides backpacks of healthy food for kids with limited or no food during weekend periods. Each food package contains kid friendly, non-perishable and easy to prepare meals with maximum nutrient value. The focus is provision of foods from each food group including five servings per day of fruits and vegetables. Not only does Food4Kids fill hungry tummies, it also fills an important gap. They offer great synergy with local Student Nutrition Programs and local hubs that provide breakfast, lunch or after school snacks. There are currently no programs in Hamilton or Halton providing healthy food for children going entire weekends without food.

# Friends of Stansted Hall
http://www.friendsofstanstedhall.com/

The Friends of Stansted Hall – The Arthur Findlay College" [herein called "The Friends of Stansted Hall] is a registered Charity under the Charities Act 1960. Its objectives are to promote education in Psychic Science and in particular to assist in the establishment and maintenance of a College for the Advancement of Psychic Science, namely Stansted Hall in Memory of J Arthur Findlay. It is all about raising the vibration, one person at a time ... mass healing that goes beyond the bounds of one person.

# Guelph-Wellington Women in Crisis
www.gwwomenincrisis.org

Guelph-Wellington Women in Crisis is a feminist community-based organization providing services to women and their children on woman abuse and sexual violence. We believe our services must be inclusive and equitable for all individuals accessing our programs while being responsive to issues of race, gender, religion, age, sexual orientation, socio-economic status and/or abilities.

## Habitat for Humanity
**www.habitat.ca**

Habitat for Humanity Canada is a national, non-profit organization working towards a world where everyone has a safe and decent place to live. Habitat for Humanity Canada's vision, mission and values are delivered by Habitat for Humanity affiliates working in over 300 communities across Canada. Habitat for Humanity Canada affiliates select and prepare partner families for home ownership, manage the construction of Habitat homes, and hold partner family mortgages. They play a vital role at the local level by engaging community volunteers, securing resources, increasing the profile of Habitat for Humanity and raising awareness about the issue of affordable housing in their communities.

## Heart & Stroke Foundation (Celebration of Life Account)

The Celebration of Life fundraiser was first launched in 2008. Its mission is to raise funds for the SPCA and for AEDs to be installed in area facilities. Vick has dedicated herself to promoting the importance of heart health after the death of her sister Cathy, who suffered a massive heart attack at the age of 40.

## Heifer Project International
**www.heifer.org**

Heifer International's mission is to work with communities to end hunger and poverty and care for the earth. By giving families a hand-up, not just a hand-out, we empower them to turn lives of hunger and poverty into self-reliance and hope. With gifts of livestock and training, Heifer projects help families improve their nutrition and generate income in sustainable ways. We refer to our animal donations as "living loans" because in exchange for their livestock and training, families agree to give one of its animal's offspring to another family in need. It's called Passing on the Gift – a cornerstone of our mission that creates an ever-expanding network of hope and peace.

274

## The Hunger Project
www.thp.org

The Hunger Project (THP) is a global, non-profit, strategic organization committed to the sustainable end of world hunger. In Africa, South Asia and Latin America, THP seeks to end hunger and poverty by empowering people to lead lives of self-reliance, meet their own basic needs and build better futures for their children.

## Kids Company
www.kidsco.org.uk

Kids Company provides practical, emotional and educational support to vulnerable inner-city children. Their services reach 36,000 and intensively support 18,000 children across London, including the most deprived and at risk whose parents are unable to care for them due to their own practical and emotional challenges. For many, the roles of adult and child are reversed and, despite profound love, both struggle to survive. Kids Company provides a safe, caring, family environment where support is tailored to the needs of each individual. Their services and support empower children who have experienced enormous challenges to lead positive and fulfilling lives.

## Mindfulness Without Borders
www.mindfulnesswithoutborders.org

Mindfulness Without Borders teaches foundational skills to manage emotions, cope with stress, strengthen character, build healthy relationships and engage communities responsibly. These vital social and emotional skills equip people to take positive action and live more fully.

Mindfulness Without Borders (formerly Between Four Eyes) is a 501(c)3 non-profit organization. In the span of two short years, it has encouraged over 650 educators and healthcare providers and more than 400 students, worldwide to bring mindful living, presence and connection to their personal and professional lives.

# The Miracle Babies Foundation
www.miraclebabies.org.au

Miracle Babies Foundation is Australia's leading organization supporting premature and sick newborns, their families and the hospitals that care for them. Since 2005, Miracle Babies Foundation has been passionate in developing and providing vital programs and resources to support and enhance a family's experience from a threatened pregnancy, hospital journey with a premature or sick newborn, the transition to home and beyond.

# The Monsinger Family Award
Email sharingcharity@outlook.com for more information.

The Monsinger Family Award is not a traditional charity. Created by Wendy Monsinger, it is an education grant/ bursary to be awarded to a young girl who, despite the struggles and hurdles, has pushed through and made it to her grade 12 graduation. It doesn't matter what her grades are, what matters is that SHE matters. It will be given to a girl who made it through the odds; whether it is some form of abuse, bullying, parental separation, depression or any other life "curve ball" she may have been thrown.

# On Butterfly Wings
www.onethousandtrees.com/wings

On Butterfly Wings is a work in progress, and the brainchild of Lisa Browning. The vision is to create an online community for girls who struggle with self-esteem issues. Lisa will partner with local organizations and individuals interested in empowering girls to become strong, confident and independent women, to create a secure, supportive online environment where girls will feel safe to be themselves, and obtain the skills and support they need to thrive.

## Power of Hope
www.powerofhopeontario.ca

Power of HOPE Community Organization is a registered not-for-profit organization that helps families in the communities of Waterloo Region, Wellington County, Perth County and Woodstock area.

Through the generosity of friends, families, local businesses and fundraising event donors, Power of HOPE is able to provide essential items needed by low income families, children and women in crisis.

## Soulworks Gifting Foundation
http://www.inspiredsoulworks.com/soul-works-gifting-foundation.html

The Soul Works Gifting Foundation's mission is to innovate, empower and inspire children, youth and adults globally through gifting books, music, materials and workshops to make a positive difference in individual lives and community.

## Spark of Brilliance
www.sparkofbrilliance.org

Spark of Brilliance, a program of the Self Help Alliance services, operated by the Canadian Mental Health Association Waterloo Wellington Dufferin Branch, is a community-based mental health initiative that promotes healing, recovery and discovery through the expressive arts. Workshops are open to people living with mental health issues and/or addictions and their supportive allies, including: family members, friends, mental health workers, etc.

## Stonehenge Therapeutic Community
www.stonehengetc.com

Stonehenge Therapeutic Community offers a long-term, intensive treatment program (4-6 months) for people whose lives have been devastated by alcohol and drug abuse, and whose reality includes the fractured relationships, derailed careers and encounters with the legal system that so often result. At Stonehenge Therapeutic Community, the members, staff and alumni comprise a supportive therapeutic community in which the whole is greater than the sum of its parts, where profound and enduring change can and does occur.

## Unity Kitchener
www.unitykitchener.com

Spiritual, but not religious? Looking for a Positive Path for Spiritual Living? Unity is a great place to start.

All ages, including children, are welcomed to Sunday services which include inspiring music, and practical talks to support you in living a life that is truly meaningful and abundant.

## University of California, Student-run Medical Clinic
http://meded.ucsd.edu/freeclinic/

The UCSD Student-Run Free Clinic Project, in partnership with the community, provides accessible, quality health care for the underserved in a respectful environment in which students, health professionals, patients, and community members learn from one another.

The clinic seeks to sustain health through free medical and preventive care, health education, and access to social services.

Are you interested in sharing your story
in an upcoming volume of SHARING?

Please contact Lisa Browning at
lisa@onethousandtrees.com,
or call 519-265-1212.

Deadline to reserve your spot for Volume 2
is July 1, 2014.

Deadline for submissions
is September 1, 2014.